PROLOGUE

By the time someone graduates from college, they have completed seventeen years of formal education. But in that time, they didn't attend a single class on how to raise a child, and they haven't been taught the first thing about how to sell—which ironically, are two of the most important functions an adult will be asked to perform in their lifetime.

—THOMAS A. FREESE

THE NEW ERA OF SALESMANSHIP

*Bringing the Art of Selling
Into the 21st Century*

Thomas A. Freese

Published by:

QBS Publishing, Inc.
P.O. Box 922933
Atlanta, Georgia 30010-2933
tfreese@QBSresearch.com

1st printing 2005
Printed in Canada
Library of Congress Control Number: 2004101757
ISBN: 1-891892-20-7

Cover design by Warren Caldwell and Jill Dible
Book design by Jill Dible

to my mother and my father

ACKNOWLEDGEMENTS

The idea for this book was actually conceived by QBS clients—former students who, after attending their initial Question Based Selling courses, pushed me to expand the QBS Methodology to get even *deeper, wider, and more strategic.* In hindsight, they were right, and I am truly grateful for their enthusiasm and encouragement over these past two years.

As with each of my other books, this project was a collective effort, and there are many people I wish to acknowledge.

For contributions in creating the book itself, I am indebted to an exceptional team of literary professionals. Thank you Jill Dible, who as a world class book designer, has been a joy to work with since the very beginning. Thank you Emily Gilreath, whose editing abilities are equivalent to that of a master crafts-person putting the finishing touches on a piece of fine woodwork. Thanks also to my literary agent, Al Zuckerman, as I am convinced that no one knows the book business better than Al.

My appreciation also goes out to our team of professionals at QBS Research, Inc., starting with my assistant Suellen Wylie. I am well aware that it takes a special person to manage the chaos that often accompanies the growth and success we have enjoyed over the last few years. Thank you, Suellen. I have also had the privilege of working with a staff of QBS trainers whom I consider to be the best and most effective trainers anywhere, including Bill Smith, Alan Rohrer, Robert Cobb, and Geoff Land.

I would like to extend a special note of gratitude to Mark Reed, Richard Sites, Jim Hardee, Roger Moore, Jerry Saunders, Chip Graddy, Scott Whitney, and Joel Hubbard. Your vision and talent has been a true inspiration. Especially during those times when I was overwhelmed by this project, and underwhelmed by results, your contributions of friendship and support were immeasurable, and words alone cannot express my appreciation.

Speaking of support, I must once again offer my most heartfelt appreciation to my three biggest cheerleaders: My wife Laura, and our two daughters, Sarah and Mary Claire. To them, the first book was somewhat of a novelty. The second book made me one of the cooler dads on campus at my daughters' school. This, my third book, has apparently put me on par (in their minds) with J.R.R. Tolkien, author of the Lord of the Rings trilogy.

It is also my privilege to take this opportunity to remember my good friend Joe Monday, whose life may have been cut short, but whose legacy lives on. Joe was undoubtedly one of the best salespeople I have ever known. He was also one of the best friends an aspiring sales trainer could ever have.

Lastly, I wish to recognize our friends at church, our New Year's Eve dinner partners, my golfing buddies at the Atlanta Athletic Club, and our extended family for replacing the daily pressures with a sense of balance that has helped me to maintain the proper perspective on what's really important.

My trilogy is now complete. It's time for your quest to begin.

TABLE OF CONTENTS

I left the corporate world after 17 successful years in the trenches of sales and management. My original intention was simple—to capture whatever had enabled me to become successful as a salesperson, and to somehow bottle it into a system that could then be transferred to increase the effectiveness of other salespeople and sales organizations. Hence, the QBS Methodology was born, and the journey I embarked on several years ago has far exceeded my wildest expectations, having published three books on sales effectiveness and had the opportunity to train literally thousands of salespeople all over the world.

This journey is far from over, however. Training other sales professionals provides an ongoing learning experience for me. In fact, I have found that my perspective on selling continues to evolve, which is why this work represents an intentional departure from my first two books, *Secrets of Question Based Selling* and *It Only Takes 1% to Have a Competitive Edge in Sales*.

Prior to this project, most of my training and development efforts were focused on raising the bar in terms of increasing the productivity of individual salespersons. In essence, improving the professional selling skills of the individual performers on a sales team can significantly increase top-line revenue generated by the larger sales organization, as well as affect the bottom-line profitability of the corporation. We have successfully proven this theory many times over at hundreds of client accounts.

There is another piece to the puzzle, however. In addition to raising the level of one's own selling skills, I have discovered that there is a similar opportunity to increase the sales effectiveness of the broader organization, which is equally important to the overall success of a company. That's why my objective with this book extends beyond the base concepts taught in Question Based Selling™, and focuses on the larger opportunity of "culturalizing" the QBS Methodology across the entire sales organization.

Human nature says that people are creatures of habit. Consequently, we tend to gravitate naturally to whatever feels most comfortable. Of course, most salespeople are going to feel most "comfortable" with whatever they have done in the past. This brings us to somewhat of a crossroads in one's own personal development as a sales professional, where you must choose to either maintain the status quo and continue using the same approach, or step back and make some conscious decisions with regard to selling strategies and techniques that will provide the greatest competitive advantage as the business environment continues to evolve.

The fundamentals of selling are still the same. Salespeople must uncover needs before they can provide solutions, and customers still need to be able to cost-justify a purchase before moving forward with a decision. And yes, relationship building is also important because people still buy from people. But, the nuances of the strategic sale have changed dramatically and differentiating yourself from the competition is now the key.

I realize that change is difficult. It's a natural reaction. Most people are averse to changing their approach because change means risk, and risk takes us out of our comfort zone. That's why I am going to use the word, 'choose'. To have a lasting impact on bottom line performance, we must choose to adapt our approach to changing market conditions, which generally requires a catalyst that will motivate salespeople to step outside the box of traditional thinking.

Truth be told, sellers are going to change their approach anyway. Market dynamics will continue to evolve over time. Product offerings will change. Even your competitors are continuously adjusting their approach in an attempt to secure a more strategic position in the marketplace. You will also change as you gain experience and mature as a professional with every business situation you face. So, the way I see it, change in sales is a given. The question is, are you open to being proactive with regard to change, which includes making some conscious decisions about maximizing your strategic effectiveness in your respective markets?

My philosophy as a salesperson was relatively simple. Give me an opportunity to succeed, give me a company that is willing to support my efforts, and most importantly, give me some control over my own destiny to differentiate myself and my company from the rest of the "noise" in the marketplace. That's what this book was intended to achieve—giving salespeople control over their own destinies, to differentiate themselves and their products, in order to achieve the highest levels of success in the profession of selling.

My strategy on this project was not to reinvent the QBS Methodology or to try and re-articulate concepts that have already been explained in previous works. Rather, the idea in this book is to build on existing concepts in an effort to merge QBS philosophy together with an implementation strategy that provides a fully integrated success formula enabling sales organizations to get deeper, wider, and more strategic within their target accounts. Action items have been included at the end of each chapter to help put the lessons learned from the book into daily practice.

Have I succeeded in creating and articulating a strategic selling model that will define the new era of salesmanship? The answer to that question will likely be revealed shortly after you finish reading this book. If your pipeline expands dramatically and something I said causes your sales results to skyrocket, then we both will have accomplished mutual objectives, and everybody wins!

CHAPTER 1

Surviving the Current Business Climate

I am a simple guy about many things. I always have been. Consequently, I have discovered that some things in life are fairly predictable. In my neighborhood, for example, the sun tends to rise in the eastern sky and set in the west. It happens this way almost every day! Other things are just as predictable. Muddy shoes tend to soil new carpets, the postman does not come on Sundays, and a light in my refrigerator comes on whenever the door opens.

But some things I don't understand. For instance, why do toasters have a setting that would burn a piece of toast to such a horrible crisp that no decent human would choose to eat it? Or, have you ever noticed that when you blow into a dog's face, he gets mad, but when you take him on a car ride, he sticks his head out the window to catch the breeze? Here's something else. Why do they put Braille dots on the keypad of a drive-up ATM?

I am equally puzzled when it comes to sales training and development. Does anyone else think it's odd that the world of strategic sales training has stayed pretty much the same over the last twenty years, while for most companies, the selling environment has changed dramatically? Why is that?

Let's start with the fact that the business climate in today's global marketplace is significantly different than what sellers experienced just a few short years ago. But the economic boom of the late 1990's has long since fizzled. Now, fiscal tightening has created a ripple effect where prospective buyers within key target accounts are more cautious with their decision-making and more judicious with their budgets and spending than ever before. Meanwhile, volatility in the face of uncertain economic conditions has caused corporations to continue looking for opportunities to cut expenses, and there is an ever-increasing sense of scrutiny over pending purchase decisions. Perhaps this is to be expected since business conditions tend to follow cyclical trends over time.

Although decision-makers within key target accounts have become somewhat gun-shy, we shouldn't blame the customer. Over the past decade, downsizing and acquisitions have burdened prospective customers with extra responsibility, oftentimes without the benefit of additional resources. As a result, workloads have increased, competition is growing fiercer, and the overall pace of business has quickened. Even if they wanted to, customers simply cannot afford to spend time with every salesperson that comes calling.

> Fiscal tightening has created a ripple effect where prospective buyers within key target accounts are more cautious with their decision-making and more judicious with their budgets and spending than ever before.

Customers are also less accessible. In the past, salespeople could invest the time to build relationships with gatekeepers in their accounts, knowing that these relationships would eventually get them in to see key decision-makers. But, electronic devices have since replaced most of the corporate gatekeepers, and you cannot build a relationship with a voice-mail system. Other technological innovations such as e-mail, fax, cell phones, digital pagers, and the Internet have also given customers the freedom to execute their job functions away from their offices. While this may help to increase productivity, it also means that potential customers are less likely to be sitting at their desks when you happen to call.

Even if a prospective customer is in the office, many decision-makers are reluctant to pick up the telephone anyway. With all the innovation in recent years, vendor companies are offering more solution alternatives than ever before. Consequently, decision-makers are being inundated with a barrage of sales callers, who are all competing for the same thing—a share of the prospect's time and attention, in order to have an opportunity to compete for a portion of their spending budget.

The shame is, the sales profession has responded poorly to these changing market conditions. Some sales organizations have tried to adapt by encouraging their sales teams to be more persistent and aggressive. "When the going gets tough," the proverbial sales manager chants, "the tough get going." The problem is, aggression is more likely to work against you. I mean, if the telephone happens to ring at your house this evening, and some salesperson decides to be "even more aggressive" with you, do their chances of selling you go up or down? Hence my concern with sales programs that base their entire approach on guer-rilla tactics or predatory marketing. Most of the customers

> The sales profession has responded poorly to changing market conditions.

I talk with don't want to be pushed, and they are no longer willing to endure a steady steam of over-zealous salespeople.

One program I recently became aware of even suggests that you should "sell like a mad-man." Really? Would you be more likely to buy from a mad-man? I'm not going to say that these approaches never work, but I can confidently say that they don't work on me.

When I talk about customers being cautious and standoffish, I should make the point that although sellers are being held at arm's-length, prospective customers don't despise salespeople. In fact, it's just the opposite. Most customers depend on salespeople—to provide industry information, innovative ideas, a vision into the future, and potential solutions. Let me say it again, customers absolutely *depend* on salespeople! But they don't depend on all of them. That's why it's so important for sellers to differentiate themselves, in order to be perceived as a valuable resource and not just another sales caller.

What Type of Salesperson Do You Prefer?

As you might imagine, the nature of my business includes a fair amount of travel, as I now work with sales organizations all over the globe. One of the perks of volume traveling is that I have achieved "relative nobility" in terms of my frequent flyer status with Delta Air Lines. As a result, I get complimentary upgrades to first class, along with free drinks and movies. It also means I usually end up sitting next to a corporate executive or manager—suffice it to say, a business person with decision making authority.

Once the plane gets in the air, that's office time for me. It's an opportunity for me to catch up on email, prepare for upcoming events, or work on my next book. But given the close proximity, I generally engage in some idle chit-chat with the person in the adjacent seat. The conversation typically begins when I break out my laptop and the other person asks, "What business are you in?" I normally take the opportunity to briefly summarize my vocation as author and sales trainer. "You're a sales trainer," they say, "Hmmm." I'm not sure what "Hmmm" means, other than it's the type of response one might give upon learning that you were a funeral director or a handler of nuclear waste.

Once the subject of sales training has been broached, however, I use the opportunity to ask, "Sir (or Madame), since you probably encounter a fair number of salespeople in your business, I wonder if I could ask you to take a minute and describe the type of salesperson you would prefer to deal with?"

I ask this question to lots of people. You should make it a point to ask this same question. The next time you are on an airplane, or you are involved in some idle chit-chat during a dinner party, ask the person beside you to profile the type of salesperson they would choose to deal with. Not surprisingly, these people *never* respond by saying they prefer a salesperson who is pushy, persistent, aggressive, persuasive, tenacious, covert, or manipulative. Let me ask, "What type of salespeople do you prefer to deal with?" The responses I receive cause me to wonder why so many salespeople are being "pushed" to be more aggressive or tenacious in the face of today's market conditions.

> Salespeople who are working hard to penetrate new accounts, often find that prospective customers are working even harder to hold them at bay.

The old, 'when the going gets tough, the tough get going' strategy may apply in football, but in the current business climate, teaching salespeople to be increasingly more aggressive is a formula for failure. In fact, we have reached the point where salespeople who are working hard to penetrate new accounts, often find that prospective customers are working even harder to hold them at bay.

One of the ways companies have attempted to improve sales productivity was to formalize their internal sales processes. This trend began back in the early 1980's and then gained momentum as the economy took off. As a result, some of the more popular sales process vendors like Miller-Heiman's Strategic Selling™, Jim Holden's PowerBase Selling™, Mike Bosworth's Solution Selling™, and Target Account Selling,™ made a gazillion dollars working with corporations to define and implement a structured approach to managing the sales process. The goal was to make sure that the players across the broader sales organization were all moving in the same direction and speaking a common language.

Some companies opted to develop their own sales processes internally. In many cases, that meant investing large sums of money to bring outside consultants in to take an objective look at the company and identify critical success factors for the sales team. This front-end analysis was usually followed by the development of specific paradigms and procedures that were then put in place to govern the operations of the sales organization. Of course, after investing all that time and money, most companies ended up with a sales approach that looked very similar to Miller-Heiman, PowerBase Selling, Solution Selling, or TAS, only with a different name.

During this formalization period, the pendulum for sales development swung way over to one side. During the 80's and 90's, companies focused most of their sales training efforts on defining their internal sales processes, in many cases, at the expense of skills development. The thought was that you could just hire good salespeople, who already had sound selling skills and a track record for success, and simply train them to follow the steps of the "all-important" sales process.

Then, the economy took a turn for the worse, sales results fell sharply, and for most companies, defining the internal sales process suddenly was no longer the problem.

Two Problems with Traditional Methods

For the record, I am not against companies having a structured internal sales process. Most of our QBS clients have a sales process in place already, and if they don't, we are happy to recommend one. But just identifying the steps of the sales process doesn't ensure that your sales team will be effective or successful.

In fact, have you ever noticed that different people on your sales team perform at varying levels of effectiveness even though they all follow the same basic sales process? You will find this to be true at every company. Top performers consistently bring in above-average sales results, while average salespeople seem to struggle through each and every deal, even though they all follow the same basic sales approach. Why? It's because there is something else, in addition to having a structured sales process, that will ultimately determine your effectiveness in sales.

The sales effectiveness discussion starts with the realization that there is a fundamental problem with traditional sales methods. Actually, there are two problems. My purpose here is not to disparage other training courses or criticize someone else's opinion. Rather, my objective throughout this book is to pick up the rug and point at reality, so we

> Have you ever noticed that different people on your sales team perform at varying levels of effectiveness even though they all follow the same basic sales process?

can have an honest and open discussion about maximizing the productivity of your sales organization.

I realize my candor is going to unnerve some people, particularly those who develop and deliver process-oriented sales programs. Lord knows I have "unnerved" a fair number of corporate ideologues over the years. But I stand firm on my position that there are a couple of fundamental problems with traditional selling approaches. So, let's step back and take a rational look at how traditional sales methods have evolved over time.

Having spent the bulk of my career in the trenches of sales and management, I have personally attended countless different sales training courses over the years. I have also read a plethora of books on the subject, listened to dozens of audio programs, and I have watched most of the popular video tapes. Every sales approach that I am aware of is foundationed on the premise that a salesperson must first uncover a need in order to have an opportunity to provide valuable solutions. This makes sense, right? If a customer does not perceive a need for your product or service, then you will not have an opportunity to provide value. I am guessing that you agree with this premise, as do I.

But, there are the two fundamental problems with this logic. In today's selling environment, just because a salesperson wants to ask questions (to uncover needs), doesn't necessarily mean a prospective buyer will want to share important information. Likewise, just because you have a good story to tell, doesn't guarantee that you will get an audience with the right people within your target accounts.

If you notice, the first step in just about every sales process calls for the salesperson to "identify" new prospect opportunities. At first glance, this makes sense, too. But how do you identify new opportunities when key decision-makers in important target accounts don't even want to talk with you? Can you see the irony? Basing your sales strategy on the assumption that prospective customers already want to engage in a dialogue is risky, if not ridiculous.

You may have noticed that some of the better-known training programs have been plagiarized over the years, to the point where many of the sales training seminars that are currently being offered now sound surprisingly similar. This creates another problem. If the goal of a sales training course is to provide a competitive advantage, why would you invest in a course curriculum that teaches your salespeople to sound just like everyone else in the industry? To me, sounding the same as everyone else is the quickest way to *commoditize* your value proposition, which is the opposite of what most sales managers and companies are trying to accomplish.

Sending salespeople to a class to learn what they already know is another miss. Particularly for companies that hire experienced salespeople, most of the people on your sales team have already attended numerous other sales training courses. Sometimes, you hear a Vice President kick-off a sales training class by saying, "Even if you only get one idea out of these next two days, it will have been worth it." To me, getting one idea from two or three days of training seems like a colossal waste of time! Unfortunately, this is an all too common scenario.

If you do a little research or visit your local bookstore, you will find that most of the material that is currently being taught was created twenty plus years ago. No wonder there are so few new ideas! Except for a relative few sales historians, most people don't care what techniques may have worked back in 1982. Frankly, it doesn't matter to me what worked in 1991 or 2001, either. Like most salespeople, I don't have any desire to go backwards. I would much rather focus on techniques and strategies that give sellers a competitive advantage moving forward. Therefore, if you are feeling challenged by fluctuations in the economy, coupled with increasing competitive pressures, then I would guess you are also looking for something that will maximize your return on invested sales effort and give your sales team a differentiable advantage in your respective markets.

The Sales Profession is Changing

When I am not actively speaking or training, I am usually on conference calls with sales managers or corporate executives talking about boosting their sales organization's productivity and effectiveness. My first question to them is always the same, "How can I help?"

It's a simple but fair question. Sales organizations face all kinds of different challenges, and if a prospective client has a problem that is outside my area of expertise, I am quick to defer to someone else. If there is something QBS can do to help, then I need some additional information about their business. So I ask, "How can I help?"

While every situation is unique, there are usually more similarities than differences when it comes to the challenges sales organizations face. Some of the most consistent requests I hear are, "Tom, we need to find a way to fill the sales forecast with more prospect opportunities." Or, "We need to do a better job qualifying forecasted sales opportunities so we don't waste valuable time and sales resources chasing ghosts."

The underlying strategic objectives of these sales organizations tend to be fairly consistent. Sales managers want to penetrate new accounts, get to the right levels of authority within those accounts, and then move opportunities through the pipeline with a greater sense of urgency. They also want salespeople to increase the size of prospect opportunities, accurately forecast potential deals, wrap up the transaction in a timely manner, and close business with higher profit margins. Do these objectives sound familiar? I bet your company has similar goals.

Salespeople in most sales organizations already have a good handle on *what* they want to accomplish. Like we just said, they want to penetrate new accounts, manage opportunities through the pipeline, close deals, and maintain the desired profit margin. Identifying "what" to do, therefore, is not the problem facing most companies. Sales managers and executives are not asking for more complex spreadsheets or additional definition with regard to their internal sales process. Most sales organizations already have an acceptable sales process in place.

Frankly, we all drank the Kool-Aid back in the 80's and 90's. As managers, it was exciting to imagine a world where sales forecasts would *always* be accurate and everyone on the team could learn to speak the same language with regard to pending opportunities. As a result, corporations spent millions of dollars over the last five, ten, and fifteen years implementing programs like Strategic Selling™, Power-Base Selling™, Solution Selling™, Target Account Selling™, Value Selling™, Counselor Selling™, or Acclivus™, all of which offer tools and spreadsheets that organizations can use to document and track sales opportunities on the forecast.

But at this point in the evolution of sales development, if you already have a sales process in place, chances are good that your salespeople have an equally clear picture of "what" they are trying to accomplish. Therefore, most sales organizations don't need additional spreadsheets, and salespeople are not out there complaining to their managers, "Boy, I wish we could get more training to help define the steps of the sales process!"

Companies have already invested heavily in process definition, identifying "what" their salespeople should be doing. In the last few years, however, the focus has shifted from process definition, to figuring out "how" to execute more effectively on these objectives. It's true. If you study business trends, you will find that sales managers today are still concerned about documentation, but they are much more focused on finding ways to boost productivity by raising the strategic effectiveness of their sales teams. What we are really talking about here is salesmanship, and the restoration of professional selling skills.

> The pendulum has swung back the other way and sales organizations are starting to refocus on skills development as a strategy to overcome turbulent market conditions.

Some people might call this a reverse paradigm shift, as the pendulum has clearly swung back the other way now that sales organizations are starting to refocus on skills development as a strategy to overcome turbulent market conditions and economic uncertainty.

To give you a better sense of the yin and yang relationship that exists between process definition and skills development, here's a simple example. Again, I am not against the idea of having a formalized sales process. Most of our clients already have a strategic sales process in place, which is fine. In fact, the first step in the sales process for most clients is the same—Step 1.) Identify new prospect opportunities. Isn't that the first step for your salespeople? So let's say you wanted to begin with Step 1. You would still face the same challenge—just because a salesperson wants to ask questions (i.e. probing for needs), doesn't necessarily mean prospective customers will want to share important information with them. And, just because you have a good story to tell, doesn't guarantee you an audience with the right people within your target accounts.

Therefore, salespeople in today's business climate had better do something to differentiate themselves from the rest of the "noise" in the marketplace because potential buyers are more cautious and judicious than ever before, and the goal of identifying new opportunities becomes exponentially more difficult when a customer doesn't even want to talk with you.

Hold on Just One Minute!

Skills development is about answering the question, "How?" You see, the questions sellers have about increasing their sales effectiveness are actually quite simple. Salespeople want to know *how* to get prospective buyers to return telephone calls, especially voice-mail messages. They also want to know *how* to uncover needs when customers are reluctant to share information with someone they don't yet know or trust. Sellers want to know *how* to recognize obstacles early in the sales process, and *how* to get past someone who may be blocking them from getting to higher levels within an account. Furthermore, *how* can you tell if a customer is even telling the truth? Basically, salespeople and managers want to know *how* to engage more prospects in more productive sales conversation throughout the sales process, and they want to know *how* to do it more consistently.

As a young salesperson, I was told that the quickest way to become proficient in sales was to seek out top performing salespeople in my industry and find out what they're doing. Then just copy their approach. I took this advice to heart and made it a practice of buying lunch in exchange for expert advice. So, whenever I had the opportunity to sit down with a top performing salesperson, I asked, "What are you doing that makes you so effective?"

It seemed like a fair question, but I was consistently disappointed in the answers I received. More often than not, I got a vanilla response, like: "Basically, Tom, I try to build mutually beneficial business relationships with prospective customers, in order to understand their needs, offer valuable solutions, handle objections, and when they are ready, I close the sale."

Hold on a minute! I was already trying to build and maintain quality relationships with prospective customers. I was also trying to uncover needs, communicate value, handle objections, and close the sale, but I wasn't enjoying the same level of success these guys were. Therefore, it became clear that some other ingredient must be contributing to their success. But, what was it (exactly) that was making these people top performers?

In time, I evolved into one of the top performing salespeople in my industry, and other aspiring salespeople started taking me to lunch. They had obviously been given the same advice, because they used the opportunity to pump me for information about how I became successful. I told them the truth—"I build mutually beneficial business relationships with prospective customers, in order to understand their needs. I also offer valuable solutions, proactively handle objections, and then close the sale."

As I pontificated to these eager young professionals, I noticed their faces reflecting the same feelings of ambiguity and confusion that I had felt years earlier. I remembered so clearly the desire to understand how to unlock the secrets of becoming a consistently successful salesperson. I have since discovered that every company struggles with the same challenge—how to duplicate the success of their top performing salespeople.

Most sales organizations I work with have an upper echelon of top performing salespeople who consistently achieve their sales objectives month after month, and quarter after quarter, while other people on the sales team are trying desperately to keep their heads above water. Identifying these top performing salespeople is easy. Just look at their results. What's difficult is identifying what it is (exactly) that gives these high performing salespeople a differentiable advantage.

Perhaps top performers in sales are just lucky. Maybe they have a knack for always getting the best territory. But don't bet on it. While I do agree that some good fortune can come from being in the right place at the right time, consistent high performance in sales cannot be attributed purely to chance. There are too many stories where an under-performing territory is given to an over-achiever, who ends up leading the team in sales the following year.

It's not the sales process that makes these top performers more productive either. Again, if you look around the typical sales organization, you will discover that some salespeople are exponentially more effective than others, even though they are all using the same basic process. Therefore, it's clear to me that we must look beyond the implementation of a standardized sales process to really understand what differentiates top performance from lackluster results.

I would add that your company's strategic sales process is probably not much of a differentiator at all. If you sell into a competitive marketplace, it's a safe bet that most of your competitors have a strategic sales process in place too—probably one that is very similar to yours. At this point, everyone is out there trying to build relationships, uncover needs, offer valuable solutions, handle objections, and close sales. Big deal!

When I discovered that the strategic sales process was not the true differentiator for a salesperson, I shifted my focus instead to trying to better understand the *execution* of the sales process, and how to become more effective at building relationships, uncovering needs, differentiating solution alternatives, proactively handling objections, and closing more sales.

When we talk about strategic effectiveness, we are really talking about the softer skills in sales, which cannot be objectively defined using a complex spreadsheet. If you want to duplicate top performance, you must first be able to identify the critical success factors that contribute to one's success. While that sounds simple enough, skills development has been on the back burner for many years now. Frankly, it hasn't even been fashionable to talk about selling skills. During the economic boom of the 1990's, it was easiest just to say, "We make it a practice to hire good salespeople." As a result, most organization focused on defining the sales process. Well, now that we have defined, adjusted, modified, and tweaked the sales process to death over the past fifteen years, I would argue that it is time to shift some of that energy back to raising the strategic effectiveness of your salespeople.

Sales Effectiveness is an Elusive Topic

Did you realize that less than fifteen percent of the typical sales manager's day is spent developing their team's strategic selling skills? In some cases, sales managers spend even less time talking directly with customers. This happens because in many sales organizations, managers are so busy tracking data that has to be reported back to the corporation, they end up spending tremendous amounts of energy on administrative minutiae, and only a small fraction of their time ends up being dedicated to the issue at hand—selling more stuff!

One of the questions I ask sales managers is, "How does your company track selling skills?" They have been asked to track deals on the forecast and opportunities as they move through the pipeline. Why not track skills development?

Truth be told, sales effectiveness has been an elusive topic. In many companies, it has been politically incorrect to even broach the subject because salespeople are expected to have excellent selling skills already. Likewise, managers are expected to have a certain level of capability, which is presumably why they have risen to their current positions. Particularly in a difficult economy, when companies are downsizing, who is going to raise their hand to a manager or executive and ask for skills training? Talk about political suicide! Perhaps we shouldn't be so surprised, then, that the issue of sales effectiveness tends to get swept under the rug.

Don't bother looking to your process vendor for help with sales effectiveness. Miller-Heiman, PowerBase Selling, Target Account Selling, Value Vision, and Solution Selling make their money by redefining the sales process and convincing companies to implement more complex spreadsheets. And frankly, I've grown weary of hearing about the importance of speaking a common language. If I could be so bold, the goal of a sales methodology is to increase productivity, and the bottom-line profitability of a company. Having a common language may contribute to this goal, but just because your sales organization speaks the same language doesn't necessarily make prospective customers more receptive to your message.

As I said earlier, identifying "what" to do is no longer the pressing issue for most companies at this point. Most salespeople already have a vision for what they want to accomplish in the sales process. The greater challenge now is upgrading your team's strategic selling skills, and then duplicating that success across the entire sales organization. This starts with giving salespeople a clear understanding about "how" to get deeper, wider, and more strategic within their target accounts. Teaching sellers how to be exponentially more effective also has the positive side benefit of increasing their confidence when interacting with customers.

For those managers who *do* want to improve the strategic effectiveness of their respective sales teams, the availability of resources dealing with this issue is surprisingly limited. Maybe that's because some of the older school skills-based programs seemed gimmicky or were short-lived in their relevance. For example, I have several sales books on my shelf right now that basically teach the art of bait-and-switch. I have other sales books that talk about how to deceive customers, and sham your way into the highest levels within your target accounts. When clients ask me to comment on some of the more radical techniques, my typical response is to ask, "Would those approaches work on you?" More often than not the answer is, "No way!" Right, so why should we expect gimmicks and tricks to be an effective means of approaching key people within important prospect accounts?

Sales effectiveness is a critical success factor for virtually every company. If prospective customers are reluctant to engage in a productive sales conversation (with your salespeople) about their needs or your potential solutions, then it doesn't matter how good your sales process looks on paper.

With QBS, we have already proven many times over that it is possible to identify and duplicate the softer skills across the broader sales organization. We have also proven that success in sales is predictable if you put yourself in a strong position to execute on the objectives of the sales process. Ironically, failure is predictable, too. The key is to understand all of the different cause and effect relationships that exist between the actions you take, and their probability of success in achieving the desired result.

> Every customer you call on is sharing their thoughts, feelings, and concerns with someone, that someone might as well be you.

Do your salespeople want to close more sales? Of course they do. Then, perhaps it's time to put them in a stronger position to ask for the order. Likewise, if you want them to uncover more needs and create a greater sense of urgency, then they must learn to craft and deliver questions that cause prospective buyers to share volumes of important information, as opposed to getting cursory responses.

Every customer you call on is sharing valuable information about their business or personal situation with someone, that someone might as well be you. The good news is, how customers respond has a lot to do with your approach. Again, my success formula in sales has always been relatively simple—give me an opportunity to succeed, a company that supports my efforts, and most importantly, give me some control over my own destiny to be perceived as a valuable resource, and not just another sales caller. That's essentially my mission throughout the rest of this book—to separate "myth and legend" from actual strategies and techniques that can be implemented to significantly raise the bar on your sales organization's overall strategic effectiveness.

This leaves you with an important decision to make. Either you continue forward with the same old approach, in which case, you can expect the same results, or you make a proactive choice to step outside the box of traditional thinking and try something that will increase your effectiveness as a sales professional.

< ACTION ITEMS >

1. Identify all of the different sales training programs your people have experienced to date. What percentage of those programs focused on process definition versus being skills-oriented? Have any of the sales training programs you've attended had conflicting goals? How do you reconcile aggressive behavior with buyer reluctance?

2. Hold a brain-storming session to identify what your salespeople are currently doing (different than your competitors) to penetrate new accounts? What are they doing differently than the competition to expand potential opportunities? And, what are they doing to differentiate their proposed solutions, increase the customer's sense of urgency for moving forward, and secure more commitments?

CHAPTER 2

Building High Performance Sales Teams

People buy from people. It's true. Prospective buyers tend to gravitate toward salespersons who are not only knowledgeable about their products, but who also come across as straightforward in their dealings, and who inspire a sense of confidence to make customers feel comfortable. The reverse is also true. People "sell" to people. And, those salespeople who are perceived by target customers as more capable and more professional than others calling on the same account tend to create more positive impressions. Consequently, they tend to have greater sales success.

Most corporate executives would agree that the human element of a company is critically important and can determine the success or failure of an organization. Yet the quality of the personnel on the sales team never appears on a company's balance sheet. That's probably because there is no good way to empirically quantify the quality of people in the sales organization. How do you put a numerical value on innovative ideas, strong leadership, commitment to excellence, and the desire to achieve, if not exceed, one's sales objectives? Nonetheless, these qualities represent the underlying cultural fabric of every company, and they will have an undeniable impact on the productivity of your sales team.

Years ago, large companies invested heavily to develop and deliver their own sales competency programs internally. The goal was to preserve the overall culture of the company by making sure that everyone in the sales organization was on the same page relative to following the same methodology. IBM, for example, was both diligent and purposeful in their efforts to instill a sales culture, especially in the early days of the technology revolution, that has since become legendary in the evolution of our current business culture.

One of the reasons companies were set on developing their own training programs internally could be that relatively few options for sales training existed back in the 1970's. The Burroughs Corporation, for example, put newly hired salespeople through a twelve-month sales insertion program, where the first 4 to 6 months were spent in a classroom setting, followed by a "promotion" to a sales assistant role to complete the rookie year. General Electric used to put salespeople through a graduated 8 to 12 week sales development program, depending on the division. Proctor and Gamble, Honeywell, Eli Lilly, Unisys, Merrill Lynch, Digital Equipment Corporation, and Xerox all had very extensive internal sales development programs. Have you ever visited the Xerox training facility in Leesburg, Virginia? My wife, Laura, graduated from the Xerox sales school, which could rival the facilities of any college campus.

In-house corporate training facilities like Xerox's were basically the sales schools of the 1970's and 1980's. The University of Florida, my alma mater, doesn't teach professional selling skills. When I attended the business school at Florida, the choice was to either major in marketing, economics, accounting, or in my case, I earned a degree in finance. Selling was simply not considered to be an academic skill. If you wanted to be a salesperson, you took a job with IBM, Xerox, Burroughs, Merrill Lynch, or Honeywell, and after graduation, they would teach you how to sell.

But guess what happened? The economy grew, and businesses expanded so rapidly late in the twentieth century, that highly trained salespeople in large corporations became easy targets for other companies who wanted to build a sales organization quickly. Smart managers figured out that it was significantly less expensive to lure away experienced sales professionals from other companies than to try and develop people from scratch. Consequently, up-and-coming companies began offering lucrative signing bonuses to sellers with IBM, Burroughs, or Honeywell experience, who were willing to jump ship. In addition to saving the upfront cost of education, companies who hired these experienced salespeople could dramatically reduce the expected ramp-up time for new salespeople, which meant realizing increased productivity much sooner. Anyone who was in sales back in the 1980's, for example, can attest that merely having the three letters "IBM" on one's resume was extremely valuable in the job market.

As time went on, the larger corporations with extensive internal training programs started bleeding salespeople, and turnover became a real problem. Not surprisingly, the mentality started to shift regarding in-house skills development. It was no longer advantageous for the cultural giants to serve as the training ground for new salespeople, only to lose them a few months later to smaller and leaner competitors who were reaping the benefits without incurring the upfront development cost.

The talent pool for instructors also evaporated over time. Back in the days of the large corporate sales schools, salespeople from the field were routinely rotated back into corporate positions to serve as internal sales trainers. In many organizations, it was an honor to be selected for this role, and it was also a good career move since it often served as a stepping stone into higher levels of management. That is seldom the case anymore. Companies who are fighting to survive in today's business environment want their best salespeople to remain in the field to maximize revenue. Talented salespeople prefer staying in the field anyway because they know they will make more money selling than training. The continuous push to cut back has also put corporate education departments on notice that overhead positions and expense budgets will be closely scrutinized. This sense of expendability has caused most of the really talented sales trainers to look for other opportunities.

As a result, very few companies offer extensive in-house, skills-based, sales development programs anymore. It's just not practical or feasible to fund the investment that would be required for companies to maintain an in-house development effort and remain competitive in today's business environment. Therefore, the practice of investing heavily in the sales culture of a company has basically ended, most of the corporate sales schools that served as the initial training ground for so many salespeople have long since closed their doors, and the old-school of selling is officially dead. That leaves us wondering, where do those companies who want to have strong sales organizations find good people?

In Search of Top Performers

One could argue that the most sensible thing companies should do is make it a practice to hire experienced salespeople—proven professionals who already have a track record of success. Simply go out and find the top five to ten percent of the salespeople in your respective industry, who have already demonstrated they are capable of over-achieving their sales goals, and bring them aboard. By hiring salespeople who have already proven themselves, your ramp-up times would be significantly reduced because they could hit the ground running, right?

Unfortunately, targeting the highest echelon of top performing salespeople has a downside. Let's start with the fact that everyone else in your industry is trying to identify and hire those same top salespeople. When I was consistently exceeding my numbers as a salesperson, I received dozens of calls per week from head-hunters and recruiters. It got to the point where fending them off felt like a full-time job. Of course, finding out who the top performers are is only part of the battle. You also have to convince them to change direction in their careers, knowing full well that their existing employers are probably very intent on retaining their services. Couple this with the fact that top performing salespeople usually don't need another job. Being tops in their field means they are probably earning large sums of money already, so why risk making a change? It's also likely that many of today's top performers are very comfortable in their current position. It's personally rewarding to feel like a "big fish in a small pond," having earned the political capital that comes from having an established track record of proven success. Top performers may also be reticent to walk away from meaningful business relationships that have been established over time, or groundwork that has been laid for future career advancement. Even when a top-performing salesperson does become available, they typically come with a healthy price tag, because they are in high demand.

Identifying who the "good" salespeople are is yet another challenge. I don't mean to overstate the obvious, but just because someone has a good looking resume, doesn't necessarily mean they are a blue-chip performer. Lots of salespeople achieved their annual sales goals when the economy was strong, which certainly was the case in the 1990's. It was easy to sell lots of goods and services when everyone had money to spend! But the question moving forward is, how will these salespeople fare now that prospective buyers are more cautious with their decision-making and more judicious with their budgets and spending than ever before?

Is it possible to find good salespeople without targeting only the top echelon of potential candidates? Absolutely! If you think about it, every successful salesperson started off as a diamond in the rough, looking for a manager or company to give them an opportunity to prove themselves. Some of these salespeople struggled at first, but after they got a few quarters under their belts, they started to blossom as professionals. The key is recognizing someone's potential early enough to have an opportunity to mold them into a true sales professional, which one might say is more of an art form than an exact science.

Good salespeople are a rare commodity indeed, but I should make the point upfront that this chapter isn't about "finding" good salespeople. Rather, our discussion here is about building high-performance sales teams, which has more to do with "developing" good salespeople. I should also make the point that the sales profession in general has

> Every successful salesperson started off as a diamond in the rough, looking for a manager or company to give them an opportunity to prove themselves.

become more of a team sport, rather than an accumulation of individualized efforts. And, the team concept changes the paradigm for small, medium-sized, and large corporations. While you still may want to hire strong individual performers, you also need to develop a corporate sales culture that rewards successful behavior, in order to duplicate these high-performance traits and qualities across the entire organization.

Experience is a Double-Edged Sword

One would assume that having sales experience is a wonderful asset. In many cases, that's true. As I said, an experienced salesperson can presumably hit the ground running and become more productive sooner. But experience is a double-edged sword, especially when your objective involves bringing together a team of people from a variety of different backgrounds. You still have to merge different levels of experience together with different selling styles and a variety of product expertise into a cohesive sales organization.

I am not a "human resources guy" by experience, and my purpose here is not to scrutinize corporate hiring practices or assess the validity of various personnel strategies. Instead, I simply want to comment first on the human aspects of building a high-performance sales team, and then on what sales managers should look for when evaluating potential talent.

Like anyone else, salespeople are creatures of habit. As such, they tend to gravitate toward whatever is most familiar. Just ask a salesperson, "Why are you doing such-and-such?" The response you will often get is, "That's the way I've always done it."

The approach a salesperson has always taken may, in fact, be the most effective way of dealing with a certain situation. But, what are the chances that all the salespersons in your company, who have come from different selling backgrounds and had different experiences, will gravitate to the same approach? The truth is, individual salespeople usually have their own way of doing things, which tends to leave the typical sales organization utilizing a mish-mash of different tactics and strategies that may or may not be congruent with the overall business objectives of the company.

The best case scenario for a sales team is to have everyone on the same page regarding the company's go-to-market strategy and the execution of that strategy. Of course, the goal isn't to turn salespeople into robotic clones, all toeing the company line. Different people do have different strengths that can be leveraged. Therefore, the goal when building high performance sales teams is to develop a corporate culture that supports the varying styles of individuals on the team, but also achieves a certain level of continuity that will maximize the effectiveness of the broader sales organization.

Evaluating the Person Beneath the Smile

It may surprise you to know that having an established track record for success doesn't actually top my list when evaluating potential sales talent. I made the point already that a one or two-page resumé can provide some indication of what occurred in someone's past, but it doesn't always accurately predict how well they will perform in the future. I could give you countless examples of people who looked great on paper, but then stepped into a sales role where there was no longer any "low-hanging fruit," or easy access to supporting resources, and quickly found themselves in over their heads. On the other hand, there are just as many up-and-coming salespeople who don't yet have the credentials on paper, but they have cut their teeth in a difficult business environment and are hungry for an opportunity and ready to succeed.

My goal, when interviewing potential candidates for a sales position, was to try and learn about the person beneath the smile in order to understand what motivates them to succeed. I also wanted to find out how interested they were in learning about me, and my objectives for growing the business. After all, when I am the interviewer, I am also the customer—in which case, a good candidate should try and understand my needs (first) in order to sell me on the value of the services they offer.

This brings us to a critical point. The most important criterion I looked for in a salesperson was whether they were question-based or statement-based. Our business culture over time has invested a lot of time and effort telling salespeople what to say, but overall, we have focused very little energy teaching salespeople how to leverage strategic questions. I talked about this extensively in my first book, *Secrets of Question Based Selling*.

I must reiterate that Question Based Selling is not just about asking questions. A "sale," by definition, is a mutual exchange of value, where both parties receive value on the way to achieving their respective objectives. The buyer wins because he acquires a valuable product or service that meets a specified need, and the seller also wins by securing the customer's confidence and then consummating a successful sales transaction. A successful sale should therefore be a win/win scenario for both parties.

In order to have a mutual exchange of value, however, one must first engage in a mutual exchange of information and ideas. In sales, a mutual exchange of ideas occurs when sellers invest the time to understand the buyer's needs, and prospective buyers invest the time to understand the value of a seller's proposed solutions. This mutual sharing of ideas and information is the result of question-based interaction, which is very different than people just coming together and blasting statements back and forth at each other. This is consistent with our focus in Question Based Selling, which is teaching salespeople how to engage more prospects in more productive conversation throughout the sales process.

If you want to get deeper, wider, and more strategic within your target accounts, your salespeople must be question-based. Sellers must have a fundamental curiosity about what is happening within their prospective customer accounts and why. This includes being interested in the goals and objectives of specific decision-makers, in addition to what may be driving their needs. They should also have the confidence as professionals to know that they will ask the right question at the appropriate time in the conversation.

I always wanted candidates who were interviewing for a sales position to ask me questions. And, I wanted them to ask before the end of the interview, when I said, "Do you have any questions?" I wanted to know that the wheels were turning up there between the ears. In fact, I wanted them to be wondering what I might be thinking, why I was asking certain questions, and what I was looking for in their responses. I wanted them to wonder about the significance of different knick-knacks on my bookshelves, and what I may have eaten for breakfast. I didn't necessarily want candidates to blurt out every question that popped into their heads, but you can tell fairly quickly if someone is genuinely inquisitive or just going through the motions of asking a few pre-scripted interview questions.

So, does this type of fundamental curiosity already exist in salespeople, or is it something that needs to be developed? Frankly, I think the answer is a combination of both. Some salespeople are inquisitive by nature. They ask good questions, communicate a sincere interest, and demonstrate good listening skills. For whatever reason, other people are not naturally inquisitive. Instead, they have more of a "show and tell" mentality. Hiring managers can and should get a sense of this very early on in the interview.

Nobody Likes the Spanish Inquisition

Salespeople are constantly being encouraged by their managers to ask lots of questions. But for many salespeople, this directive (to ask lots of questions) puts them at odds with how we have been conditioned over time. From a very early age, children are taught *not* to question authority. On many occasions, we were told by adults to be quiet when something sparked our curiosity, and we were quickly subdued if we made the mistake of asking too many questions. Remember how in school, you could only ask a question if you were willing to raise your hand, and run the risk of being labeled as either a slow learner or teacher's pet?

In sales, however, there is a great deal of information that needs to be acquired. Salespeople must ask questions to understand the customer's needs, as well as the underlying implications that are driving those needs. Sellers must also qualify prospects to ensure that the opportunity is indeed mutually beneficial. They must understand the timeframe for the project, how the decision

> It's more important for a salesperson to be a proficient asker of questions than to be a prolific deliverer of statements.

will be made, and who else will need to be involved. They must also understand what other alternatives the customer is investigating should they choose not to buy. But there is always a fine line between asking enough relevant questions to understand the customer's situation, and making customers feel as if they are being interrogated. As Monty Python used to say, "Nobody likes the Spanish Inquisition!"

It has always been my opinion that it is more important for a salesperson to be a proficient asker of questions—to gather valuable information about the client, than to be a prolific deliverer of statements—just to provide information about your product or service.

Lots of people can provide information about the most appropriate solution once enough is known about the customer. But, getting customers to open up and share volumes of information about their current situation and needs is rapidly becoming a lost art.

In addition to being directed to ask lots of questions, sellers have also been taught to be energetic and highly enthusiastic about the value of their products and service offerings. We talked extensively about this in each of my first two books. But, I have discovered that in sales, always positive is not always most productive. Therefore, sellers who put on the big smile and romp around the countryside espousing all the wonderful benefits of their product or service, actually limit their opportunity to communicate value. While some fraction of your customers are interested in the positive aspects of your product or service, others aren't necessarily motivated by "wonderful benefits." We know that prospective buyers are motivated differently. Consequently, there is often a huge difference in perceived value between providing wonderful benefits and solving important business problems.

Being always positive and conveying a false sense of enthusiasm doesn't fool potential customers anyway. Unless you work for Walt Disney, you probably don't sell happiness. If you answer the telephone at home during dinner, for example, and a super-charged, highly enthusiastic salesperson is on the other end of the line, does that make you more likely to take their call? I submit that the most valuable part of a sales conversation actually happens after you get past the initial pleasantries and everyone wipes the proverbial smiles off their faces. As a salesperson, I wanted to be perceived as genuine and earnest as opposed to highly enthusiastic, in order to foster a more candid and open discussion with prospective customers about what things were most important to them.

I am of the same mind when interviewing potential candidates during the hiring process. Everyone smiles big and acts nice during a job interview. As a sales manager, I was never interested in evaluating whether or not a candidate was friendly or congenial. Instead, I looked for three specific qualities that customers want from salespeople. I looked for candidates who conveyed high levels of competence, credibility, and value.

Prospective customers who perceive high levels of competence, credibility, and value from a salesperson are much more likely to engage in a mutually beneficial business conversation. On the other hand, when a salesperson is not perceived as being competent, credible, or valuable, their chances of making a sale are greatly reduced. And, none of these important qualities gets communicated by demonstrating a false sense of enthusiasm.

This brings us to another important point. To be successful in sales, potential customers must "want to" share valuable information about their current situation and needs with you, rather than the many other salespeople who are also posturing to earn their business. While that sounds easy, customers have learned how to fend salespeople off. Don't take it personally. It's not *you* they are fending off. It's the perception that you might end up wasting their time, just like the last forty-seven salespeople who called did. Like it or not, we (as sellers) inherit all the negative baggage from other salespeople who have called previously, relentlessly probing for needs with a customer who didn't want to be "probed." Perhaps we shouldn't be so surprised. People in general don't want to be probed. Go to your local hospital, ask around. People don't want to be probed! It's no wonder, then, that many of the older-school selling strategies have actually increased buyer resistance.

There Are No Magic Bullets

Earlier this year, I received a call from a well-known sales and marketing magazine. They wanted me to be the subject-matter expert for an article they were planning for an upcoming issue. "Sure," I said, "Happy to help." An interview was scheduled the following week where I would talk with two of the magazine's senior editors.

The conference call began, and we exchanged a few pleasantries before one of the senior editors opened the official part of the meeting. "Tom," he said, "we have skimmed through some of your materials, although to be honest, we haven't had time to read your books. To expedite

> Customers are more cautious and standoffish than ever before, and it is very difficult to sell to someone who is holding you at arm's length.

our purpose in this call, however, we were hoping you could start by sharing the four or five *magic* questions you teach salespeople to ask in Question Based Selling."

"Magic questions?" I wondered to myself. I was suddenly intrigued by where this conversation was headed. I responded by saying, "Guys, I don't have any 'magic' questions."

"Hmmm," they pondered, "Surely, you must have a few zingers?"

"Nope," I responded playfully, "the prospects and customers I am used to dealing with don't want to be *zinged*!"

The direction of the conversation opened the door for me to inquire, "Gentlemen, I have been a subscriber of your magazine for several years. And every month, an article appears somewhere in your publication that talks about the importance of asking questions. It's no surprise that a sales and marketing magazine would want to focus on questioning strategies. Everyone who has anything to do with sales stresses the importance of asking questions! But, I have to ask, why is it that I have never seen an article about what causes a customer to *want to* share valuable information?"

I made the point at the very start of this book—just because we want to ask lots of questions, doesn't mean prospects and customers will "want to" share valuable information with you. Customers today are more cautious and standoffish than ever before, and it is very difficult to sell to someone who is holding you at arm's length. Too often, people try and boil the success formula for selling down into something simple, like: you should treat customers the same way you would want to be treated. While the Golden Rule may be a good formula for daily living, just being kind and considerate does not guarantee you a more receptive audience within target accounts. In fact, prospective customers are so predisposed to responding negatively to sales calls that they sometimes turn off before they even know what it is that you are selling.

Remember that these same customers, who are holding you at arm's length, don't despise salespeople. As I said earlier, most customers depend on salespeople—for information, ideas, potential solutions, and to get a vision into the future. They just don't depend on every salesperson who comes calling. Therefore, since customers are going to be

> If a prospective customer doesn't "want to" share important information with you about their current needs or environment, then it doesn't matter what you ask.

sharing their thoughts, feelings, and concerns with somebody, that person might as well be you. Fortunately, that has a lot to do with your approach.

Let me make it easy for salespeople everywhere. If a prospective customer doesn't "want to" share important information with you about their current needs or environment, then it doesn't matter what you ask—you are not going to have a productive sales conversation. On the other hand, if someone does "want to" share valuable information with you, then you won't have to work so hard to facilitate a mutually beneficial exchange of ideas.

Now we must ask the question: what is it that causes prospects and customers to "want to" share important information about their current status, environment, and needs with you, rather than the many other salespeople who are competing for mindshare in your same accounts? Couple the answer to this question with the inquisitive nature that comes from being fundamentally curious, and you start to leverage a very powerful strategic combination that will help differentiate you and your sales team from the rest of the "noise" in the marketplace.

The Quickest Way to Commoditize Your Value

The last sales training course I attended before leaving the corporate world was one of the "leading" name-brand courses. I won't mention which one, because I don't want to pick on any one course.

If my memory serves, however, this particular course was broken down into a series of two-hour time blocks (called modules), spread over three days. On the morning of the first day, the instructor opened with some introductory comments about the course, and then started into the first module entitled, *Managing Internal Politics*.

He talked about the importance of taking a proactive approach with regard to managing the political landscape within key target accounts. Then he flipped through a dozen or so PowerPoint slides showing various organizational structures we might expect to encounter. An hour and forty-five minutes into the discussion, I raised my hand and said, "I agree with everything you just explained. Managing internal politics and being proactive within prospective customer accounts is definitely important! My question is: What should I be doing differently to gain a competitive advantage in the marketplace?"

The wide-eyed instructor looked at me for a moment and said, "That's an excellent question." He added, "My job, however, is to explain the various components of the sales process and why they are important. And, it is our belief that managing internal politics is very important." Then, he said, "Your job, as the professional salesperson, is to know how to deal with the different situations that could arise."

"Really?" I challenged. "You didn't have to tell me that managing internal politics was important. I knew that a long time ago! What we need is some guidance on how to be more effective than our competitors."

Apparently, I stumped the panel. So, he simply moved onto the next module—*Getting to Higher Levels Within your Target Accounts.* The same thing happened! His presentation began with a dissertation about why it was important to get to higher levels within our prospect accounts. My hand flew up into the air. "Does everyone in this room agree that it *is* important to get to the right levels within your prospect accounts?" Everyone nodded, and a few even chuckled. "Can you see where I'm going with this?" I asked the instructor, who at this point realized that he was in for a very long three days.

My guess is most of us could quickly agree on what is important when it comes to managing the strategic sale. What we (as salespeople) really want to know is how to increase our strategic effectiveness with regard to executing the sales process, in order to get better and more consistent results.

Seriously, what advice would you give someone who wanted to improve their sales effectiveness? Would you advise them to just put their nose to the grindstone and work harder? Would you enroll them in one of the popular name-brand sales training courses that has been around for twenty plus years? Just like watching a movie for the second or third time, the argument could be made that you can always take "something" away from a training class. But, the counterpoint is also valid, where sending experienced salespeople through a training course they already attended would have limited value in terms of expected increases in sales productivity. If a salesperson didn't buy into the material the first time around, why should we expect them to buy into it now?

Honestly, does anyone think it makes sense to try and teach salespeople what they already know? Furthermore, if the recognizability of a training program is its main selling point, does it make sense to train your salespeople to sound just like everyone else who has participated in these same courses for the last twenty years?

Again, sounding just like everyone else is the quickest way to commoditize your value proposition. Likewise, teaching salespeople what they already know is another miss. This is the opposite of what salespeople and companies are trying to accomplish. Most salespeople are trying to differentiate themselves and their products in order to gain a competitive advantage in their respective markets. That's good, because customers don't want to buy lackluster products from an average company, and certainly they don't want to take advice from an "average" salesperson.

Sales Effectiveness is a Different Story

What *do* you say to the inexperienced young salesperson who eagerly wants to improve his or her selling skills? Do you send them to a bookstore to buy the same sales books you read as a fledgling salesperson? Do you enroll them in the same courses you attended ten years ago and hope the messages still apply in today's business environment? Or, perhaps you should just pat them on the shoulder and send them back out into their territory to gain more hands-on experience? By the way, what should we tell the seasoned professional who has years of practical sales experience under their belts, but has grown frustrated now that the business climate has changed and they are no longer experiencing the level of success they once enjoyed?

We could just provide another round of training to reinforce the current sales process, making the existing spreadsheets larger and even more detailed. This approach has been the default for many years. But, as I have said many times, adding complexity to a company's sales process doesn't necessarily increase your sales organization's strategic effectiveness, or your top-line sales productivity.

What salespeople are thirsty for is a set of strategies and techniques that will give them a competitive advantage in their respective markets, and traditional sales training programs are not the answer. Don't take my word for it. Try a simple experiment. Mention to your salespeople that you are thinking of scheduling some additional sales training over the next few weeks. Note the reaction. "More sales training? Arrrgh! Do we have to?" You can literally watch mature adults dissolve into childish hissey-fits, as if you were asking them to sit through their big sister's dance recital.

> I bet some salespeople in your organization are faring better than others, even though they are all following the same basic sales process.

It's not that sales training and professional development are no longer necessary. They are. I don't know your specific situation, but I bet a quick glance at last year's performance statistics would reveal that some salespeople in your organization are faring better than others, even though they are all following the same basic sales process. That means some salespeople are more effective than others, and I would argue that something other than the sales process is making these top performers consistently more effective than those who are struggling.

If you see a need to revamp your sales process, fine. Choosing a sales process is relatively easy and straight forward. Once a need is identified, you simply contact the four or five leading process vendors, send out a request for proposal (RFP), and evaluate their responses to determine which process model would provide the best fit for your company. Raising the bar on your company's professional selling skills and strategic effectiveness is a different story, however.

When we talk about high-performance sales teams, we have to talk about skills enhancement—specifically, developing the softer skills. What do I mean by soft sales skills? Basically, I am talking about the intangible nature of sales activities like rapport building, establishing credibility, piquing the prospect's curiosity, leveraging relationships, and differentiating the value proposition of your product, service, and company. These elusive concepts are always thought to be an important part of the strategic sales process, yet they are very difficult to harness and then replicate across the broader sales organization.

Not only are sales skills hard to replicate, they are also difficult to measure. Softer skills like rapport building and the ability to differentiate yourself in a competitive market are impossible to quantify. How do you measure the strategic effectiveness of a salesperson? Clearly, there are some statistics that can give you an indication of whether there may be a problem. You can measure sales activity, for example, by tracking the number of face-to-face sales calls per week, which is certainly a leading indicator of your team's relative effectiveness. If you manage an inside sales organization, you might be able to measure talk-time. Monitoring someone's sales activity, however, is not the only factor that determines whether or not they are on the right track. After all, companies don't pay salespeople just to stay busy, and filling the day with customer appointments or talk-time doesn't always translate into transactable revenue.

The most common measuring stick managers use to evaluate sales effectiveness is results. Right or wrong, if a sales territory produces a large amount of revenue in any given year, that salesperson is presumed to be highly effective. Be careful with this kind of logic, however. As Shakespeare would have said had he been in sales management, "One good year 'doth' not an effective salesperson make!" All we have to do is look back to the 1990's when everyone sold lots of stuff. How many companies back then were patting themselves on the back for blowing away their sales numbers and claiming to have the "best" sales organizations in the world? A few months later, these same companies started laying salespeople off and putting others on performance plans because the economy turned and results dropped significantly.

Granted, sales results do tend to fall off when the economy gets soft, but selling skills didn't change overnight. A sales organization doesn't suddenly forget how to sell. It's more likely that the skills gaps that existed back in the 1990's were being masked by an irrationally exuberant economy. And, now that we have come back down to earth, managers are discovering how effective their salespeople are in times of normalcy—when the job of selling includes prospecting for new opportunities, justifying to customers that your proposal should take precedence over other projects, and beating out competitors who are hungrier than ever to win the business.

If sales effectiveness is the issue, then sending salespeople through another round of training to revisit each of the desired steps in the sales process is a miss. As we've said, most salespeople already know "what" they are trying to accomplish in the sales process. The more pressing question in today's business climate is, "how" can we accomplish these objectives more consistently? Salespeople want to know "how" to penetrate more new accounts, given that potential buyers are more cautious and standoffish than ever before. And, when they reach a customer's voice-mail, they want to know *how* to get more return calls. Once they make it past the gatekeeper, they want to know *how* to pique the prospect's interest, and uncover more needs. They also want to know *how* to differentiate their value proposition from competitive alternatives, *how* to deal with possible objections, and *how* to increase the prospect's sense of urgency for moving forward with a decision. Essentially, sellers want to have a clear picture of *how* to engage more prospects in more productive conversation about the customer's needs and their corresponding solutions.

> Lots of people talk about selling skills, strategic effectiveness, and execution, but talk is cheap.

Lots of people talk about selling skills, strategic effectiveness, and execution, but talk is cheap. I would be frustrated too if someone tried to convince me that adopting methods from fifteen or twenty years ago was going to give my sales team a differentiable advantage in today's business environment. Frankly, managers today don't want their salespeople to sound just like everyone else, and I would push back against anything that added complexity without adding value to the sales effort.

The goal is not to change for the sake of change. Sales managers are looking for tangible ways to ramp newer salespeople up more quickly, and at the same time, re-invigorate their experienced veterans with a renewed sense of confidence and differentiation that they once commanded. Is this even possible given the obstacles sales-people currently face? The answer is yes, but it may require a few adjustments in strategy, which is what we will talk about next.

< ACTION ITEMS >

1. Create a skills inventory for the sales organization. For each person on your sales team, identify five selling skills or qualities that contribute to their success, as well as five areas where there might be an opportunity to improve their sales effectiveness. This exercise is an excellent way to identify critical success factors and then duplicate individual strengths across the broader organization.

2. Include skills development in your continuing education plan. Ask the question: What are we doing in the next three months that will increase our effectiveness as individuals, and the effectiveness of our sales team? You should also ask: What am I doing to increase my sales skills this month? What about this week? What are you doing to give yourself a competitive advantage today?

3. For every opportunity posted on your sales forecast, make a list of three things you are doing differently than other salespeople who are competing for that same piece of business. Make it a point to engage in think-tank discussions with the rest of your team about what else you could be doing to create additional separation.

CHAPTER 3

Culturalizing the QBS Methodology

Sales managers are paid to bring in revenue. As a result, they spend a great deal of time tracking deals and forecasting sales results. On a quarterly, monthly, and sometimes weekly basis, they have a responsibility to review the individual opportunities of each salesperson on their team, and then roll this data up into a comprehensive sales forecast that can be used by the corporation to manage expected revenue for the business. Accordingly, sales managers are supposed to ask their team members tracking questions like, "How are we doing on the such-and-such account? What are the outstanding issues? Have we identified potential next steps in the sale? Who are the key players? Has a timeline been established for wrapping up the transaction? Is there any possibility of closing the business this month?"

Maintaining an accurate picture of anticipated revenue is important because it provides the larger organization with critical information that ultimately affects many other areas of the business. For example, projected sales revenue can impact decisions regarding budgeting, manufacturing, inventory, marketing, advertising, capital investments, headcount, and services. Consequently, managers should absolutely be tracking deals on the sales forecast.

It's an expected part of every sales manager's job. But, who is responsible for tracking sales skills—specifically, the softer skills like your sales team's ability to secure mindshare in target accounts by piquing the decision-maker's interest, or their ability to establish credibility in order to differentiate themselves and your company in the marketplace? At the end of the day, someone needs to have responsibility for creating a corporate culture that will increase productivity across the organization and maximize the company's overall return on invested sales effort.

In the old days, in-house education departments were tasked with the job of building a cohesive internal sales culture. As I mentioned, large corporations like IBM, Xerox, Burroughs, and Honeywell all invested heavily in building long-term sales insertion programs that were designed to shepherd a newly hired salesperson through their first twelve to eighteen months on the job. The goal of these programs was broader than just teaching salespeople how to sell. IBM's in-house training school, for example, wasn't just teaching people about IBM's technology solutions; they were tasked with teaching newly hired salespeople how to become an "IBMer." The goal at IBM (and at other companies that developed their own in-house sales insertion programs) was to create an internal sales culture that maximized production and also propagated the company's commitment to delivering the highest levels of excellence and performance.

When business conditions changed in the late 1990's, and the economy took a turn for the worse, corporate executives suddenly faced a series of economic trade-offs, one of which involved the decision of whether to continue cultivating sales expertise in-house or bring experienced sellers in from the outside. These decisions, coupled with expense control measures and pressures to reduce headcount, have in many cases, eliminated the resources needed to sustain the development of this type of homogeneous sales culture internally.

Of course, without the benefit of a standardized internal sales culture, companies are now finding themselves at the other end of the spectrum, managing a new era of cultural randomness that has resulted from bringing together sales professionals with a wide range of different backgrounds and experience.

Different salespeople all have their own unique personalities and personal styles. As such, it's not surprising that individual sellers will gravitate toward whatever their experiences have taught them in the past. While one could argue that companies can benefit from this type of diversity, bringing disparate groups of salespeople together can also create some unique challenges in terms of building a cohesive sales team.

> The best-case scenario for maximizing your return on invested sales effort is to make sure everyone on the sales team is on the same page relative to managing the strategic sale.

In my view, the best-case scenario for maximizing your return on invested sales effort is to make sure everyone on the sales team is on the same page relative to managing the strategic sale. Trying to get salespeople to all move in the same direction is a little like herding cats, however. In addition to managing the human elements of individuality and personal preference, managers also have to account for the fact that every customer opportunity is different, and the business climate overall remains in a constant state of flux. Establishing a high standard for performance, execution, and professional consistency throughout the sales organization is desirable nonetheless.

There is no magic in the formula for being a successful salesperson. The key to consistently performing at the highest levels of excellence in sales is having a repeatable system—a methodology that can be introduced, implemented, and then culturalized across the entire sales organization as the defacto standard, whether you are managing existing customer accounts or approaching new prospect opportunities.

Notice I use the word "culturalize" as a verb. Human nature causes people to gravitate naturally to wherever they are most comfortable. And in most cases, people are most comfortable with whatever they find most familiar. Different salespeople tend to have different comfort zones, so they will likely approach the sales process in different ways. Therefore, if you want to culturalize a methodology across the sales organization, either to change the way salespeople manage their geographic territories or how they approach specific customer situations, then you must alter their comfort zones. This means causing salespeople to gravitate toward the desired behavior, rather than whatever happens to be most familiar or comfortable.

Altering a salesperson's comfort zone requires managers to start thinking beyond just tracking deals on the forecast. It requires a renewed focus on strategic positioning and skills development, which includes introducing salespeople to a new

> Altering a salesperson's comfort zone requires a renewed focus on strategic positioning and skills development.

wave of business logic and sales philosophy that will ultimately give them a competitive advantage in their respective markets.

Quantitative vs. Qualitative

If developing and tracking sales effectiveness is so important, how do you assess whether or not a salesperson is truly effective? It's a valid question, and one that I am often asked as the subject matter expert. In many cases, I get the feeling that the asker is looking for an easy answer, some simple way to measure the current competencies of their salespeople and direct them on how to enhance professional selling skills where needed. The good news is, sales effectiveness is quantifiable, but not necessarily with an empirical formula.

As I mentioned in the last chapter, the most common means of assessing sales effectiveness is to look at results. If someone wins a sale or achieves their sales quota for the year, they are assumed to be an effective salesperson. But results can be misleading. Just because a salesperson experienced success when economic conditions were favorable, doesn't necessarily assure their survival when economic conditions change and things get tough.

Even when tracking specific deals, results can be misleading. Say someone closes a $100,000 deal, for example. Is that good? Your initial reaction might be, "Of course, that's good." Be careful though, because if a more strategic approach could have expanded that same opportunity into a $250,000 deal, then only getting $100K may not be so "good." On the other hand, if an innovative salesperson leveraged his or her skills to turn an initial $50,000 opportunity into that $100K order, then it's time to ring the bell!

Sometimes companies and managers measure component parts of the sales process as indicators of a salesperson's effectiveness. For instance, corporate call centers often have automated telephone systems that measure the number of dials made and the amount of talk-time for inside sales teams. Inside salespeople are then measured against a minimum number of dials per day, or a minimum talk-time requirement. While I do agree these measurements can provide useful statistics, this type of quantitative data doesn't always tell the whole story. If someone spends large amounts of time chit-chatting with their most amiable customers, or they make dozens of calls that don't ever get past the introductory blurb, their call statistics might be favorable, but one wouldn't necessarily label them an effective salesperson.

A salesperson out in the field might be measured on making a certain number of required calls per week—the logic being that a busy salesperson is likely to be more productive. Busyness alone does not define someone's ability to fill the forecast with qualified prospect opportunities, however.

> One of the reasons it is so difficult to duplicate the success of top performing salespeople is because the softer skills cannot be empirically measured.

One of the reasons it is so difficult to duplicate the success of top performing salespeople is because the softer skills cannot be empirically measured. We have always heard that sales is a numbers game. If you want to make more money, simply make more sales calls. The logic seems simple. With a success rate of 10%, for example, making twice as many calls would double your results. I can't argue with the math. But what about the quality of these calls? What if it were possible to raise the bar in terms of your team's effectiveness such that salespeople succeeded in twenty percent of their calls, or thirty percent?

Essentially, there are two ways to increase sales results. One is to simply work harder. If you are lying around smoking cigars instead of making sales calls, then get to work! But I know this is not the case with most salespeople, especially in today's business climate. Most salespeople are already working hard. Therefore, asking people to "work harder" has very little upside in terms of raising sales productivity. The other way to increase sales results is by working smarter. But, I hate clichés. Rather than just saying work smarter, let's be specific. To me, working smarter means increasing your sales effectiveness. It means increasing the quality of your sales conversations to make the sales funnel wider, so a greater percentage of opportunities that come into the sales process (i.e. the top of the funnel), flow through and come out the bottom as forecastable and closeable revenue transactions.

What's Important to Your Customers?

An effective salesperson is someone who knows how to convey value to customers. The tendency has always been to believe a salesperson's greatest opportunity to convey value lies in their ability to provide valuable information, usually in the form of communicating good news about their respective product or service. The problem is, whatever a salesperson might say about their product or service is completely irrelevant unless it is being communicated against the backdrop of what's important to the customer. Consequently, I would argue that a salesperson's primary role is to understand the customer's needs, in order to then be in a position to offer more valuable solutions. With this in mind, it is imperative to make a distinction between the potential value provided by your product or service, and what is truly important to your customers.

By reviewing your company's website or product brochures, a prospective buyer can probably gain some insightful information about the value of your offerings. That's good, because your marketing materials should paint a picture of the solutions you bring to the table. But, I have discovered that painting a picture of the value your company offers doesn't necessarily help a salesperson understand what's important to their customers. This creates an interesting paradox for salespeople. How can you be perceived as a valuable resource in the eyes of prospective customers if you don't have a clear picture of what things are most important to them?

Of course, the argument could be made that sellers are not clairvoyant. True. It is impossible to know exactly what's going on in a customer's head until you actually engage in a dialogue with them. But, couldn't we leverage our depth of experience to hypothesize in advance about what *might* be important to your next customer?

In my second book, *It Only Takes 1% to Have a Competitive Edge in Sales*, I introduced a strategic positioning model called PAS, which talks about about the importance of bonding with customers on what's most important to them, as opposed to what's important to us (as sellers). So, let me reinforce the point by asking a very specific question. What would you say is more important to prospective customers when you first engage—their problems or your solutions?

Most analytical thinkers would agree that customers are much more interested in their own needs than they are in hearing a salesperson's pitch. Therefore, the logical starting point when initiating a sales conversation is to focus on uncovering the customer's needs, right? After all, if a customer doesn't have a need, then you cannot offer any value. We will talk more about this concept of PAS positioning later. For now, I just want to make the observation that needs development is the traditional starting point for most sales training programs.

We are all in agreement that a salesperson has to uncover needs in order to then provide valuable solutions. Starting with needs development poses a bit of a problem, however. Customers are definitely more focused on their own problems, issues, and concerns. But that doesn't necessarily mean they are willing to share their thoughts, feelings, and concerns with every salesperson who comes calling. This was one of the misconceptions we discussed earlier, where just because a seller wants to ask probative questions (to uncover needs), doesn't necessarily mean prospective buyers will choose to share information with them. And, even when a salesperson succeeds in getting someone to open up, prospective customers usually share only some fraction of their needs, which limits your opportunity to provide value.

Here's another problem. How do you uncover needs if the customer doesn't know what they need? Is it possible that what the customer really needs is someone to help define their requirements?

In my view, it's a big mistake to assume customers already know what they need. Some do. Other customers think they know, but don't. Here's an example when I was the customer who didn't necessarily know what he needed. Several months ago, I headed off to the local audio outlet to purchase a big screen television. An energetic young salesperson spotted me from across the room and scurried over. He introduced himself and said, "How can I help?"

"I'm here to buy a big screen TV," I said.

"Do you know what kind you want?" he asked.

"Yes," I said confidently. "I want a big one!"

I thought I knew exactly what I wanted—a big screen television. What I really needed was someone to help me understand all the different technical elements and decision factors that need to be considered when purchasing a home theater system. The truth is, when I first walked in the store, I didn't know anything about HDTV, digital reality, S-video, monster cables, RF jacks, comb filters, convergence, plasma screens, or the many other features which should be considered when making this kind of decision.

What about the corporate customer who calls a technology vendor about upgrading their current data base onto its own separate server? Does that customer know what they need? It's possible that they know exactly what they need—a data base server. But, have they considered all the implications of moving a large data base? Have they considered the inter-operability issues, since hardware compatibility is often dependent on software? Are they in need of professional services to complete the implementation?

For that matter, there are a significant number of other questions a salesperson might ask to fully understand the customer's needs. Questions like: How large is your existing data base? Where does your data currently reside? How many users does your IT department support? In how many locations? Is your data mirrored across multiple sites? What other server options are you considering? What is your timeframe for making a decision?

The same thing could happen if a prospective client called an insurance broker and said, "I want to investigate health insurance options." What is it that they need? They need health insurance, of course. But what type of health insurance? That's going to depend on the answers to some specific questions. Is the person married or single? Do they have children? Where are they currently employed? Do they currently have coverage under another health insurance policy? If so, which one?

If the health insurance prospect was a corporation, you might want to ask: How many employees in your company? Who is your current provider? Where is corporate headquarters? Do you have multiple office locations? In how many states? And, the list goes on. There are dozens of pertinent questions to be asked.

Our objective in asking these questions is not just to "probe" for information. Rather, we are trying to understand the customer's specific situation in order to make a recommendation that best satisfies their needs. Think about it this way: How can you

> How can you give valuable advice if you don't specifically know what the customer is trying to accomplish?

give valuable advice if you don't specifically know what the customer is trying to accomplish? And, if you don't bother to ask detailed questions, customers won't necessarily share their specific needs.

For these reasons, I tell audiences all over the world that a salesperson's job is no longer to *uncover* needs. I know that statement goes against the grain for traditional thinkers who have been taught and conditioned for years that one of their primary functions as a sales-person is to "uncover" needs. Yes, I understand. But a salesperson's job is more than just extracting information from potential buyers, in the hopes that some fraction of them will have an existing need for your product or service. The real opportunity to be a valuable resource is to help prospective customers think through the needs development process, which goes way beyond just probing for infor-mation that customers already have.

In that vein, sellers must do their homework in advance, not just to know something about the account before calling, but also to arm themselves with an understanding about what prospective customers "might" truly need before picking up the telephone and making sales calls. In that understanding lies one of the secrets to top performance, which starts with putting yourself in a position to actually be a valuable resource, not just another sales caller.

What Concerns Your Customers Most

If a salesperson wants to be perceived as a valuable resource, then they need to have a fundamental understanding of the challenges, issues, and concerns that potential customers in their respective ter-ritories might be facing. Notice I am intentionally qualifying my comments by referring to needs that customers "might" have. Unless you are psychic, you cannot know a customer's specific situ-ation (or needs) before you engage them in an actual dialogue. But, if you want to be perceived by customers as a valuable resource, you must equip yourself in advance with a fundamental knowledge of what those customers' needs might be.

To explain, let me reintroduce the metaphor I used in Chapter 29 of my second book. That chapter was called, *Re-Engineering the*

Elevator Pitch. Basically, I concocted a fictitious scenario where we supposed you and I suddenly changed careers and took sales positions with a company that manufactured and sold water pumps. We also supposed that our target market was property owners who might have to deal with flooding in the basement of their homes when pipes burst in the winter, or if there was an excessive spring-time thaw, or during the summer rainy season.

Continuing this hypothetical scenario, suppose you and I were asked to follow up on a lead where a potential customer was experiencing a flooding problem. Tomorrow, we planned to make a joint call on the homeowner. But, before we actually left to go on the sales call, let's assume we spent a few minutes strategizing in advance.

I use this metaphor during "live" QBS Methodology Training programs because it enables sales audiences to think outside the box of their normal routines. In fact, not having to worry about your specific product offerings frees you up to start focusing on how you can use strategy and technique to differentiate yourself in an increasingly competitive business environment.

The first question in our strategy session should be, "What problem does this homeowner have?"

That's an easy one! The customer has a flooded basement. For some reason, water has come into an area where it should not be!

We think we have successfully identified the problem, but guess what? Water in the basement is *not* the primary catalyst that causes homeowners to purchase water pumps! Did you get that? Most homeowners will *not* be compelled to make a purchase decision just because they have a flooded basement. Instead, it's the implications of having a basement full of water that creates a sense of urgency and motivates prospective customers to take action. These underlying implications are what ultimately drives the customer's need, and they also represent a salesperson's true opportunity to provide value. So, we had better not stop our strategy session here, by assuming that the problem we are trying to solve is a flooded basement.

To strategize further, let's ask ourselves the next question. "Why might water in the basement be a problem for this homeowner?"

Again, there is no way to know exactly what a customer's specific buying motivations are until you actually talk with them. But, couldn't we hypothesize in advance? Couldn't we arm ourselves with a mental list of possible implications that could be important to a homeowner?

For example, a homeowner might be concerned about potential odor or mildew issues that could result from standing water. They might also be concerned about the cost of repairs or possible structural damage to the foundation of the home. They may also be concerned about any number of other implications like their insurance coverage, damage to other systems in the house (i.e. furnace, air conditioner, electrical), possibly having to replace furniture, potential health risks, safety hazards, or not being able to use the space. That's a quick list of ten potential implications, off the top of my head.

Here's my question to you. How many reasons do you want customers to have to buy from you? One or two? In this scenario, I would want homeowners to have many reasons to buy from me, knowing that multiple implications will translate into a greater sense of urgency for making a decision. Well, then, someone needs to bring these other implications into the conversation.

Ironically, the default for most salespeople is to assume that the customer's specific hot buttons will be uncovered as a natural by-product of the needs development conversation. This is a bad assumption, however, because most customers will only share some portion of the implications driving the broader need. For example, during the sales call, you might say, "Mr. Homeowner, besides the obvious objective of getting the water out of your basement, what specifically are you most concerned about?"

Asking, "Besides the obvious…," is a wonderful technique that eliminates your risk of sounding too rhetorical. The last thing you want is to ask something like, ""Mr. Customer, is value important to you?" As my five-year-old daughter would say, "Duh!" Of course value is important to a customer! Why bother even asking that? What we really want to know is *why* the broader issue is important. This requires us to take the needs development conversation to the next level of depth—to identify potential implications.

Therefore, I would ask, "Mr. Customer, besides the obvious, getting the water out of your basement, what are you most concerned about?" Remember, it's the underlying implications of a problem that ultimately drive the customer's need and create a sense of urgency for taking action.

Please note that most customers will *not* rattle off all of the different implications that you have assimilated on your mental list. Human nature is fairly predictable; so you can expect customers to bring up some subset of the larger list—generally naming one, two, or three implications.

In the case of the water pump analogy, the homeowner might respond by saying, "I am concerned about two things, mildew and structural damage to the foundation."

Bingo! Now, we're getting somewhere. The homeowner isn't just worried about flooding, he's concerned that water in the basement will lead to other implications, like creating a mildew problem or long-term structural damage to the foundation of the home.

Should we assume these are the only two things that are important to the customer? A lot of salespeople do make this assumption.

I guess they figure, "we asked the customer about the implications of flooding, and they named two: mildew and structural damage. Therefore, mildew and structural damage must be what's driving the customer's need."

Now, let me pose the same question again. As a salesperson, how many reasons do you want customers to have to buy from you? Personally, I want prospective customers to have lots of reasons to move forward with a favorable decision. Therefore, my goal in the discovery process is to expand the needs development conversation into a broader list of potential implications, thus creating more opportunities for me to provide value.

Some sellers continue to drill down, asking, "What else (is important)? What else? What else? What else?" Be careful, because there is a fine line between facilitating a mutually beneficial needs development conversation, and making customers feel they are being interrogated.

> My goal is to expand the needs development conversation into a broader list of implications, thus creating more opportunities for me to provide value.

Again, the goal in the needs development process is not to "uncover" needs. If you want to be perceived as a valuable resource, then one of your greatest opportunities to provide value is to actually help *define* the customer's needs. After all, you're the expert on water pumps (or data base servers, or health insurance).

If you arm yourself in advance with a repository of *all* of the different issues and implications that might be important to prospective customers, that empowers you to be proactive in helping to identify their needs. In the case of the homeowner with a flooded basement, preparing a mental list of ten implications that would be relevant to most homeowners makes it easy to expand the needs development conversation by raising other implications like, "Mr.

Customer, do we need to be concerned about the potential health risks brought on by standing water? What about safety—do you have any children or small pets? Where is the water in relation to your furnace or electrical box? Does your homeowner's insurance policy cover water damage?"

A few well-placed implication questions give sellers an opportunity to make the problem "bigger" by raising awareness that there may be multiple reasons to take action. Broadening the conversation to include multiple implications essentially expands your opportunity to provide value. Expanding the scope of the problem also increases the prospect's sense of urgency by giving them multiple reasons to move forward with a purchase decision.

> Expanding the scope of the problem increases the prospect's sense of urgency by giving them multiple reasons to move forward with a purchase.

Once you understand that the underlying implications of a problem or issue are ultimately what drives the customer's need, then it is incumbent on you (as a sales professional) to "arm" yourself in advance with a knowledge base of potential issues and implications. This strategic approach allows you to facilitate better conversations about what issues are most important to your customers, and why those issues might be important.

Building a Repository of Business Issues

If you want customers to have a sense of urgency for moving forward with a favorable decision, then you will want them to have a number of reasons to buy from you, rather than just one or two. Sellers actually have a responsibility, as subject matter experts, to expand the conversation by raising other possible implications.

Some of these other implications that could come from having a flooded basement might include: odor problems, cost, safety risks, potential heath hazards, damage to personal property, recurrence, inconvenience, cleaning up the mess, or not being able to use the space. Taking your sales conversations to the next level of detail is, in fact, your opportunity to be seen as a consultative resource, not just another sales caller. Your chances of making a sale are also significantly increased when customers have multiple reasons to buy from you. Additionally, the more implications that get raised during your needs development conversations, the more opportunities you have to provide value with your product or service.

This strategy of getting deeper, wider, and more strategic in your sales conversations isn't limited to selling water pumps, however. Whatever you sell, be it technology, pharmaceuticals, financial services, or manufactured goods, the same logic applies. The water pump analogy is just a metaphor that teaches sales-

> Woody Allen once said, "Ninety percent of being successful in life is just showing up." That may be true. But in my view, the other ten percent determines whether or not you win the sale.

people to think strategically about needs development, as opposed to being locked into traditional probing strategies. So, let's talk more specifically about what might be most important to *your* customers.

Every salesperson wants to be perceived (by their customers) as a consultative resource, as opposed to just another pesky salesperson. What action steps are required to accomplish this goal? Woody Allen once said, "Ninety percent of being successful in life is just showing up." That may be true. But in my view, the other ten percent determine whether or not you win the sale.

The key to positioning yourself as a consultative resource starts with making a physical list of what's important to your customers and why. It goes back to the concept of "arming" yourself in advance. This is one of the most important action items students take away from our "live" QBS training programs.

Basically, you make a physical list of what things might be important to target customers (i.e. their business issues) and why those issues might be important (i.e. implications that are specific to their business or industry). Essentially, you end up creating a repository of topics and sub-topics that can and should be further explored in your needs development conversations.

There's no need to make this exercise overly complex. Just take out a piece of paper, think about your customers, and make a list of what business issues and implications might be most important to them. Here are a few examples.

FINANCIAL SERVICES	TECHNOLOGY SALES	PHARMACEUTICAL SALES
Return on Investment	Availability	Clinical Efficacy
Safety of Principal	Performance	Trials/Studies
Growth of Capital	Scalability	Exclusions
Risk/Diversification	Cost Effectiveness	Possible Side Effects
Monthly Reporting	Disaster Recovery	Contra Indicators
Market Updates	Manageability	Precaution Warnings
Estate Planning	Ease of Use	Drug Interactions
Cash/Liquidity	Interoperability	Multiple Indicators
Trust in Advisor	Customer Satisfaction	Cost Effectiveness
Access to Information	Upgradeability	Alternative Generics
Hedge Against Inflation	Maintenance	Formulary
Retirement Planning	Support/Services	Paperwork Required
Year-End Reporting	Time to Market	Managed Care
Income Stream	Company Viability	Ease of Use
Cost of Services	Industry Leadership	Samples Available
Confidentiality	Data Integrity	Continuous Learning
Prompt Service	Education/Training	Company Image
Integrity of Company	Implementation	Rep. Availability
Consistent Performance	Remote Locations	Patient Satisfaction

If you sell financial services, matters like retirement planning, confidentiality, and regular financial updates regarding market conditions might be key issues for some clients. Other clients might be more interested in diversification, growth of capital, or hedging against inflation. How can you know in advance what business issues are most important to the next customer? You can't. That's not the objective. The goal is to be prepared to facilitate a discussion regarding any of the business issues on the broader list. Then you can easily gravitate toward those issues that are most important as the conversation unfolds. Whether the conversation goes in the direction of retirement planning, financial updates, diversification, growth of capital, or hedging against inflation, it is both prudent and logical for a professional salesperson in the financial services industry to be ready to discuss any of these topics.

Similarly, if you sell technology, customers will have a variety of different business issues. In the corporate arena, for example, different people within a targeted prospect account often have different agendas for a decision, and therefore, they have different hot buttons and concerns. As a result, some people in an account could be interested in issues like availability, disaster recovery, or data integrity, while other people in the same account are more interested in security, upgradeability, and managing remote locations. Again, wouldn't it be prudent for a technology salesperson to be able to facilitate a robust discussion on any or all of these issues?

This brings us to an important point. It is vital for sellers in today's competitive selling environment to be keenly aware of all the potential business issues their prospects and customers could possibly be facing. After all, if you don't have a clear understanding of what's important to your customers, how can you possibly be perceived by them as a consultative resource, not to mention someone who can offer valuable advice or differentiated solutions?

It only makes sense that sellers should have an appreciation for the different business issues that "might be" important to prospective customers in their respective markets. Note that I am specifically talking about having an awareness of what's important to customers, not what customers should like about your product or service. This is an important distinction. We'll talk about the value of your products and services later. For now, customers have problems, issues, and concerns, whether your company exists or not! If you want to differentiate yourself as a valuable resource, then you must have a clear understanding of what things matter most to prospective customers long before the features or benefits of your products and services ever come up in the conversation.

Ironically, this is where traditional sales approaches break down. Old-schoolers tend to fixate on arming themselves with product knowledge, figuring the more a salesperson knows about their product, the easier it will be to make a sale. They also rely on probative questions to uncover needs—incorrectly assuming that customers already know what they need. Again, how do you uncover needs if a customer hasn't yet defined their requirements? Likewise, how can you facilitate a robust needs development conversation unless you have a fundamental understanding of what business issues might be important to your customers, and why?

What Problem Do You Solve?

Zones, Inc., is one of the world's leading providers of technology solutions, headquartered in Seattle, Washington. Zones' Chief Operating Officer, Scott Koerner, recently brought me in to train their entire tele-sales organization on the QBS Methodology.

One of the ongoing challenges Zones' sales organization faces is keeping up to date with regard to product knowledge. As a large technology reseller, Zones represents dozens, if not hundreds, of different vendors offering computer hardware, printers, wireless and telephony solutions, software, network connectivity, computer accessories, and more. In fact, the list goes on to include thousands of different products. As you might imagine, it would be impossible for a salesperson in this environment to be fully versed on all of the different products and services Zones offers.

To help with this challenge, Zones routinely invites vendor representatives to come to their main offices and deliver product presentations, as a way to educate the sales force. In fact, several times a week at Zones' headquarters, different vendors provide a free lunch or host a happy-hour event, as a strategy for securing mind-share from the sales team. Of course, having a captive audience over lunch enables vendors to present a few dozen PowerPoint slides that highlight their respective solutions.

Everyone agrees that product information is important, but the complaint I kept hearing from Zones' salespeople was that these vendor presentations all sound so similar. Once a Zones salesperson has attended a few pizza-and-beer sessions, the value propositions from different vendors all seem to run together, in which case the sales team is no better off than before.

"Here's what I would do," I told Zones' salespeople in my training class. The next time a vendor starts an educational presentation on the value of their product or service, I would raise my hand and say, "I very much want to hear about all the wonderful things your solution does, but first I need you to help me understand what problem your product solves?"

You see, I believe that all the product information in the world won't help a salesperson to be more effective if they don't have a fundamental understanding of the problems or issues they are trying to solve.

I found out later that my advice to the group created somewhat of a new sport at Zones. Salespeople would wait for vendors to jump into their product presentations, and then fifty hands would shoot up, all wanting to know what problem the vendor's product was attempting to solve.

Vendors were often caught off guard by these requests. Vendor representatives were so used to talking about their products, that many were unprepared to intelligently discuss the problem they were actually trying to solve. Sometimes, the vendor rep would counter by saying, "Let me give you a brief overview of what we do, and then we can talk about the customer's problem." With all due respect to vendors, the answer should be, "No." Once again, if a salesperson doesn't have a clear understanding of what problems they are actually trying to solve, then whatever a vendor might tell them about features, benefits, or product functionality is essentially worthless.

Frankly, it would be impossible for a salesperson on the floor at Zones, Inc. to have comprehensive knowledge about all of the products and services being offered. But it is absolutely possible for these same salespeople to gain an understanding of what's important to their customers, in order to then bring the appropriate resources and solutions to bear.

So, here's the action item with regard to developing a more effective knowledge base for your sales organization. First, I encourage you to challenge your entire sales team to be able to name fifteen to twenty business issues off the top of their heads, representing those things that "might" be important to prospective customers. Start by asking each of the members on your team to create their own physical list of potential business issues. Be sure to document the lists on paper. Then, at your next sales meeting, combine lists. It's a wonderful opportunity for the sales team to proactively arm themselves with a repository of business issues that can then be used to fuel their sales conversations. I would recommend against designating someone to create a master list and then forward it to everyone on your team, however. Just like in school, having a copy of someone else's work doesn't necessarily make you more effective.

Also, resist the temptation to prioritize this list of business issues. Granted, it is natural to think, "These two or three issues are probably most important to customers, so let's just focus on these." Certain issues may have a greater impact or come up more frequently, that's true. But, you still want to empower yourself and your sales team with the ability to expand opportunities by raising implications that could provide additional momentum toward a purchase. In fact, be sure to make yours a "living" list, where new business issues can be added as they come up. Again, if the goal is to culturalize an expanded knowledge base throughout the sales organization, you must start with a fundamental understanding of what's important to your customers, so you can facilitate a more productive conversation about how you can provide value.

And why is that important?

Once you create a physical repository that identifies "what" is important to potential customers, there is another level of detail to explore in your needs development conversations. To engage more prospects in more in-depth conversations about their needs and your corresponding value, you must condition your sales team to think beyond the general business issues, and focus more on the specific implications that are actually driving the need.

If we refer back to our water pump analogy, the issue home-owners were facing was water in their basements. But, I made the point that "flooding" is generally not what causes prospective buyers to move forward with a purchase decision to buy a pump. Instead, it's the implications of flooding that creates a sense of urgency to resolve the issue. These implications could include concerns about cost, structural damage, odor or mildew, insurance coverage, damage to the furnace or other systems in the house, damage to personal property, potential health hazards, safety risks, and as we said, not being able to use the space.

This same logic can be applied to any sale. If you sell financial services, a business issue like "return on investment" has a whole list of underlying implications ranging from broader market index comparisons, to maximizing wealth, diversification, liquidity, risk, dividends, retirement planning, income supplementation, and tax planning.

If you sell technology, a popular issue like security also has many implications. Basically, *why* might the issue of security be important to customers? Security is important because customers might want to protect intellectual property, confidentiality, customer privacy, data integrity, or protect against downtime, lost information, viruses, or diverting valuable resources from other important projects.

After arming yourself with an understanding of what's important (i.e. business issues), you can expand your opportunity to provide value by arming yourself with a more detailed understanding of "why" those business issues are important. The easiest way to accomplish this is to think of a potential business issue, and ask yourself, "Why might this issue be important to a customer?" Then push yourself by asking, "Why else?"

Identifying the broader list of business issues and their corresponding implications enables salespeople and sales organizations to dramatically expand the size and scope of their value propositions. As I have said many times before, if you want customers to have a sense of urgency for moving forward with a purchase decision, then you need to give them many reasons to buy from you. Therefore, it is incumbent on you, as the valuable resource, to raise issues and underlying implications that may ultimately be driving

> Identifying the broader list of business issues and their corresponding implications enables salespeople and sales organizations to dramatically expand the size and scope of their value propositions.

the customer's need. What's the alternative? If you aren't going to bring this level of detail to your sales conversations, you leave the door wide open for competitors to come in and define the customer's requirements in a way that favors their solutions.

Management Must Play a Leading Role

One approach to becoming more strategic as a sales organization is to assume that individual salespeople will be motivated enough to arm themselves (in advance) with a repository of business issues and implications. Another approach would be for managers to take a leadership role, in order to culturalize this thinking throughout the broader sales organization.

In terms of managers being leaders, one of the secrets to raising the effectiveness of your sales team is to be specific in your conversations with sales reps when strategizing about specific accounts. Because of the ratio of sales reps to managers, strategy conversations about specific accounts tend to be somewhat abbreviated. When a sales manager asks, "What are the key issues at such-and-such account?" it's not unusual for a salesperson to comment on the two or three key issues the customer mentioned in their last sales call. For example, a salesperson might say, "The customer's key issues are availability of information, upgradeability, and cost." That's often as deep as the conversation gets.

Sales managers who practice what they preach must delve deeper into the conversation during these strategy sessions. "Why are these issues important to your customer?" This one simple question will tell you a great deal about how much your rep really knows about their accounts. Don't settle for a cursory response. Reps ought to be able to explain why "availability of information" is important to this customer, and the answer should contain multiple implications. If it doesn't, you simply ask, "Why else is availability important to this customer?" Again, how many reasons do you want customers to have to buy from your salespeople? If you want more versus less, then it's your responsibility as a mentor to help reps start thinking deeper, wider, and more strategic within their prospect opportunities. That's what top performers do!

By the way, knowing that customers often have more than just two or three concerns, I encourage sales managers to ask, "What other issues might be important to your customer?"

I can see salespeople reading this section and cringing at the thought of sales managers asking even more questions about their accounts. Sorry, guys! The tactical significance of these questions is buried in their subtlety. You see, if a salesperson knows their manager is going to probe into "why" specific issues are important, that salesperson has a built-in incentive to take the conversation deeper when talking with prospective customers. What's the incentive? Looking good in front of the boss! Likewise, managers, when sales people know that you are going to ask, "What else is important to this decision maker?", they will naturally start to expand their sales conversations with customers. Some people call it behavioral conditioning. I call it culturalizing the methodology.

Ultimately, you want your salespeople to ask themselves these questions. During a sales call, it is extremely strategic for sellers to constantly be thinking, "I wonder why such-and-such is important?" That leads to, "I wonder what else might be important to this customer?" How can you teach salespeople to think like this? It's not something that gets learned in a classroom, rather this mindset is a conditioned behavior that needs to be instilled and supported as part of the daily culture of your sales organization.

The bottom line is this: if you want salespeople to identify more opportunities, then they must have a basic understanding of the business issues customers face, and the underlying implications that are ultimately driving those needs. Too often, we

> If your salespeople don't proactively participate in the needs development process, your competitors will.

associate needs development with the act of probing for information, expecting customers to raise all of the salient points in the conversation. But, guess what? They won't. Most customers will only offer some fraction of what's really important to them, in which case, if your salespeople don't proactively participate in the needs development process, your competitors will.

< ACTION ITEMS >

1. Challenge your sales team to build a repository of business issues and implications, identifying "what" issues are most important to prospective customers, and "why?" Start by asking each of the

individuals on your team to create their own list. Do not worry about duplication of effort. The goal is to create a thought process, not just a physical document. Later, you can combine their efforts into a larger repository and share the wealth. Building this repository is one of the most important action item students take away from QBS training.

2. If you are a salesperson, you should constantly be asking yourself, "Why is that important?" Sales managers strategizing about specific deals should constantly be asking salespeople, "Why is that important? Take the time to drill down even further by asking, "And why is that important?" Strategic wins and losses typically happen at the next level of detail in the conversation. Therefore, you might as well condition yourself and the rest of your sales team to gravitate there naturally.

CHAPTER 4

The Effectiveness Triad™

My first two books, *Secrets of Question Based Selling* and *It Only Takes 1% to Have a Competitive Edge in Sales*, were intended to widen the sales funnel by increasing the effectiveness of the individual salesperson. We did this by focusing on strategic selling skills like leveraging curiosity to secure more mindshare within target accounts, establishing credibility to increase the salesperson's perceived competence, escalating the value of sales questions to facilitate a more in-depth discussion about the customer's needs, and implementing a positioning strategy that allows customers to be more receptive to your value messages. We also talked about getting to the right person in your accounts, reducing the risks of buyer reluctance and rejection, and creating a sense of momentum in the marketplace as a way to communicate that the trail to success has already been blazed.

Each of these concepts implemented separately can have a positive impact on sales performance. But now it's time to focus on the broader opportunity, which comes from adopting a cohesive sales strategy and then integrating the QBS methodology into the operational fabric of the entire sales organization. That's where your potential return-on-investment in terms of increased sales productivity suddenly becomes exponential.

To have an intelligent discussion about enhancing sales performance, we must break the broader topic of selling effectiveness down into its component parts. When I deliver QBS Methodology training programs, I draw three interlocking circles on a whiteboard to represent the three components of an effective sales approach. Essentially, to be successful in sales, sellers must have the following: 1.) a depth of knowledge from which to add value, 2.) a strategic approach that enables them to repeat their successes, and 3.) professional selling skills that will cause them to be seen as a valuable resource in the eyes of target customers. In Question Based Selling, we call these three components the Effectiveness Triad™.

The Effectiveness Triad™

Each circle in the effectiveness triad represents an important ingredient in the formula to raise sales performance across the broader organization. Our objective in this chapter is to more closely examine each of these component parts in order to gain a better understanding of the critical success factors that will ultimately determine the success of your QBS implementation.

The discussion about sales effectiveness actually started in the previous chapter, with our conversation about your sales team's depth of knowledge regarding *what* is important to their customers, and *why*. You may have noticed that having a knowledge base from which to add value is the first component in the effectiveness triad. I will make the point again that building one's depth of knowledge doesn't refer to product knowledge alone. For years, much of the training salespeople received focused primarily on product education, where companies hosted boot camp training courses that taught sellers about all the features and benefits of their product offers. But, value doesn't always get communicated by salespeople espousing wonderful benefits about their product or service.

I am *not* suggesting that product information is unimportant. Having a depth of knowledge regarding one's product offerings is absolutely important, and those salespeople who know their solution alternatives inside and out have a definite advantage. My goal in Chapter 3, however, was to raise awareness that something else may be even more important than knowing one's product. To me, that something is having a keen awareness of what things might be most important to prospective customers.

Customers are much more interested in what's important to them than what's important to a salesperson. As such, "arm-

> Customers are much more interested in what's important to them, than what's important to the salesperson.

ing" your sales organization in advance with a fundamental awareness of potential business issues (*what* things are important to customers), and the underlying implications (*why* those issues might be important), puts your sales team in a strong position to develop a broader range of needs and create a greater sense of urgency for customers to move forward with a favorable purchase decision. Hence, the first component in the effectiveness triad is having a robust knowledge base from which to engage more prospects in more productive sales conversation about their needs and your corresponding solutions.

Your Execution Strategy

Once your sales team is appropriately armed with a depth of knowledge regarding the business issues and implications that are important to prospective customers, the next component in the effectiveness triad is your execution strategy.

One's overall effectiveness as a sales professional has a lot to do with how they approach the strategic sale, which is a study that extends far beyond the basics of penetrating new accounts, qualifying opportunities, uncovering needs, communicating value, and closing deals by the end of the month. Having good intentions is certainly a plus, but good intentions alone won't increase your sales effectiveness.

As a career salesperson, I remember feeling frustrated whenever the trainer leading a sales course would pound the table, preaching the importance of obvious goals like account penetration, getting to the right person, and uncovering customer needs. This was hardly "new news" to us. As I've said, most salespeople already have a clear picture of "what" they are trying to accomplish in their target accounts. Of course it's important to penetrate new accounts, qualify opportunities, uncover needs, communicate value, and close sales! The bigger question is, "how" can sellers upnotch their sales effectiveness to more consistently accomplish these objectives?

Now that I'm one of those sales trainers, if I'm going to talk with salespeople about account penetration, I ask detailed questions like,

"What is your current strategy for broadening the needs development conversation?" Or, I might ask, "How do you currently differentiate yourself from the rest of the "noise" in the marketplace?" If I really want to get specific, I might ask, "What are you doing to generate a higher return-call rate when leaving voice-mail messages?"

You see, I don't want to talk generically about the topic of account penetration. I want to talk more specifically with sales reps about their approach. I want to know their *strategy* for penetrating accounts and how they plan to fill the sales forecast with new prospect opportunities.

I also ask other questions like, "What challenges do you expect to encounter in such-and-such account? And, "What is your strategy for dealing with those challenges in a proactive manner?" I might even ask for suggestions by saying, "Is there anything the company can do to better support your efforts out in the field?"

There is a big difference between questioning your team's work ethic and talking with them about sales strategy. At this point in the business world, the potential upside that can come from telling salespeople to work harder is predictably small. People are already working hard. Instead, the key to increasing the return on your invested sales effort is developing a more effective sales approach. You might say, "Working smarter."

Before we go further on the issue of sales strategy, I want to briefly revisit some of the strategic concepts that were introduced in my first two books, and are now an integral part of the Question Based Selling methodology. These strategies run the gamut from how best to position yourself in the marketplace to tactical ideas sellers can implement to enhance the quality and depth of their face-to-face sales conversations. To build a solid foundation, let's begin with a look at your broader positioning strategy.

Conversational Layering

Most sellers have certain goals for the sales process. When first penetrating new prospect opportunities, for example, they want to understand the customer's needs. They also want to qualify the opportunity and communicate the value of their potential solutions. That's fine, it's important to have clear goals in the profession of selling. But, if you want to consistently accomplish these objectives, you must realize that certain prerequisite conditions must first be met on the way to achieving your goals.

What do I mean by prerequisite conditions? Any experienced salesperson will tell you that if you want to close a sale, you must first earn the right to ask for the order. Likewise, if you want to uncover needs, then you had better earn the right to ask probative questions. You will find that the sales process is a continuum of cause and effect relationships that exist between the objectives sellers are trying to achieve, and the prerequisite steps that will allow you to achieve those objectives. In Question Based Selling, I developed a visual representation of these cause and effect relationships into a model we call Conversational Layering™.

Conversational Layering™

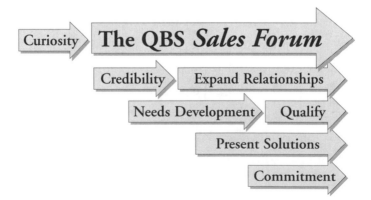

The visual created by this diagram serves as an engagement model that provides a backdrop for every conversation you will ever have with a prospect, customer, or reseller partner. The true value of this model is its ability to identify each of the prerequisite conditions that must be satisfied on the way to achieving your desired goals in the sales process.

Working backwards from the bottom of the Conversational Layering diagram, for example, you will notice that in order to secure a commitment, a salesperson must first present a viable solution. I think most sellers would agree that presenting a viable solution is a fundamental prerequisite on the way to securing a purchase commitment. Good! So, let's continue working backwards.

Before you can present a viable solution, however, the Conversational Layering model suggests that you must first uncover a potential need. Identifying customer needs is another fundamental prerequisite, in this case, on the way to presenting a viable solution, and then securing a commitment. Can you see a trend?

You will notice that the discovery process in this model actually has two component parts. One is needs development—your product or service has to be good for the customer. Qualification is the other component—the opportunity you are pursuing should also be good for your company.

Thus far, we have merely stated the obvious. Uncovering customer needs gives you an opportunity to present solutions and close a sale. But, the sales process does not begin with needs development. Salespeople can't expect to just pick up the telephone and start firing probative questions in the direction of prospective customers.

Therefore, in the Conversational Layering model, you will notice that establishing a relationship is an important prerequisite to having a productive needs development conversation. I should make the point that in Question Based Selling, we define the word "relationship" very differently than most sales trainers. Many sellers have been taught that it's important to build rapport with customers, in order to have relationships. I would disagree, on the grounds that we live in a much more cautious society, and prospective buyers are normally reluctant to chit-chat with someone that they don't know or trust. For example, if your telephone rings tonight during dinner, and the salesperson on the

> Sellers can't expect to just pick up the telephone and start firing questions at prospective customers.

other end tries to build rapport by asking how your day is going, does that increase your desire to take the call? For most people, the answer is no. Therefore, it is my opinion that the concept of rapport building is over-rated in today's selling environment.

To establish relationships with prospective customers, you must first earn the right to engage them in a productive conversation about their needs and your corresponding value. So, the question I end up asking salespeople and sales managers is: What is your strategy for causing prospective customers to *want to* engage in a productive conversation about their needs and your potential value?

If we continue working backward to the very beginning of the Conversational Layering diagram, you will notice that two foundational prerequisite conditions must be satisfied in order to engage prospective customers in a productive conversation. These two prerequisite conditions include: piquing the prospect's curiosity and establishing credibility—which I believe, are two of the best kept secrets in the sales profession.

I should make the point that my goal here is not to re-explain the QBS Methodology, along with all of the strategies and techniques that have already been covered in each of my first two books. I am simply using this opportunity to reiterate a few core competencies, which should allow you to step back and make some conscious decisions about how you want to be perceived by target customers in your respective markets. In fact, let's start with the discussion with some thoughts about leveraging curiosity.

Leveraging Curiosity to Increase Mindshare

Since I began studying the sales process, I have invested a great deal of time and effort in the idea that "curiosity" is the *genesis* of every sale. Ironically, I have never seen a sales training course that even mentions curiosity, even though it is the single most important factor that determines whether or not you will succeed in getting a share of your prospective customer's time or their attention.

Think about it this way. If a prospect is *not* the least bit curious about who you are or what you can do for them, then it becomes very difficult to engage them in a productive conversation about their needs and your corresponding value. Fortunately, the converse is also true—as prospective customers become more curious about who you are and what you can do for them, it becomes easier to secure mindshare (i.e. time and attention) from key people in important target accounts.

So, the question needs to be asked, what are you currently doing to leverage curiosity in the sales process? I pose this question to salespeople, sales managers, and executives all over the world. Interestingly, the most common response I hear back is, "Huh?"

The role curiosity plays in the strategic sales process has essentially been ignored by traditional sales approaches. Isn't that odd? Virtually everyone I meet agrees with the premise that if a prospective customer is not the least bit curious about who you are or what you can do for them, then you will not succeed in securing their time or attention. Still, the subject never seems to come up, even though curiosity is ultimately the catalyst that causes prospective customers to "want to" engage.

To understand the strategic significance of curiosity in the sales process, voice-mail is a good starting point. For many salespeople, voice-mail has become a major obstacle. It's the gatekeeper that often stands in the way of having "live" conversations with key decision-makers. In fact, depending on what article you happen to read, it's reported that only 2% to 5% of the voice-mail messages left by salespeople ever generate a return call, which significantly narrows the window of opportunity for engaging new prospects.

Now that we've identified the problem with voice-mail (not getting enough return calls), let me share that there are two motivations that cause people to return voice-mail messages. One is obligation. The other is curiosity. Let's start with the easy one—obligation. If your sales manager calls and leaves you a voice-mail message, you would probably return the call, because it's from your boss. If your mother calls and leaves a voice-mail message, you would call her back too. She's your mom!

But, what percentage of prospective customers feel obligated to return voice-mail messages left by salespeople? The answer if very few. That's where curiosity comes in. If someone does not become even the least bit curious when they listen to your

> What percentage of prospective customers feel obligated to return voice-mail messages left by salespeople?

voice-mail message, your chances of receiving a return call are greatly reduced. On the other hand, if you succeed in piquing the prospect's curiosity with your voice-mails, then you are likely to receive a return call, and it will probably happen sooner rather than later. Why? Because action items like returning telephone calls get prioritized based on two things: obligation and curiosity. If a customer feels a strong sense of obligation, they will probably return your call. Likewise, if something in your voice-mail message piques their curiosity, they will call you back just as quickly. It's that simple!

Here are some examples of curiosity-inducing voice-mail messages:

1. *"Hi, Mr. Prospect, this is Jamie Hudson, District Manager from XYZ Company, in central Ohio. I was trying to solve a problem for your company regarding maintenance for your current hardware platform and I've come up with an idea that could save you a significant amount of money. When you get a minute, could you please call me at (777) 666-5544. I should be here today until around 4:30pm."*

2. *"Hi, Ms. Prospect, this is Pat Stone, client manager from ABC Company handling southern California. I wanted to reinitiate contact because we've had thirteen new announcements in the last three and a half months, two of which would have an immediate impact on your business, and I wanted to see if it would make sense to bring you up to speed. If you get a chance today, give me a call on my direct line at (333) 222-1100."*

3. *"Hi, Mr. Strategic Partner, this is Dana Hutchens calling from JKL Chemicals. I am planning to call one of your larger accounts later in the week and I was hoping to catch you for a minute to strategize in advance, so I don't step out of bounds on the call. If you get a chance, can you please call me at (666) 777-8899. I should be in the office this morning until around 11:30am."*

I want to stress that leveraging curiosity to increase your return call rate is not an exercise in using clever one-liners. If I were to leave ten voice-mail messages with ten different prospect accounts, I might use ten different sets of words, depending on the information I had about the account and my objectives for the call. Different words, but same strategy. As a result, my expectations for getting return calls after leaving a voice-mail message are in the neighborhood of eighty to ninety-percent, and yours can be too.

Achieving dramatic results is simple once you understand the following paradigm: *Curious prospects will choose to engage, while those who are not curious won't.* Your ability to pique the prospect's interest with curiosity-inducing voice-mail messages is the single most important factor that will determine whether or not your calls are returned. This raises an important question: What are you currently saying in voice-mail messages to pique the prospect's curiosity?

Curiosity is a strategy that can be leveraged in other areas of the sales process as well. Escalating the priority of the email messages you send is another example. Similar to voice-mail, email messages that pique the recipient's interest will receive greater priority and generate more robust responses than other email messages that don't. So, what are you currently doing to leverage curiosity with the email messages you send?

For that matter, what are you doing to bolster attendance at product presentations or industry seminars? What are you doing to pique the curiosity of higher-level executives within your target accounts? What is your strategy for penetrating accounts where the incumbent vendor is a strong competitor? And, what are you doing to expand the size of your deals, or pull them into the current quarter or sales year?

Most salespeople have never thought about all the different opportunities to leverage curiosity in the sales process, or the strategic impact curiosity can have in terms of securing more time and attention from prospective customers. As I said, most sales training courses don't even mention curiosity, let alone teach salespeople "how" to increase mindshare within their target accounts. My intent here is simply to point out that curiosity is one of the two most important prerequisites to engaging prospective customers in a productive conversation about their needs and your corresponding value. Basically, I'm saying that if you aren't currently leveraging curiosity in the strategic sales process, then there is a huge upside opportunity for you and the rest of your sales team.

Diagnostic Questions for Instant Credibility

In the Conversational Layering model, credibility is the other prerequisite condition that needs to be satisfied if you want to engage prospective customers in a robust needs development conversation. We already said that people are more cautious and stand-offish today than ever before. As a result, prospective customers don't just open up to every salesperson who wants to ask questions. In fact, there can be a significant amount of risk associated with probing for too much information, too soon. Therefore, if the goal is to understand what customers need, then it is incumbent on salespeople to first "earn the right" to ask probative questions.

My first experience with strategic sales training occurred back when I was a rookie salesperson and I attended one of the old Xerox sales courses. The big "thing" Xerox taught was opening a dialogue with open-ended questions.

Though I was not an experienced salesperson at the time, I was a logical thinker, so this made sense to me. I did want to open a dialogue with prospective customers, so asking open-ended questions seemed to be a logical approach. Therefore, I went out into my sales territory asking all the open-ended questions I could think of. But, guess what? Many of the customers I asked were reluctant to openly share information, and I quickly realized that people are generally reticent to "open up" with someone they don't yet know or trust.

If you were on the receiving end of a sales call at home, and the salesperson started off by saying, "Hi, Mr. Boyd, this is Joe Salesperson with Equity Life Insurance Company, what are your financial goals and objectives over the next five years?" Let me ask, are you open to sharing this type of information with sales callers? While you probably do share your financial goals and objectives with someone, most people are reluctant to openly share with someone they don't even know. That's why open-ended questions can indeed be valuable conversational tools, but only after you've earned the right to probe for this type of information.

One of the techniques I introduced in Question Based Selling was specifically designed to sidestep this risk of asking for too much, too soon. The logic is simple. If open-ended questions increase a salesperson's risk of failure by asking for too much information too soon, then perhaps we should go down the opposite path. The idea is to establish credibility early in the sales conversation in order to earn the right to probe more deeply into what's really driving the customer's need. QBS accomplishes this objective by teaching salespeople to ask a series of diagnostic questions, as a stepping-stone strategy to kick-off a more productive needs development conversation.

Diagnostic questions are short-answer queries that ask about the status of a customer's current business environment, or in the case of a consumer sale, their personal situation. Since Chapter 8 in Secrets of Question Based Selling explains this technique in detail, I won't re-examine all of the logic that supports this idea here. But, I do want to give you a quick illustration of how this strategy works.

Suppose, for example, you sell high-tech solutions. At the appropriate time in the conversation, when you sense that it's the right time to ask questions, here's a condensed sample of the diagnostic questions one might use to initiate the needs development conversation:

Seller: *"Mr. Prospect, can I ask you a couple specifics about your current IT environment?"*

Prospect: *"Sure."*

Seller: *"Is your current IT platform centralized or distributed?"*

"How many servers to you currently have installed?"

"What about your operating system, are you currently using UNIX, NT, or some combination?

"How many users do you support?"

"In how many different locations?"

Of course, you would pause after each question to allow the prospect to respond. But, by opening with a series of short, easy to answer, diagnostic questions, give a salesperson an opportunity to accomplish four very strategic objectives in the first sixty seconds of their needs development conversations.

First, this technique provides sellers with a non-threatening way to kick off the needs development conversation, which is critically important. If the prospect has been verbally accosted by previous callers, they will be quick to start playing defense at the first sign of an impending interrogation. Secondly, a series of short-answer diagnostic questions will yield some valuable information that will help to guide the rest of the conversation. You would talk differently with a prospect who supports two hundred end-users, than a customer who currently supports twenty thousand. Thirdly, asking diagnostic questions gives sellers a unique opportunity to establish credibility early in the needs development conversation. It's simple really. If you demonstrate an ability to ask relevant, intelligent ques-

> If you demonstrate an ability to ask relevant, intelligent questions, the other person in the conversation will assume you have knowledge in those areas.

tions, the other person in the conversation will assume you have knowledge in those areas. It's human nature to make this assumption. We already said that knowledge was one of the three components in the effectiveness triad—not just having knowledge, but having the ability to convey it. Hence, in the sample dialogue above, the customer will automatically begin to form the impression that you know something about centralized and distributed IT environments, server hardware, operating system software, and configuration. Asking relevant and intelligent questions early in the sales process is critical because that's when customers are forming their impressions about whether or not to share their thoughts, feelings, and concerns with you.

Lastly, opening with a series of short-answer diagnostic questions creates many wonderful opportunities to expand the needs development conversation into a broader and more in-depth discovery about the customer's problems, issues, and concerns. The best part is, all four of these strategic objectives can be accomplished in the opening seconds of the discovery process, which makes this strategy of asking diagnostic questions a very good investment of time.

Of course, an old-school traditionalist could argue, if the goal of needs development is uncovering customer needs, why not just cut to the heart of the matter and start the conversation off by prob-ing for problems, issues, and concerns? The answer is you can try and probe for whatever you want. But that brings us back to the roadblock we talked about earlier—just because a salesperson wants to probe for problems, doesn't necessarily mean prospects and cus-tomers will open up and share that information with you.

The truth is, you don't need a strategy for those prospects who already want to share important information with you. You need a strategy for all the other prospects who won't open up until you establish credibility as a knowledgeable resource.

Using diagnostic questions to establish credibility is a proven technique for getting deeper, wider, and more strategic within your target accounts. What's the alternative—using a random approach, which puts sellers at risk of asking for too much information, too soon? As a salesperson, I wanted to identify strategies that worked and then duplicate my successes. Therefore, I tended to gravitate away from random approaches, in favor of consistency.

To help salespeople become more consistent, one of the action items I recommend to students during our training courses is to prepare a master list of diagnostic questions that can be used over and over in conversations with customers. I tell them to think of it like this: If you had unlimited access to prospects who were willing to share information, what questions would you ask?

Creating a master list of potential questions is a great idea. But, it can be an intimidating task. For whatever reason, thinking of possible questions that could be asked during the needs develop-ment conversation doesn't always come naturally. Therefore, I rec-ommend instead that you create a list of data points. If you had "carté blanche" to ask anything you wanted, what would you want to know about the account? It is so much easier to manage a sales conversation if you have a repository of questions from which to choose, rather than trying to reinvent the wheel in every new account situation.

So, what is your strategy for needs development? At the first whiff of opportunity, do you start probing for problems? If so, you are taking a big risk. I bet you don't readily share information with people you don't know or trust. So, why should we expect it to be any different for prospective customers?

Escalating the Value of Your Sales Conversations

If you read my first two books, then you know Question Based Selling is *not* just about asking questions. Rather, QBS is about the strategy of teaching salespeople how to engage more prospects in more productive conversation, throughout the entire sales process. Needs development is a critical component of the strategic sales process, which is why we talked about using diagnostic questions as a risk reduction strategy. But, what's your strategy in the needs development conversation after the first sixty seconds?

One of my primary goals in QBS was to simplify the needs development process. In doing so, I found that sales questions fall into one of four categories based on their level of mutual value in the conversation. Essentially, needs development questions either probe the current status of an opportunity, or they seek to uncover potential issues that may exist, or they explore the implications of those issues, or they focus on the potential for providing a solution. To that end, needs development questions can be characterized as Status Questions, Issue Questions, Implication Questions, and Solution Questions. Note the graphic on the next page.

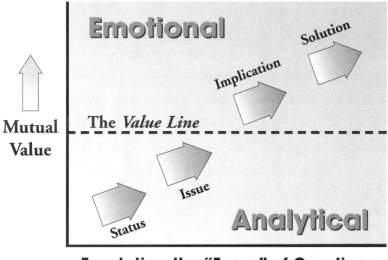

Escalating the "Focus" of Questions

If you remember, the diagnostic questions we just talked about are intended to probe the status of the opportunity, which is why they appear in the lower left-hand corner of the diagram. Questions that probe the status of an opportunity tend to be low in mutual value. That's because the customer already knows the status. Status Questions are great tools for kicking-off the needs development conversation, but you'd better have an escalation strategy for getting into more depth. The formula is simple. If you want to escalate the value of your sales conversations, then you need to escalate the value of your questions.

Once you kick the discovery process off with a series of short-answer diagnostic questions, the next step is to transition to the more highly valued Issue Questions.

Getting a business issue on the table for discussion is not difficult. You simply say, "Mr. Customer, to what extent is _____ important in your business?" Of course, the context of the question will vary depending on the customer, and your target industry. An insurance salesperson might say, "To what extent is estate planning important to your longer term financial goals?" Someone selling pharmaceuticals might ask a doctor, "To what extent do recent changes in managed care affect your prescription choices?" Basically, you just fill in the blank with a relevant issue, and that topic is open for further exploration. Notice also that the phrase "to what extent" is intentionally used to broaden the scope of the question in order to generate a more in-depth response from the customer.

Be careful, though. Once you raise an issue for discussion, it is critical that you escalate the conversation further to get into more depth on that specific issue. As I said earlier, you don't just want to talk about the customer's issues, you want to talk "beyond" their issues. In our water pump analogy from Chapter 3, for example, we didn't want to talk with homeowners about having a flooded basement. We wanted to talk with them about the implications of flooding, which included possible structural damage, mildewing, damage to personal property, insurance concerns, safety risk, displacement, cost, and so on.

If you want customers to have multiple reasons to buy from you, then you have a responsibility to be proactive in the needs development conversation, which includes raising potential implications that customers may not bring up on their own.

How do you know in advance which business issues and implications are relevant? You start by using the repository we recommended you build at the end of the previous chapter. A salesperson cannot possibly know what's most important to prospective customers before actually talking with them, but they can absolutely "arm" themselves in advance with a pretty good sense of what business issues might be important and why. This formula can then be repeated to escalate the value of your needs development conversations.

Soliciting More Accurate Information

Our discussion about strategy continues with a look at the quality of the information we receive from prospective customers. When asking questions, how much of the input we receive from customers is quality information? I have heard sellers say, "buyers are liars." To me, this seems a bit harsh. It is true, however, that just because a potential customer shares information, doesn't necessarily mean the information is 100% accurate.

As sellers, we tend to blame the customer. We probe for information, and then presume that customer responses will be accurate and complete. This seems reasonable enough to us. But, consider the customer's point of view. Perhaps there is an underlying reason or specific catalyst that causes customers to share less information, and less accurately than we would like.

If you look at how the sales profession has evolved, salespeople have been conditioned over time to be energetic, enthusiastic, and always positive. As a result, sellers tend to ask questions with a positive tone. Examples of positive questions include: "Mr. Customer, would next Tuesday work for a conference call?" Or, "Does your boss like our proposal?" A typical closing question might sound like, "Are we still in good shape to wrap this deal up by the end of the month?" If you listen carefully, these questions all have a certain built-in hopefulness. Say them out loud and you will feel your head bobbing up and down. In fact, some questions are delivered with such a hopeful tone that the asker is almost begging the customer to, "Please tell me what I want to hear." In Question Based Selling, these hopeful questions are said to be positively dispositioned.

Most sellers gravitate naturally to asking positively dispositioned questions. People who are measured on revenue production do want to hear good news. The problem is positively dispositioned questions tend to cause prospective customers to share less information, and less accurately. Why? Because people in general don't like to be the bearers of bad news.

Here's a simple example to illustrate the point. Suppose you were invited to a friend's house for dinner, and your host came in at the end of the meal and asked, "So, how was dinner?" If it was the worst food you ever put in your mouth, would you tell them? Most people wouldn't. Why not? Because it's easier to say nothing or sidestep the truth than to say something you know the other person would not want to hear.

So when an eager salesperson asks a question like, "Ms. Prospect, are we still in good shape to wrap this deal up by the end of the month?", what answer do you think the salesperson wants to hear? Obviously, the seller wants to hear good news. But, suppose the budget had been recently cut or someone on the executive committee is leaning toward some other solution. Human nature says that customers are just as quick to sidestep the truth. Therefore, rather than share bad news, customers are more inclined to give a lukewarm response like, "I have your proposal on my desk, and we are still working through the selection process, but will keep you posted."

When a salesperson hears his or her proposal is still on the customer's desk, to them, that might sound like they are in "good shape" to get the deal, when in fact, the customer's budget may have been slashed or one of the key decision makers is favoring some other proposal. I would argue that not knowing where you stand in the deal puts your entire sales team in an extremely weak position. How can you manage an opportunity all

> How can you manage an opportunity through the sales process if you are not aware of obstacles that might exist?

the way through the sales process if you are not aware of potential obstacles that might exist?

In QBS, we teach salespeople how to solicit more accurate information using a strategy that is designed to neutralize the disposition of your questions. The goal is to remove the hopefulness. Hopefulness is your enemy because it injects a level of expectation into your questions that you only want to hear good news. This expectation causes prospects and customers to respond with less and less accurate information. Let me ask you, if there is a problem brewing in one of your accounts, do you want to know about it? What about the opposite? If there are opportunities developing somewhere within your accounts, I'm guessing that you would want to know about those, too.

My goal when asking questions is simple—I want people to respond with more information (rather than less), and I want that information to be as accurate as possible. Consequently, the question I would have asked in the previous example is: "Ms. Prospect, do you think we are still in good shape to wrap this transaction up by the end of the month, or do you think something might cause this deal to get pushed out?"

Unless the customer is going to blatantly lie (which most won't), if a problem is brewing in the account, you will likely find out that something is not right. You can leverage this same technique even more directly by saying, "Mr. Customer, is there a problem with this transaction that I'm not aware of?"

Critics of this strategy could argue that you are giving the customer an out. Technically speaking, that's true. But I believe customers already have an out. I believe most customers already know that they are under no obligation to buy from you. Therefore, I will trade all the "outs" I would otherwise give for the increased accuracy and the volumes of information I receive by neutralizing the disposition of my questions.

So, what is *your* strategy for soliciting more, and more accurate, information from prospects and customers? Oddly enough, no one talks about this technique of neutralizing your sales questions, which creates a huge upside opportunity for yourself and the rest of your sales team, to have a competitive advantage when managing prospect opportunities.

Gold Medals & German Shepherds

A similar opportunity for differentiation exists in the way sellers position the benefits of their products and services. In my first book, *Secrets of Question Based Selling*, I made the point that different types of buyers have different buying motivations. It's true. People have different priorities and hot buttons, which often creates different agendas for a decision. Therefore, let's step back and evaluate how you can adapt your sales strategy to accommodate a broader range of buyer motivations.

Most salespeople do try to adjust their sales approach to accommodate different types of buyers. Traditionally, the most common method for accomplishing this was using a behavioral approach that categorized the personality profiles of prospective buyers into various sub-groups—identifying people as either drivers, amiables, kinesthetics, judgers, thinkers, feelers, etc. The theory was, if you can identify which type of buyer you are dealing with, and you can position yourself accordingly, this knowledge would presumably help you "connect" with prospects earlier in the sales process.

But, as I pointed out in my first book, there are several problems with these behavioral approaches. Let's start with the fact that when you first engage, it is very difficult to accurately assess a prospect's true motivations in the first few seconds of a sales call.

Even if you do get a sense for someone's behavioral category, you can't always judge a book by its cover. Furthermore, if you are dealing with multiple decision makers or a decision committee, whose personality profile should you mirror?

> Prospective buyers are motivated to make decisions in one of two ways—either to take advantage of some positive reward, or to avoid a negative consequence.

Rather than make this issue of buyer motivation overly complex, Question Based Selling boils it down into two fundamental behavioral influences. We have found that prospective buyers are ultimately motivated to make decisions in one of two ways—either to take advantage of some positive reward, or to avoid a negative consequence. To illustrate this point, we use a simple metaphor in QBS that says: While some people are motivated to run fast toward *Gold Medals* (positive reward), many other people run even faster from *German Shepherds* (negative aversion).

Positioning your solutions in terms of both *Gold Medal* and *German Shepherd* benefits is a strategy that can provide a significant competitive advantage within your target accounts. Say performance is one of the key benefits your product or service offers. In addition to highlighting obvious *Gold Medal* benefits like enhanced productivity or happier end-users, you should also be sure to point out that increased performance will protect against shipping delays between distribution centers (*German Shepherds*).

The tendency for salespeople is to position the value of our products and services positively, because we have been conditioned to believe that benefits are good things. Benefits *are* good things. But you must be careful not to limit your value proposition. While customers may want to take advantage of positive benefits, they may also want to avoid negative consequences. Recognizing that customers are actually motivated in two ways enables sellers to step outside the box of traditional thinking and realize that any benefit, for any product, in any industry, can be positioned in terms of both, *Gold Medal* and *German Shepherd* benefits.

Here again, what's *your* strategy with regard to positioning the value of your products and services? Do you want to be seen as an organization that provides only positive benefits (*Gold Medals*), or do you also want to help protect customers against undesirable circumstances (*German Shepherds*)? If you are like me, then you want to maximize your value proposition which means providing both positive reward and negative protection.

The Herd Theory™

In Chapter 3 of my first book, I shocked the selling establishment by suggesting that, "traditional reference selling is highly overrated." Please understand that I was not speaking out against the use of success stories to support your presentation. Satisfied customer references can absolutely help raise a prospect's confidence in a proposed product or service. But references can also hurt your sales efforts. Therefore, I am once again going to pick up the rug and point at reality when it comes to using references as a differentiation strategy.

> Even when you do produce a list of happy customers, customers tend to discount their significance.

The problem with traditional reference selling is twofold. First, if you sell in highly competitive markets, which most salespeople do, then you must assume your competitors also have good references, just like you. Most viable companies can produce a list of happy customers. Consequently, producing a list of satisfied customers is usually not a competitive differentiator.

Plus, even when you do produce a list of impressive references, customers have a natural tendency to discount their significance. When salespeople use references, they are basically making the argument that because these customers have been successful with their solutions, "you" will be successful too! This brings us to the second problem with traditional reference selling. It's related to the age-old lesson our parents taught us, "Just because your friend Jimmy jumped off a bridge, doesn't mean you should jump off, too."

Potential buyers in today's economic climate need to feel comfortable that they are indeed making the right decision in order to pull the trigger on a purchase. How can you make prospective customers feel more comfortable? Well, using forcefulness or manipulation is clearly not the answer. No one wants to be pushed by an overly-aggressive salesperson. But, sellers can absolutely cause prospective buyers to feel more comfortable by creating a sense of momentum in and around the sale. The underlying strategy is to lower the buyer's risk by showing them that the trail to success has already been blazed.

The Herd Theory (Book 1, Chapter 3) is a strategy for leveraging momentum in the sales process. Besides providing individual references where appropriate, The Herd Theory lets customers know that other clients have already paved the way. At the appropriate time in your sales conversations, rattle off an impressive list of customer names (financial services companies, for example), including: Citibank, Citicorp, American Express, Allstate Insurance, State Farm, Merrill Lynch, Bank of America, Bank of Boston, First Union, Wachovia, Transamerica, Goldman Sacs, Wells Fargo, Northwestern Mutual Life. Most customers will quickly form the impression that *something about your product or service must be valuable*. Basically, The Herd Theory puts you in a position to say, "Mr. Customer, do you want to know why all these other companies are doing business with (our company)?"

Of course key decision makers will want to know why the rest of the "herd" is all moving in your company's direction! That sets you up perfectly to explain or reiterate key points that will help differentiate your value proposition from the rest of the "noise" in the marketplace.

Navigating to the Right Person

"Calling high" in target prospect accounts has become somewhat faddish over the last ten years. Frankly, some people are surprised to hear me say that I am not a huge fan of top-down-only selling strategies. I feel this way because purchase decisions don't always happen from the top-down. By the way, I am not a big fan of bottom-up-only strategies—for the same reason. Purchase decisions aren't always influenced from lower levels in the organization either.

There are pros *and* cons for targeting higher levels within an account, and there are also pros and cons for calling low. If you can get in at a senior management level, for example, someone at the top generally has the budget, the authority, and the ability to shorten the sales process by dictating decisions to people at lower levels. The downside to calling high is that top executives aren't always aware that a problem exists or they might not see opportunities for improvement, which is why they have subordinates. Furthermore, if a higher level executive rejects your initial advances, succeeding in the account becomes exponentially more difficult.

Targeting lower levels within a prospect account has strategic advantages as well, starting with the fact that it may be easier to gain access into lower levels. You can also get lots of valuable information from people who aren't final decision makers. The downside to calling low is that people in lower levels usually don't control the purse strings or the timing of decisions. You may also increase your risk of being blocked politically.

In Chapter 13 of *Secrets of Question Based Selling*, I made the point that it's difficult to know how the internal politics of an account will play out before actually making the first contact. Therefore, my strategy was always to penetrate new accounts somewhere, and then navigate to the appropriate person—influencers and key decision makers. How do you identify the appropriate people? By asking questions like, *"Are you the person I should be talking with about _____?"* Or, *"Who else needs to be involved in the decision?"* You might also want to ask, *"Who will ultimately need to sign off on a purchase?"* If you want to uncover potential adversaries within the account, you might even ask, *"Is there anyone who might oppose this proposal?"*

There's nothing mysterious about these questions, but they do bring to light the idea that you can have a repeatable strategy for identifying key players and getting to the right person within your target accounts.

Four Keys to Closing More Deals

Yet another opportunity to be strategic exists at the end of the sales process where we can put some "methodology to the madness" to increase your effectiveness with regard to closing sales.

The truth is, there is no magic formula for closing a sale. If a prospective customer, for whatever reason, is *not* ready to move forward, then it will be very difficult to wrap up a sales transaction. That's why we spend a lot of time in QBS strategizing about getting opportunities ready to be closed. What do I mean by getting prospects "ready?" If you want to close a sale, there are five prerequisite conditions that must be satisfied. Those five prerequisite conditions are as follows:

1.) The buyer must recognize the existence of a need.

2.) The seller must be offering a viable solution.

3.) The perceived value of the purchase must justify its cost.

4.) The customer must have the authority to make a decision.

5.) The buyer must have a sense of urgency for moving forward.

Put it this way: If a potential buyer does *not* recognize the existence of a need, or if your solution is *not* viable in the eyes of the customer, or if the value of your product does *not* justify its cost, or you are *not* dealing with someone who has the authority to pull the trigger on a purchase decision, or the prospective buyer does *not* have a sense of urgency for moving forward, then you probably won't succeed in finalizing a sales transaction. On the other hand, if these five prerequisite conditions have been fully satisfied, then closing a sale can become as simple as, "Press hard, five copies."

Even when these five prerequisites are indeed satisfied, sellers still have an opportunity to fine tune their strategic effectiveness with regard to closing sales. I talked about this in Chapter 15 of my first book, where we simplified the "art" of wrapping up a sale into a strategy called: The Four Keys for Closing More Sales.

The first key to closing more sales is knowing where you stand in the sales process. And, the only way to find out where you really stand is to ask for the order. Asking for the order is the moment of truth in the sales process where you either get some indication that your customer is ready to move forward with a purchase, or you find out that your sales efforts to date are at risk.

Of course, there are multiple ways to ask for the order. You can take the direct approach, by asking, *"Mr. Prospect, are you ready to make a decision?"* Or, the opposite works just as well: *"Mr. Prospect, is anything preventing you from moving forward on this deal?"*

Another way to find out where you stand in a sale is to reverse roles by asking, *"Ms. Prospect, if you were in my shoes, what would you do?"* You can also take your conversation off the record, by asking, *"Mr. Prospect, can I ask you something—off the record? How does your management really feel about the proposal we submitted?"* I don't know who's keeping a "record," but it's amazing how much information you can get once you are off it!

You might even try being honest. *"Mr. Prospect, can I ask your advice on something? In the morning, I'm supposed to have a conference call with my sales manager. I have been forecasting this opportunity to close in April, but I would rather be accurate than optimistic. Do you think April is still a reasonable target, or should I tell my boss something different?"*

The first order of business when closing a sale is to find out where you stand in the opportunity. Then you can either move forward toward wrapping up the deal, or work through any outstanding issues that may be holding the customer back.

The second key to closing more sales in QBS is reiterating your value proposition. Complex sales often have a longer duration, lasting several weeks or months, and include multiple players who come in at various stages of the sales process. Even if customers pay very close attention to every word you say, retention rates are typically less than 100%. That said, how long do you think it takes for a customer to forget half of the points you made during your initial sales presentation? In today's hustle and bustle world, I bet the answer is, "not long." Therefore, I point out to salespeople that your job is no longer just to represent your company and products. Rather, your responsibility is to "re-present" your company and reiterate your proposed solutions, so the value messages that get communicated during the sales process are fresh in the customer's mind when it is time to make a purchase decision.

> Complex sales often have a longer duration, lasting several weeks or months, and include multiple players who come in at various stages of the sales process.

The third key to being an effective closer is providing emotional reassurance. Customers are more cautious with their decision making and more judicious with their budgets and spending than ever before. Consequently, decision makers need to feel comfortable that they are indeed making the right decision. Ironically, the traditional mode of pushing harder and harder at the end of the sales process actually tends to make customers less and less comfortable, which is the opposite of our objective. Buyers are worried about the downside risks. What if they make the wrong decision? As the time for commitment draws nearer, buyer resistance tends to creep into the sales process as decision makers start to think of possible problems that could arise. It's called getting cold feet.

One of the best ways to increase a prospective buyer's comfort level is to reduce their downside risk, using *The Herd Theory*. Basically, if you can foster a sense of confidence in the sale by showing potential buyers that the trail to success has already been blazed by many other customers, then the customer's risk of making the wrong decision can be greatly reduced.

Another way to reduce a prospect's downside risk is to give them multiple reasons to buy from you. This is one of the reasons it was so important to expand the needs development conversation, as we discussed earlier. If you sell technology solutions, for example, you would want customers to see that in addition to being cost effective, your proposed solution also improves productivity, enhances system performance, assures end-user satisfaction, *and* provides data protection. Having multiple reasons to buy from you gives customers a greater sense of value, which increases their comfort level. Even if a purchase decision ends up yielding only some fraction of the proposed benefits, buyers can still rationalize that it was a smart purchase.

The fourth key to closing more sales in Question Based Selling is a negotiating strategy, called, "Tit-for-Tat." Simply put, if a prospective buyer asks you for something, you have the right to ask them for something else in return.

I have always viewed the sale as a mutual exchange of value. (The operative word here is mutual.) It's unhealthy to think customers are doing us a favor by sharing their needs, evaluating our products, or making a purchase commitment. Nor are we sellers doing them a favor by marketing our wares. Rather, each party in a transaction seeks a desirable outcome—customers want a valuable product or service, and sellers want revenue from closing a sale. When things go well, both parties win.

This tit-for-tat sense of mutuality should be prevalent throughout the sales process. For example, if a customer says, "Tell me about your products," you have every right to ask them for something in return. In this case, "Mr. Customer, I would be happy to tell you about our product offerings. Since our solution portfolio covers a broad spectrum, would you mind if I asked a couple specifics about your business?" This simple question takes a salesperson out of benefit recital mode, right into discovery.

The same principle applies later in the sales process. A prospective buyer might ask for a discount, saying, "Can we get a better price?" A good question back would be, "How much of a discount are you wanting?" Gaining some additional perspective from customers will generally tell you whether or not you are even in the ballpark. If their expectations are reasonable, I might say, "Mr. Customer, if I can get this discount approved, would you be willing to move forward with a purchase?" Basically, if a customer asks you for something, you earn the implicit right to ask them for something in return. It's tit-for-tat!

Two out of Three

A salesperson's chosen strategy is critical to their success. I'm not just talking about the need to identify the various steps in the sales process, but also the more detailed strategy of how you plan to execute on target objectives, and then repeat your success in the future.

Strategy is only one of three interlocking rings that make up the Effectiveness Triad, however. As we discussed, sellers also need to arm themselves with a base of knowledge that enables them to be perceived by potential customers as a valuable resource. This includes being knowledgeable with regard to the solutions being offered, and also, having a fundamental understanding of what business issues might be important to prospective customers.

The third and final piece in the sales effectiveness triad is the professional selling skills component. Even if you have a tremendous base of knowledge, and a bullet-proof strategy, you still need to develop the skills and the ability to consistently execute. That's what we'll talk about in the next chapter.

< ACTION ITEMS >

1. An effective sales strategy deserves to be repeated across the broader organization. Repetition requires documentation, however, as strategies tend to look very different once they are on paper. Therefore, invest the time to document your strategy for leveraging curiosity to penetrate new accounts. Also document your strategy for establishing credibility, creating momentum, qualifying opportunities, and securing commitments on the way to closing more sales transactions.

2. Make the investment to build another repository, this time of possible diagnostic questions that could serve to kick off your needs development conversations. Start with a wish list of what you want to know about your account. It's easier to choose from an existing inventory of appropriate questions, than to reinvent the wheel on each and every sales call.

3. Go back and reread *Secrets of Question Based Selling*, particularly chapters six through twelve, which contain much of the foundational detail that I did not attempt to re-explain in this book.

CHAPTER 5

Someone has to "Pedal the Bike"

The third component in the sales effectiveness triad is professional selling skills. Even after a salesperson is armed with a robust knowledge base, and they make some conscious decisions regarding sales strategy, they still have to have the skills and ability to execute on the desired objectives.

What does it mean to be a sales professional? By definition, the word professional characterizes someone who upholds the highest standards of aptitude and ability within their respective discipline. Therefore, at the risk of stating the obvious, those sellers who are committed to raising their selling skills to the highest levels will have a considerable advantage over other salespeople who rely mostly on happenstance, good fortune, or their experiences to date.

It's easy to confuse professional selling skills with strategy, knowledge, and experience. People tend to bunch them all together, figuring that if a salesperson has been successful in the past, then they probably are highly

skilled. That may, in fact, be true. But, just because a salesperson had a good year, or their sales were strong when the economy was hot, doesn't necessarily mean they have the skills to succeed in the future.

To fully appreciate the difference between knowledge, strategy, and skills, consider the phenomenal success of Lance Armstrong. Lance is a five-time winner of the Tour-de-France, and arguably one of the greatest athletes that has ever lived. I have never competed professionally in a bicycle race, but I am reasonably certain that strategy and knowledge (i.e. experience) played an important role in Lance Armstrong's success. But even with a great strategy and tremendous depth of experience, someone still has to pedal the bike. Lance Armstrong still had to possess the skills and conditioning required to succeed.

Salespeople must also have skills and conditioning to succeed in today's business environment. From a strategy perspective, most salespeople already understand that it is important to penetrate new accounts. We also know that it's important to uncover needs, understand the political landscape within a target account, and navigate to the right people who are going to make the decision. From a skills perspective, however, the real desire is maximizing your effectiveness with regard to accomplishing these objectives.

In Question Based Selling, I made the point that a vendor cannot offer any value, to any customer, at any time, unless there is a recognized need. This makes sense because in today's business climate, very few customers move forward toward a purchase decision without first recognizing the existence of a need. Whose job is it to uncover needs? Needs development is a salesperson's responsibility, of course! Salespeople are supposed to ask questions, right? Not so fast. As I stated earlier, just because a salesperson wants to ask probative questions, doesn't necessarily mean prospective customers will "want to" share valuable information about their needs.

Questions are excellent tools for gathering information. And one can learn a great deal by using them. Questions can also be valuable strategic tools for securing mindshare within your target accounts, for establishing credibility early on in the sales conversation, and for qualifying account opportunities. Questions can also help sellers expand the customer's need, and by doing so, create a sense of urgency for moving forward.

Questions are valuable conversational tools indeed. But, human nature would suggest that a person's behavior and abilities are largely attributable to their education and conditioning. That said, much of the education salespeople have received over time has conditioned them to be statement-based, as opposed to question-based.

As the sales profession evolved over the last thirty years, companies have spent millions of dollars telling salespeople what to say. With a seemingly continuous roll-out of new products, salespeople have been deluged with updated value propositions and marketing messages that they are supposed to absorb and communicate to their target customers. But, many of these same companies that invested heavily in telling salespeople

> A conscious effort to upgrade the professional selling skills of your sales organization could yield a significant increase in revenue production.

what to say, have invested little in developing the proficiency of their sales teams with regard to the strategic use of questions. Consequently, a conscious effort to upgrade the professional selling skills of your sales organization could yield a significant increase in revenue production.

To me, using a question-based approach is more than just probing for needs. Being question-based means having the confidence and skill to know that you are going to ask the right question at the right time in the sales conversation. It also means being conversationally fluent in the strategic use of questions.

What do I mean when I say that a salesperson is fluent in the strategic use of questions? The concept of fluency is generally used to describe someone's ability to converse proficiently using a second language. Being fluent in a second language, for example, means that you can comfortably speak and understand that language. The true definition of fluency, however, is that having the ability to actually "think" in terms of the second language, as opposed to doing the mental gymnastics that would otherwise be required to translate back-and-forth between different languages in your mind.

As an example, I took two years of Spanish in high school, and didn't do so well. Most of time, I didn't have a clue what other people were saying. Someone would turn to me, for example, and ask a simple question like, "Como sé llama?"

Then I would have to think to myself, "Oh boy, what does that mean? Let's see…como means *what*. Sé llama…means *your name*. *What's your name?* I eventually figured it out that the other person was asking my name. OK, I would think, *my name is Tom Freese*…Me yamo Tomas." Whew!

Having to work this hard to translate a conversation in your mind makes it extremely difficult to communicate effectively. Similarly, if a salesperson is working hard to think of the right question at the right time in the conversation, then facilitating a needs development conversation can be equally difficult. On the other hand, having the confidence to know that you will ask the right question at the right time is empowering for a salesperson.

The innate ability to "think" in terms of strategic questions is not a gift; rather, it is a skill; and it's a skill that must be developed. So, here's a question for you: How much time have you spent thus far in your professional sales career conditioning yourself to be fluent in the strategic use of questions? I probably already know the answer.

I understand that some people are set in their ways. It's natural to be averse to change, especially since some changes in life can be quite difficult. If you would like to be more proficient in the strategic use of questions, however, I have good news. Learning to be a question-based salesperson is an easy skill to acquire. It won't happen without some effort on your part, but if you are willing to invest ten minutes per day, for three consecutive days, developing your questioning skills will change the way you interact with people. More importantly for salespeople, becoming question-based will change the way other people interact with you. In QBS Methodology training programs, we teach salespeople how to become fluent in the strategic use of questions using a simple exercise we call, "Ten Questions."

Ten Questions Exercise

If you want to acquire the confidence to know that you will ask the right questions at the right time in your sales conversations, then you must learn to think in terms of question marks, rather than statements.

In order to facilitate this questioning exercise, we need some topics to ask questions about. For our purposes here, I usually encourage sellers not to think about their daily routine. Don't worry about what questions you might want to ask a prospective customer during an actual sales call. We have already talked about content and strategy as the two other components of the sales effectiveness triad. For now, let's just focus on skills and becoming more proficient in the strategic use of questions.

Thomas A. Freese

When I first led this exercise in the corporate arena, I asked the audience to help me think of three obscure topics that we could ask questions about. The three suggested topics were: Sailing, Yugoslavia, and Nuclear Physics. Pretty obscure, huh? I wrote them on the whiteboard in the front of the room.

Then, I asked everyone to stand up and select a partner. The object of this exercise is simple—one person counts on their fingers while the other person asks ten questions about their respective topic. (Hence the name, Ten Questions.)

If you had to ask ten questions about the topic of sailing, for example, how many different questions could possibly be asked? Dozens? Hundreds? Maybe even thousands? You only have to come up with ten. Sounds easy, doesn't it?

Now, there are a couple of ground rules for the exercise. First, you want to condition yourself to ask questions with a certain popcorn-credibility. Popcorn credibility, you ask? Well, what does popcorn sound like when it's popping really well? You hear a rapid fire popping that sounds like…pop, pop, pa-pa-pop, pa-pop-pop, pa-pa-pop, pa-pa-pop. When it's almost done, it begins to slow and you hear an intermittent…pop….pa-pop…pop………pop. In the QBS model, we say that a salesperson gains credibility so long as their popcorn keeps popping. Therefore, if your popcorn isn't popping, and you are having to think too hard to come up with the right question at the right time in the conversation, orchestrating a sales call becomes much more difficult.

The second ground rule in this Ten Question exercise is that you want to teach yourself to think on the periphery of your assigned topic. If your topic is sailing, for example, it doesn't help to think of questions like: Does your *mother* like sailing? Does your *brother* like sailing? Does your *sister* like sailing? Does your *father* like sailing? If

118

every question is about "sailing," and you can only ask questions about a subject that is already on the table for discussion, you forfeit a huge opportunity to expand your conversations to include a broader range of business issues and implications.

Let me give you an example of what I mean by teaching yourself to ask questions on the periphery of a topic. A few weeks ago, one of the topics that came up in a "live" QBS training program was greek mythology. One of the many questions that got asked was, "How do you spell Zeus?" Can you see that this question is about greek mythology, but does not depend on the topic phrase as a crutch. Another topic that came up was Disneyworld, and someone asked: "Have you ever been to Orlando?" Another question was, "How often do you take family vacations?" Certainly, it isn't wrong to ask questions that zero-in on a certain topic. But, if we consider that a salesperson's opportunity to increase the customer's sense of urgency is by raising implications that extend way beyond the issue, then it is to your advantage to think on the periphery of the subject. In fact, I usually tell students that in this exercise, they can only use their topic in four or less questions (out of ten).

Sometimes participants complain when they have to think of questions about a topic with which they are unfamiliar. "Photography?" they complain. "But, I don't know anything about photography!" Well, doesn't that mean you should have lots of questions?

Now it's your turn to give the exercise a try. After I assign a topic, take a few seconds to collect your thoughts, and then (out loud) ask ten questions about the topic. Be sure to count on your fingers so you know when you get all ten. Ready? Your topic is: Bicycles. Go!

Did you try it? For many people, this seemingly simple exercise of coming up with ten questions about a specified topic is much more difficult than they would have guessed. Usually, the brain goes blank somewhere along the line, and it's easy to get off track. Most people tend to think of questions in spurts—usually, two or three at a time. Many times, after making it to ten questions, people realize that they are having to work much harder (to think of questions) than they would like. Herein lies the opportunity to sharpen one's professional selling skills.

The initial exercise of asking ten questions about a certain topic is just the tip of the iceberg. Teaching yourself to become fluent in the strategic use of questions requires a slightly larger investment. I usually recommend three days, ten minutes per day. In ten minutes, you can easily run through the exercise of asking ten questions about a selected topic three times, with three different topics. In fact, you will find that this exercise of asking ten questions about a given topic becomes progressively easier.

What topics should you choose for practice? Anything. You could ask ten questions about violins, road signs, or fertilizer. If you happen to be in a funky mood, ask ten questions about hair styles, or leather. You can select any topic that is unrelated to your business. Remember that we're developing a personal skill, which will be merged back into your daily business routine shortly.

The secret to easily formulating a sequence of questions about a given topic is to compartmentalize your thoughts, as opposed to just randomly thinking up questions that are related to a given topic. If your topic was sailing, for example, rather than ask questions about the broad topic of sailing, this exercise becomes significantly easier if you think of related subtopics. For sailing, you could ask questions regarding different types of boats. You could ask about climatic conditions, weather patterns, or oceanography. You could also ask about historical aspects of sailing, or the future of sailing as an Olympic sport, or the cost involved with getting started in sailing as a hobby. There must be dozens of different subtopics surrounding the broader topic of sailing. By the way, each of these subtopics can then be further divided into even more specific subcomponents. If you wanted to think of questions regarding different types of boats, for example, you could ask about hull design—mono-hull versus catamaran, or trimaran. You could also ask about the materials used to build a boat, like the advantages of fiberglass versus wood or composite material. You could even ask about the potential tradeoffs between size, function, and speed.

Once you realize that broad topics can easily be broken down into smaller subtopics, and then each of those subtopics can be broken down (again) into even more subcomponents, the reservoir of possible questions that could be asked expands dramatically.

It's important to note that the goal of this exercise is not to teach people how to *ask* specific questions. Rather, the goal is to teach you how to think, so you develop the confidence to know that you have the ability to easily formulate valuable questions in your conversations with customers. You are essentially conditioning yourself to think in terms of question marks. Like Lance Armstrong, you can have the greatest strategy in the world and the most experience, but you still have to have the skills required to pedal the bike.

If you follow my advice and practice this exercise for three consecutive days, you will discover that formulating ten questions about a topic becomes easier and easier with each pass. In fact, it won't take you ten minutes to run though three topics on the second day. It should only take you six or seven minutes. That's because of what I said earlier—learning to become question-based is an easy skill to acquire. In fact, by the third day, it will probably only take five to six minutes to complete the exercise.

After doing this exercise for three consecutive days, I recommend that you practice this technique when talking with customers. But rather than thinking of unrelated topics like sailing or Yugoslavia, you will be using your newfound skills to create a reservoir of possible of questions in your head regarding issues that are relevant to technology, healthcare, manufacturing, or financial services, and the implications of those issues.

People often ask me, "Tom, why is it so easy for you to think of the right question at the right time?" The truth is I don't try to think of the "right" questions to ask. Instead, I use this same technique to formulate a mental list of questions that "could" be asked. At that point, choosing the most relevant question from a broader list of possibilities is relatively simple.

Again, learning to become fluent in the strategic use of questions is not difficult. This will require some effort on your part, but I encourage you to invest the time and see if it doesn't change the way you interact with prospects and customers. More importantly, becoming question-based will change the way other people interact with you!

Putting it All Together

Becoming fluent in the strategic use of questions is an important skill to acquire and one that will impact your overall sales effectiveness. It's clear that a question-based salesperson has a significant advantage in today's business environment. But, just having the ability to ask questions is not enough. You must also be "armed" with a base of knowledge that enables you to facilitate robust conversations with customers, and a strategy that will differentiate you from the rest of the "noise" in the marketplace.

Have you ever noticed that in your best accounts, you aren't actually "selling" customers on the value of your products and services as much as you are trying to help them make a good decision? That's what should be happening, because people don't want to be *sold* anyway. Therefore, when the sales process goes well, you are helping customers make sound business decisions. This requires all three components of effectiveness triad—a knowledge base about what things are most important to customers, a strategy that causes prospective customers to "want to" engage in a conversation about their needs and your potential solutions, and the professional selling skills that allow you to be perceived by customers as a valuable resource, as opposed to just another sales caller.

So, have you created a repository of business issues and implications? What are you doing to leverage curiosity in the sales process? What are you doing to establish credibility early in the sales process, broaden the need, and increase the prospect's sense of urgency? What's your strategy for securing a commitment at the end of the sales process? Are you fluent in the strategic use of questions? Tracking deals on the forecast is still important, but so is the development of your team's professional selling skills. While selling may have been easy back in the days when customers had lots of money to spend, times have changed and it is incumbent on sales organizations to look inward and make an honest assessment with regard to your organization's current abilities, and the opportunity to raise your selling skills to the next level.

Whether you are the top performing salesperson in your company or you have struggled over the last several months, your effectiveness in the future will be directly related to the investment you are willing to make in yourself and the rest of your sales team. By the way, I am yet to meet a professional salesperson who didn't want to enhance their skills and escalate themselves to the next level of success.

< ACTION ITEMS >

1. Commit to setting aside ten minutes over three consecutive days to complete the Ten Questions exercise. In addition to increasing your confidence when interacting with other people, it will also change the way customers interact with you in sales conversations.

2. Make it a goal to adopt two or three QBS habits every week. Rome was not built in a day, and you cannot expect to transform 100% of your sales team's behavior overnight. "Divide and conquer" is a very effective implementation strategy, realizing that your focus needs to be equally divided between enhancing your team's knowledge base, their strategy, and their professional selling skills.

CHAPTER 6

Solving Problems vs. Providing Solutions

Do you want to hear something funny? Your prospective customers are spending millions of dollars every year hiring high-powered consultants to help them understand their business needs and make good buying decisions, and here you are, the expert on your product, offering to help them for *free*.

> While some salespeople are indeed excellent resources, the perception exists that other salespersons are trying to help themselves more than they are trying to help the customer.

Salespeople are more than ready to help prospective customers understand their business requirements in order to then recommend solution alternatives. But, customers are often reticent to rely on salespeople for this kind of help. We shouldn't blame the customer. It's natural to be skeptical. You are probably just as wary when you are in the customer's shoes. Haven't you ever walked into a car dealership, and cringed when the over-enthusiastic salesperson came up and said, "Can I help you today?" It's so easy to respond with a non-committal, "No thanks, I'm just looking."

Frankly, customers have a right to be cautious. While some salespeople are indeed excellent resources, the perception exists that many other salespersons are trying to help themselves more than they are trying to help the customer. Unfortunately, this perception is probably true in many cases.

The pressure on salespeople to bring in new customer accounts and increase revenue has escalated significantly in recent years. Companies are pushing sales managers to accomplish more with less, and the message has clearly been communicated that if a salesperson doesn't produce, they are gone. The net result is predictable. If a salesperson inherently knows they have to make their numbers in order to feed the family, then we shouldn't be surprised when self-preservation manifests itself into a sales approach that sounds self-serving, as opposed to being customer-oriented.

Let me ask you. Do you think the typical customer is more interested in your needs as a salesperson, or their own needs as the customer? Clearly, customers are much more interested in their own needs, which could include a broad range of problems, issues, or concerns. That's why it would be absurd to expect customers to make a purchase decision just because a salesperson wanted (or needed) to make a sale.

Of course, the idea of being customer-centric is not new to sales organizations. Companies have been talking about it for years. Just revisit the PowerPoint slides from your last sales kick-off meeting. I'd be willing to bet that one of the underlying themes of meeting had something to do with being "customer-focused."

I agree with the idea of being customer-centric. Everyone does! But, at the risk of being the "bad-guy" here, someone needs to step back and point out that our actions, in many cases, have become incongruent with this message of maintaining a strong customer focus. As a result, good intentions are too often being superseded by the drive to close the sale. That reinforces the perception that we (as sellers) are more interested in pushing our own solutions than solving the customer's problems. Of course, anything that creates this type of self-serving perception with customers is going to be counterproductive to your selling efforts.

What Your Current Message Communicates

The first few lines of any company's product literature usually say a lot about whether that company is being perceived as customer-centric or product-centric. You may even want to take a moment and click on your own website. Is it all about you, your company, and your product offerings, or does your product's marketing literature focus more on what's important to your customers?

Let me give you an example.

Suppose you open a product brochure that starts off: *"Our next generation family of medical devices leads the industry in both function and cost efficiency. As the proud holder of 35 technical patents, our commitment to research and development has enabled us to grow as a company and thus expand our product offerings in the medical industry."*

These may indeed be impactful messages, but can you see that this verbiage is not about the customer? Contrast that message with a product brochure that reads: *"Patient demographics are changing rapidly. As a result, the demand for state-of-the-art medical technology is climbing at a rate that exceeds the industry's ability to deliver new services, and today's doctors, nurses, and specialized clinicians cannot afford to be left behind."*

The second literature sample still sounds "cutting edge," and it will undoubtedly go on to talk about the vendor's product offerings, but notice how the way it starts out has nothing to do with the host company or its products. The initial verbiage is purely intended to

127

set the stage regarding the current medical environment and the need to take action. The underlying philosophy of these two samples is ultimately driven by what the writer believes is most important to customers—their problems or your solutions.

Sales presentations offer another example of our tendency toward self-promotion. Have you ever noticed how the first six to ten slides in a formal sales presentation often have nothing to do with the customer? Instead, the opening script for many presentations tends to focus on the vendor's products or their track record for success. I'm not suggesting that you shouldn't be proud of your company's history or the solutions you bring to the table. I am merely pointing out that our business culture has caused sellers to have a tendency toward being inwardly focused.

This philosophical dichotomy of being vendor-focused as opposed to being customer-centric isn't limited to product literature or sales presentations. Voice-mail offers another example. When customers listen to voice-mail messages, they form impressions based on what they hear. The question is: what impression do you want prospective customers to form about you?

One of the exercises we facilitate during a QBS methodology training course is to capture a sample of each student's outgoing voice-mail message, so we can gain a more realistic perspective on what is actually being communicated to their customers. Here is a sample of the type of voice-mail messages we typically hear: *"Hi, Mr. Prospect, my name is Pat Wilson with XYZ Company and I am calling to introduce myself as your account representative. I was hoping to get a few minutes of your time because I wanted to understand your business and then tell you about the many valuable solutions we offer. If this sounds valuable to you, I would appreciate a call back at (404) 569-1000. Have a great day!"*

This verbiage is a representation of the typical voice-mail messages that are being left by salespeople. Unfortunately, there are some real problems with this approach. Let's start with the fact that the sample verbiage on the previous page is bland at best. I always say that generic words are your enemy, particularly on voice-mail. That's because key decision makers in important prospect accounts receive tons of voice-mail messages that sound just like this one— boring diatribes from salespeople, all wanting to introduce themselves, understand the prospect's business, and recommend potential solutions. Big whoop! Sounding just like everyone else who has also left a voice-mail is the quickest way to cause your messages to be erased, as opposed to having customers return your calls.

In my first book, I talked at length about the fact that there are two reasons people return voice-mail messages. One reason is obligation. If your boss calls and leaves a voice-mail message, you would probably feel some sense of obligation to respond. That's because it's from your boss. But very few prospective customers feel "obligated" to return sales calls. As a result, the average success rate for salespeople getting return calls when leaving voice-mail messages has declined to somewhere between two and five percent.

The other reason people respond to voice-mail messages is curiosity. If a prospective customer listens to a voice-mail message, and they are *not* the least bit curious about who you are or the value you bring to the table, they probably won't return the call. On the other hand, if someone who listens to your voice-mail message does become curious about what you can do for them, your chances of getting a return call increase dramatically.

Ironically, most of the voice-mail messages that are being left by sellers actually do more to satisfy the prospect's curiosity, rather than pique it. Plus, if your voice-mail message makes you sound just like the last 50 callers, you automatically forfeit your competitive advantage. Can you see why I'm not a fan of "standard" voice-mail messages?

I have realized that there is another problem causing voice-mail to be less productive than desired, however. It's the fact that messages being left by salespeople tend to sound self-serving. It's very common, as in the sample voice-mail verbiage above, for sellers to say things like, *"I am calling to introduce myself,"* or, *"I was hoping to get a few minutes of your time,"* or, *"I wanted to understand your business."* That's great! Now we know what your objectives are for the call, but what's in it for the customer?

If we step back and take a broader look at your positioning strategy, which would you say is more important to potential customers, their problems or your solutions? Don't you think prospective buyers are much more interested in themselves than they are in the salesperson who calls on them? Particularly when you first engage, customers are definitely focused on themselves. I can guarantee that 99% of the customers you encounter will be much more interested in their own problems, issues, and concerns than they are in your potential solutions. Yet, 99% of the time, sellers are chomping at the bit to tell customers about *all the valuable solutions* they offer.

> If customers are more interested in their own problems than they are in hearing about a salesperson's solutions, why don't we spend more time talking about the problems we solve?

That leads me to wonder, if customers are more interested in their own problems than they are in hearing about a salesperson's solutions, why don't we spend less time talking about the solutions we provide, and more time on the problems we solve?

You might think I'm splitting hairs with this discussion. One could argue that "solving a problem" and "providing a solution" are, in fact, the same thing. I agree, which confirms my point. If the act of "solving a problem" and the act of "providing a solution" are indeed the same, then why not be customer-focused and talk in terms of what's most important to the customer—their problems.

A customer-centric voice-mail message, therefore, would sound more like this: *"Hi Ms. Prospect, this is Francis Dodson, Regional Manager for ABC Company, handling Southern California. I was hoping to catch you for a minute because I am trying to solve a problem relative to your current inventory management system. I'm not sure exactly who I should be dealing with, and the last thing I want to do is step out of bounds in your account. So, if you have a moment today, can you please call me back at (310) 555-6677."*

Because it's true that prospective customers are much more interested in their own problems than a salesperson's solutions, this slight adjustment in positioning tends to generate a much higher return call percentage.

Leveraging curiosity to increase your call back rate is not a trick, and I don't use gimmicks to "lure" customers into returning my calls. Instead, I am simply using logic. If a customer is not the *least* bit curious about who you are or what you can do for them, then you probably will not receive a return call. Likewise, if customers are more interested in their own problems, issues, and concerns, why not focus on what's most important to them? Hence, when I leave a voice-mail with someone saying that, *"I am trying to solve a problem for your company relative to _____,"* the first thought that pops into the customer's mind is, *"What problem?"* They're curious.

The next question salespeople ask is: "Tom, if this is the first time you are attempting to contact a new prospect, how would you know what their problems are?" Good question! Again, let's apply some simple logic.

I think we would all agree that customer situations differ from account to account, and from person to person within the account. Given these differences, there is no way a salesperson can know for certain what a customer's specific business issues or hot buttons are before actually contacting them. But if you invest the time to "arm" yourself in advance with a mental repository of business issues and implications, as I suggested earlier, you may know more about target customers than you think.

Prospective customers do have certain uniquenesses, but they also have many similarities. Let me give you an example. If you sell into the financial services industry, and you have done your homework, then you would know that the vast majority of potential customers probably want to maximize their return on investment. You would also know that diversification is important, along with other issues like risk management, capital growth, estate planning, hedging against inflation, year-end reporting, and confidentiality.

If you sell technology, then you should know that customers face a wide range of business issues from performance, to availability, security, scalability, customer satisfaction, upgrades, documentation, and disaster recovery. If you target manufacturing companies, you probably know that potential customers deal with business issues like operational effectiveness, inventory control, supply chain management, capital equipment, in-house engineering expertise, time to market, and cost of goods sold.

If you have done your homework and created a repository of what's important to customers and why, then you probably have a reasonably clear picture of what people in your industry are concerned about. At that point, it's relatively easy to leave a customer-centric voice-mail message, as in the example above, where the salesperson was trying to be proactive in order to help solve a potential problem. If you think about it, the only reason a salesperson would ever pick up the telephone and call a customer is to help them solve a problem.

A skeptic could still contend that sellers also contact customers to provide solutions. That's true. As I said, you can't do one without the other. A salesperson cannot provide a solution without also solving a problem. Likewise, the only way a salesperson can solve a problem is by providing a solution. Again, the act of solving a problem and providing a solution are one in the same.

Now, let me hold up a mirror. Earlier, I asked the question: which do you think is more important to prospective customers, their problems or your solutions? If you agree that customers are much more interested in their own problems, issues, or concerns, then why not position your message in a way that sounds more customer-centric, as opposed to sounding self-serving.

Re-engineering the Elevator Pitch

Earlier in the chapter, I said prospective customers are quick to form impressions when they listen to voice-mail. That's how they prioritize messages and ultimately decide whether or not to return your calls. Potential buyers are just as quick to form impressions in a "live" sales call, or during your sales presentation. That's why it's important to be customer-centric throughout the entire sales process.

In my second book, *It Only Takes 1% to Have a Competitive Edge in Sales*, Chapter 29 was appropriately called, *Re-Engineering the Elevator Pitch*. In that chapter, I unveiled what has proven to be a startling revelation for many salespeople and managers. The revelation I'm referring to is the simple fact that every year, companies continue to invest millions of dollars, yen, euros, pounds, kroners, francs, and pesos, trying to create impactful messages that will hopefully provide their sales organizations a differentiable advantage in the marketplace. As a result, marketing departments all over the world are hard at work trying to craft next-generation messages into a corporate sales pitch that can be distributed to the sales force at the upcoming sales kick-off meeting or product launch. The problem is, starting with an enthusiastic elevator pitch tends to put a salesperson or sales team in an extremely weak position. This raises the question, why would you want to invest millions of dollars, yen, or euros, only to put your sales team in a weak position?

Are you familiar with the term elevator pitch? An elevator pitch is a colloquialism that has been around the sales world for a long time. Picture a salesperson who suddenly finds himself (or herself) standing on an elevator with a decision maker from one of their important prospect accounts. After the button gets pushed, the salesperson realizes that he or she only has a limited window of time (basically, until the doors open) to make their pitch, hopefully by saying something—anything—that will fuel the conversation or justify their asking for a subsequent appointment.

When first contacting new prospects, whether face-to-face or over the telephone, sellers have a similarly limited window of opportunity. There is significant pressure on an initial sales call to either say something that's impactful enough to further the conversation, or endure the consequences of being dismissed as just another pesky sales caller. Consequently, the goal for companies has always been to create an elevator pitch that sales-

There is significant pressure on an initial sales call to either say something that's impactful enough to further the conversation, or be dismissed as just another pesky sales caller.

people can use to initiate conversations with prospective customers that will hopefully generate new sales opportunities.

The elevator pitch is traditionally filled with impactful messages about the viability of the host company, and the value offered by their products and services. As salespeople, we so desperately want to say something that will differentiate our value proposition in a way that puts us head-and-shoulders above the competition. Consequently, the voice-mail, email, and boardroom airwaves are being filled with claims of greatness intended to generate a positive reaction from prospective clients. Unfortunately, the reaction sellers receive is often very different than what they are seeking.

There's a reason potential customers no longer respond favorably to these introductory elevator pitches. Actually, there are two reasons. First, claims of greatness tend to cause salespeople to sound braggadocious or arrogant. Have you ever come across someone who started off by bragging about themselves when you first met? Does this type of person make you want to continue the conversation or run away? Since there is a fine line between describing your position in the marketplace and sounding arrogant, blasting someone with claims of greatness may not be the best way to initiate a productive conversation, especially with a prospective customer.

The second problem with the traditional elevator pitch is that everyone claims to be the "best." You think you have great products and services? Well don't look now, but I bet your competitors are claiming to be market leaders, too. I bet they also claim to have the best products and services, the best value, the best people, and an impeccable track record of success.

If you sell in a competitive marketplace, I would argue that there is nothing you can say in an introductory blurb (or elevator pitch) that is significantly different from what your competitors are saying about their products, services, or company. Essentially, everyone claims to be the best, and in most cases, your competitors are claiming they are better than you!

The truth is, you don't win by sounding the same as everyone else. You win by differentiating yourself, your company, and your proposed solutions from the rest of the "noise" in the marketplace. Therein lies the problem when first initiating contact with prospective customers—starting with the elevator pitch puts a sales team in a weak position because it is the quickest way to commoditize your value proposition. Simply put, if you sound the same as everyone else, you forfeit your competitive advantage.

> Starting with the elevator pitch is the quickest way to commoditize your value proposition.

To sprinkle some additional salt in the wound, these introductory blurbs that are designed to initiate sales conversations, usually focus on the value proposition being offered by a company's product or service. But, let's go back to the question of what's more important to the customer when you first engage, their problems or your potential solutions? The answer is still the same—customers are exponentially more interested in their own problems, issues, and concerns, than they are in hearing another similar-sounding elevator pitch.

What if there was a way to step outside the box of traditional thinking, and sidestep the risks associated with starting with the traditional elevator pitch? Is it possible to differentiate yourself with an even more impactful customer-centric message? Well, buckle your seatbelt because we are about to change the way your sales team interacts with customers. More importantly, we are about to change the way prospective customers interact with your salespeople, and the resulting upside in terms of sales productivity that comes from being customer-focused is phenomenal.

SPA vs. PAS Positioning

After spending the bulk of my professional career in the trenches of sales and management, plus having trained thousands of salespeople in all different industries, I have observed that most sellers use an SPA approach to position their products and services.

What do I mean by S-P-A? SPA is an acronym we use to characterize the overall flow of a strategic sales conversation. When a salesperson first initiates dialogue with a prospective customer, for example, the tendency is to open with some version of the traditional elevator pitch, in order to make an impact on prospective customers with some powerful messages about their proposed solutions (S). The hope is that saying something impactful about the company or product will lead to a more in-depth conversation about the customer's problems (P). Then at some point in the conversation, or later in the sales process, the conversation will transition naturally to a comparison of your solution versus other alternatives (A) in the marketplace. Hence, the acronym SPA.

I already mentioned two of the risks associated with starting with the traditional elevator pitch. In addition to sounding just like everyone else, claiming your own greatness increases your risk of sounding braggadocious, which actually increases buyer resistance. And it's very difficult to sell to someone who is holding you at arm's length.

The broader risk of an SPA approach has to do with how you are being perceived by potential customers. Let me ask you this question. If it was up to you, would you rather be seen by key decision makers in your target market as a company that solves problems or provides solutions? Seriously, if you had to choose one or the other, would you rather be perceived as a problem solver or a solutions provider?

I now pose this question to salespeople all over the world. The responses I hear back are surprisingly consistent. Most people are very quick to say that they would rather be seen as someone who solves problems. Me too. I suppose that feeling comes from what we agreed earlier, that customers are much more interested in solving their own problems (P), than they are in hearing about a salesperson's potential solutions (S). Can you see why starting with an elevator pitch that focuses primarily on your solutions (S), may not be the best way to initiate a productive conversation with prospective customers, who are actually much more interested in (P)?

In Question Based Selling, one of the ways salespeople get an immediate boost in sales productivity is by re-engineering their current elevator pitch into more of a PAS positioning approach, versus SPA. Let me take a few moments to explain the differences between SPA and PAS positioning.

The first thing you should notice about the PAS positioning model is the letters have not changed. To me, it makes no sense to ask salespeople to throw away all the valuable knowledge they have gained thus far in their careers. Instead, my thought is to leverage the experience a salesperson has acquired over time, knowing that a few small adjustments in positioning can produce a significant net increase in sales effectiveness. It all has to do with how you want to be perceived in your respective marketplace.

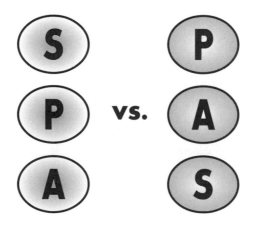

What do I mean by P-A-S? PAS is a positioning strategy where the salesperson starts off by bonding with customers on what's most important to them—their problems (P). Once a need is identified, the seller then has an opportunity to differentiate themselves by positioning away other alternatives (A), as not the best approach. This, of course, paves the way for a more robust conversation about the customer's needs, and your corresponding solutions (S). Hence, the acronym PAS.

With regard to product positioning, people often ask me, "Tom, what does it feel like now that you are no longer in sales?"

No longer in sales? How am I no longer in sales? I have to market my products and services just like anyone else. In fact, my target audience has become extremely skeptical when it comes to sales training. Salespeople have been through umpteen other courses already, and sales managers aren't necessarily excited about taking their salespeople out of the field for another class. Plus, it takes a significant return on investment to justify education when a company is trying to cut costs. So, I am basically in the same boat as you.

Especially in today's business climate, buying decisions need to be cost-justifiable in the mind of the decision maker before they can feel comfortable enough to move forward with a purchase. Knowing this, I integrated the PAS model into my own sales approach a long time ago. Now, when a prospective QBS client says, "Tell me about Question Based Selling," I respond in a way that is intended to maximize my opportunity to be seen as a valuable resource, rather than risk sounding like just another sales trainer.

Sure, I could just deliver a standard elevator pitch about QBS, like the following:

Sample QBS Pitch: *"Question Based Selling is a high-end strategic sales methodology that helps salespeople and managers increase pro-*

ductivity by penetrating new accounts, uncovering needs, filling the pipeline, qualifying prospect opportunities, increasing the prospect's sense of urgency, identifying key players…blah, …blah, …blah…"

But, isn't this what every sales trainer says about their programs? QBS is very different than traditional sales methods, but that may not matter. If you start down the path of SPA, you end up sounding just like everyone else, which is the quickest way to commoditize your value proposition and forfeit your competitive advantage.

To avoid falling into this trap, I look for an opening to shift the conversation in the direction of PAS. I do this by focusing on the customer's problem (P), rather than just trying to articulate my own solutions (S). For example, I might ask a VP of Sales, "Do you have salespeople who are trying to penetrate new accounts, making lots of sales calls and leaving lots of messages, but not being called back?" Since buyer resistance is a common challenge among sales organizations, the answer is predictable. Sales executives who want to penetrate more accounts will say, "Yes, absolutely!"

I might go on to ask, "When you bring new salespeople on board, do you find that some of them ramp-up in a relatively short time-frame, while others struggle along, and in some cases, never make it over the hump?"

Again, sales managers who want to increase sales performance respond by saying, "Yes."

Notice that the focus of the conversation is intentionally directed at the customer's challenges, as opposed to jumping into a diatribe about all the features and benefits of my product or service (in this case, QBS training). My point is that you bond with customers on their problems (P), not your solutions (S).

Bonding with people on what's important to them (their problems) is a very effective way to generate additional conversation. In this case, virtually every sales manager's next question is, "How do you solve that?" If you were the sales manager and I had just mentioned two of *your* biggest challenges, wouldn't you want to know how QBS could help?

Here's the best part. Once you start talking about real problems (P) that are impor-

> Once a prospective buyer realizes that you may be able to help them, they start helping you help them.

tant to a customer, you will notice the tone of your conversations changing from a feeling of cautiousness, to prospects being more receptive to your message. Why? Simply put, when a prospective buyer realizes that you may be able to help them, they start helping you help them.

Once it's established that QBS might be able to help solve the prospective client's problems (P), that's my queue to start talking about our value proposition. But, don't misunderstand. It's not yet time to jump into a litany about your solutions. That's because the "A" in the PAS model gives you an opportunity to position away possible alternatives, as a differentiation strategy that paves the way for you to introduce your recommended solution (S).

When delivering QBS Methodology training in a live setting, I usually ask the audience, "How many of you want to successfully differentiate your proposed solutions?" I know it's a loaded question. Predictably, everyone in the room raises their hand. Well, if you want to differentiate your solutions, you must differentiate them from other alternatives in the marketplace. Hence, the importance of (A) in the PAS model.

The VP of Sales will ask, "How do you solve these problems?"

"Well, Mr. Vice President, there are a couple of ways to deal with the issue of sales training and development. One option is to bring in a motivational speaker. And, while motivational speakers can be quite entertaining, if your salespeople go back to using their same approach, they will likely get the same results—since hype tends to wear off relatively quickly."

This technique of positioning away potential alternatives is called *subtly poisoning*. We're not trying to make customers feel stupid or disparage someone else's offering, but if you want to differentiate your products and services, you must differentiate them from other options they may be considering.

With a Vice President of Sales, I may also want to differentiate QBS from traditional sales methods. If so, I will say, "Mr. Vice President, another option with regard to sales development is to revamp your existing sales process. There are plenty of process vendors who would like to augment your existing sales process with sophisticated spreadsheets and management roll-ups. There's only one problem. Just because a salesperson has a sophisticated spreadsheet doesn't mean his or her prospects will want to engage in a mutually beneficial business relationship. That's why in QBS, we do something very different." Can you see how the "A" in the PAS positioning strategy paves the way for me to propose a different solution?

If you bond with customers on their problems (P), it's so much easier to communicate the value of your product or service against the backdrop of their issues, than it is to deliver a generic elevator pitch.

Taking Advantage of the Missionary Sale

Another opportunity to be customer-centric is to work with customers to help develop their needs. Customers aren't always familiar with your value proposition, and in some cases, they may not even understand their own needs. That's why education is such an important part of the sales process. And it's incumbent on sales-people to educate prospective customers as to how their products and services will benefit them.

It has long been the case that whoever defines the customer's need, usually ends up winning the sale. Have you ever received an RFP (request for proposal) that was clearly written in a way that gave one of your competitors a distinct advantage? On the other hand, have you ever helped develop criteria for an RFP that clearly favored your product or service? If your proposed solutions (S) are ultimately going to be evaluated against the customer's problems (P), then defining the criteria for a decision gives you a significant advantage when it comes time to match your value proposition to the customer's needs.

Top performing salespeople know that one of the keys to success is getting in early. In addition to positioning your product or service in its best light, you can also create obstacles that will make it more difficult for the competition to meet the customer's requirements. In other words, if you can convince a customer to build certain exclu-sions into their RFP (i.e. product features that should be avoided), you can significantly distance yourself from, and sometimes elimi-nate, your closest rivals very early in the selection process.

Let me give you an example.

When I sold superserver technology for NetFrame Systems back in the early 1990's, our closest rival was Tricord Systems. Generally speaking, the Tricord people hated NetFrame. In all hon-esty, we had a healthy disrespect for them as well. Some people call this friendly competition. I call it, one salesperson ends up winning the sale, and the other one doesn't get a commission check.

My strategy was to get in early and offer to help customers write their RFPs. I knew that NetFrame didn't have a technical advantage over Tricord on every line item in the RFP. In fact, much of the criteria in a requirements document can be satisfied by multiple vendors. In the case of NetFrame and Tricord, there were many items where we could both check the "*Yes*" box. But, there were several technical features, like Functional-Multiprocessing, hot-swap connectivity, and ninth bit parity checking, that virtually guaranteed a NetFrame win—if we could get them included into the RFP.

At NetFrame, we didn't always win on technical superiority, however. Sometimes, decisions came down to buyer preference. For example, one of the criterion we used to encourage customers to insert into their RFPs was the fact that the server should open from the front, as opposed to from the top or sides. You might be thinking, who cares which way a superserver opens? Ah, but after a few simple positioning questions, this rudimentary product feature suddenly became a hingepin that could sway a purchase decision.

I would simply ask, "Mr. Customer, do you plan to rack-mount these servers?" I knew most customers did prefer rack mounted systems. So when they said, "Yes," I explained that their RFP should include a firm requirement that the server must open from the front. This made sense because you cannot access a rack-mounted server from the top or sides, which would make it very difficult to maintain, upgrade, or trouble-shoot if there was a problem.

Who wouldn't agree with that logic?

If the customer seemed indifferent to rack mounting their servers, I went on to ask, "Mr. Customer, do you want to have the option to rack mount your servers in the future?" Since everything was moving toward rack-mounted technology, the answer was always yes. "If so, Mr. Customer, you should make it a point to specify that the selected product must open from the front, or you will rob yourself of having this flexibility down the road."

Guess what? Our biggest rival, Tricord Systems, built their superserver products to open from the top. Oops!

What percentage of your sales opportunities are driven by a request for proposal (RFP)? It might depend on your industry and the products and services you sell. But, I would argue that 100% of the opportunities you encounter are driven by decision criteria of some kind, whether it's written down in a formal request for proposal, or not. The question is: Who is responsible for crafting the decision criteria that will ultimately determine the selected vendor? Too often, sellers rely on prospective customers to formulate their own criteria, thinking that customers already know what they want. Sometimes, sellers assume customers who don't know what they want aren't qualified prospects, in which case, they are reticent to invest lots of time in these accounts. Unfortunately, this view forfeits a significant opportunity to gain a competitive advantage, and potentially, shorten the sales process.

Education has always been an important aspect of the sale. The primary focus of the traditional missionary effort was to educate customers about the value of your goods and services. As salespeople, we want to share good news about all the wonderful benefits our proposed solutions bring to the table. But, it's important to realize that whatever information you share about your product or service is only valuable if it is being positioned against the backdrop of decision criteria that is important to the customer.

Again, do you want to be viewed by potential buyers as someone who solves problems or provides solutions? Personally, I want to be seen as someone who solves problems, for two reasons. First, given that relationships in sales are very important, talking with customers about their problems, issues, and concerns is a bonding opportunity. Customers tend to do business with people who make them feel comfortable, and one of the things that makes people feel comfortable is the recognition that you understand and care about the challenges they face. Secondly, if a customer doesn't have a problem that needs to be solved, then your solutions are essentially valueless to them. If, on the other hand, a customer is wrestling with several issues, then you have multiple opportunities to add significant value. Also, the larger the problem seems, the greater the prospect's sense of urgency will be for making a decision.

For salespeople, the strategic opportunity for education extends far beyond just giving customers an elevator pitch about your product or service. The larger opportunity is helping customers identify and better understand the full extent of the issues that need to be addressed, which takes us to the next level of detail in the needs development conversation.

Implication, Implication, Implication...

When we talk about solving problems in the PAS model (as opposed to a traditional SPA approach), we must remember that the goal is to facilitate an in-depth conversation about what's important to the customer, and why. That brings us back to the idea of talking beyond the issue, in order to get deeper, wider, and more strategic in your needs development conversations.

Is security important to one of your prospective customers? If so, then you will want to broaden the conversation to explore *why* security is important to them. In every type of sale, business issues are important to different customers for different reasons. So, what are the implications of security to this particular customer? Are they concerned about theft? What about the confidentiality of information? Do they need to protect intellectual property or ensure the privacy of their client base? Are they worried about the possibility of someone hacking into their computer systems, or the unscheduled outages that could result? In addition to giving you insight into "why" security is important, broadening the conversation expands your opportunity to make a sale by giving you multiple opportunities to provide value.

With good preparation and a sound strategy, facilitating an effective needs development conversation becomes relatively easy. Just raise a business issue, and then explore the next level of detail using implication questions. It's a simple technique—raise an issue, and then focus on implication, implication, implication. After you exhaust one issue, simply raise another, remembering to focus on the specific implications of each.

Once again, how many reasons do you want customers to have to buy from you? Just one? Will two or three reasons suffice? If I was the salesperson, I would want prospective buyers to have many reasons to move forward with a favorable purchase decision.

> Ultimately, I want customers to have so many reasons to buy from me that cost-justification is a mere formality.

Ultimately, I would want customers to have so many reasons to buy from me that cost-justification is a mere formality. If you feel the same, then I recommend you heed the advice to "arm" your sales organization with a comprehensive list of what things are important to prospective customers. Forget about your products and services. If your company didn't even exist, there would still be a list of business issues that are important to target customers. What issues do they talk about at staff meetings? What problems are keeping them up at night, and why? Most customers are going to share their thoughts, feelings, and concerns with someone; that person might as well be you. Fortunately, whether or not customers choose to share information has a lot to do with your ability to bond with them on their problems (P).

Leveraging the Rest of the Herd

Helping customers identify potential problems, or opportunities to improve their existing condition is somewhat of a delicate task. As you know, people are not always open to talking with a salesperson, especially when there is a potential risk that issues or problems might be exposed. Much of this risk can be sidestepped using The Herd Theory, which in addition to being used as an associative technique to generate momentum, can also be an invaluable tool for needs development.

> Helping customers identify potential problems, or opportunities to improve their existing condition is somewhat of a delicate task.

As I explained earlier, having a successful needs development strategy requires a basic knowledge of possible business issues and implications, so you know in advance what things might be important to customers, and why. Much of this effort comes from knowing what's important to other customers. This puts you in a strong position to associate needs from "the rest of the herd" with potential needs a prospective client might also be experiencing. Basically, the technique sounds like this:

Salesperson: "Mr. Prospect, you mentioned that productivity and asset management are key issues for you. I recently worked with another customer who is also having to keep close tabs on inventories. Do we need to be concerned about current inventory levels in your business?"

The format when using The Herd Theory is to simply say, *"Mr. Prospect, other customers we work with are focusing on issues like _____ and _____. Do we need to pay attention to those for you?"*

Or, you could say something like, *"Another thing customers often struggle with is _____. Is that a concern for you as well?"*

This technique gives prospective customers an opportunity to associate their own needs with problems, issues, and concerns that other customers are currently facing or have already encountered. Basically, leveraging the rest of the herd softens the conversation, thus reducing the risk that customers might feel threatened or exposed by sharing their problems or concerns with you. This technique makes it easy for potential buyers to conclude that if other customers have already dealt with these challenges, perhaps there is an opportunity to benefit from their experiences.

Gravitating Away from Whatever Feels Most Comfortable

How you are perceived in today's selling environment has a lot to do with how you choose to position yourself with prospective customers. The natural tendency for salespeople is to try and differentiate their company's offerings by describing their products and services as the best in their respective markets. But, once again, everyone claims that their products are the *best*.

Many years ago, the school of hard knocks taught me that if you sound the same as everyone else, then you forfeit your competitive advantage. That's why the SPA approach is so problematic. In today's business climate, claims of greatness tend to fall on deaf ears. As a result, starting with the elevator pitch is one of the quickest ways to commoditize your value proposition, not to mention sounding braggadocious, which is the last impression you want customers to form in a competitive selling environment.

Once we realize that customers are much more interested in solving their own problems (P), than they are in hearing about our potential solutions (S), the opportunities for bonding on what's most important (to them) increase significantly. And, if you arm yourself in advance with a repository of business issues and implications, you are in a strong position to use PAS to facilitate a more detailed conversation about what's important to your customers and why. You are also in a strong position to steer the conversation in the direction of issues that give you the strongest competitive advantage. After all, sometimes the difference between winning and losing a sale can be as simple as whether your product conveniently opens from the front, or only opens from the top.

One more note about PAS. We talked about bonding with customers on their problems (P). We also talked about being proactive to differentiate yourself from alternatives in the marketplace (A). But, we haven't spent much time on the positioning of your solutions (S). That's what we talk about next.

< ACTION ITEMS >

1. At your next weekly sales meeting, ask someone to name a business issue that might be important to your customers. Then, go around the room and have everyone on your sales team identify an implication of that issue. In other words, "why" might that issue be important to prospective customers? Keep going until you fully exhaust the issue. Note how many implications your team can name before running out of gas. You should be able to come up with at least 10 implications per business issue. Then, do the exercise again by raising another issue.

2. Make a list of technical or functional requirements that would give you a competitive advantage if they were written into a request for proposal. Also create a list of possible exclusions, that

if written into an RFP document, would make it difficult for competitors to meet the selection criteria.

3. Revisit your product literature and sales presentation. Does the support material you use in your daily efforts focus more about what's important to you (S), or what's important to the customer (P)?

CHAPTER 7

The Paradox of Value

I have begun to notice that life is a continuum of intriguing paradoxes. Just when you think something should be one way, you discover it's completely the opposite. Have you ever noticed, for example, that some of the richest people in the world are also some of the most unhappy? Just check out the next issue of People magazine at your local newsstand. Here's another example. Isn't it strange that we vaccinate humans against chronic diseases like polio and small pox by injecting them with small doses of the actual disease?

Do you like sports? Have you ever wondered why deer hunters carefully dress in camouflaged clothing, but just before they go into the woods, they strap on a florescent orange vest and cap? If you play golf and you want to curve the ball to the right, then you must swing to the left. Of course, there are usually legitimate underlying reasons to support these behaviors. Since deer are color blind, for example, hunters know that wearing a bright orange vest doesn't expose them to their prey, but it does identify them to other hunters who may also be in the woods. In golf, swinging to the left creates clockwise spin on the ball, which makes it curve to the right when the ball encounters normal air resistance.

I can keep going. Have you ever noticed that the more anxiously you look forward to Christmas, the slower it seems to come? Or, isn't it odd that parents who want to maintain close relationships with their children must be willing to let them go off and make some of their own mistakes.

Things are not always what they seem in sales, either. For example, don't you think it's strange that the introduction of sophisticated communication tools like voice-mail, e-mail, fax, and pager systems have, in many cases actually made it more difficult for salespeople to get through to new prospects? There are many paradoxes in sales. Here's another example. Prospective buyers in today's business climate are more cautious and standoffish than ever before. But, isn't it strange that some sellers have responded by becoming even more aggressive and tenacious, causing customers to retreat even further?

In *Secrets of Question Based Selling*, we exposed the fact that several of the mindsets salespeople have been conditioned to accept over time are no longer valid. For example, salespeople are often thought of as being supercharged and highly enthusiastic. But you will find that top performing salespeople in most companies are generally not the cheerleader type. In fact, top performers are usually quite analytical, always looking for a strategic advantage or potential obstacles that could undermine a successful sale. That's why one of the first premise concepts I introduced as part of the QBS methodology was, "Always positive is not always most productive."

To illustrate, sellers have long been conditioned to ask questions with a positive, even hopeful, tone. Therefore, typical sales questions tend to sound very optimistic, like: *"Mr. Prospect, would next Tuesday work for a conference call?"* Or, *"Does your boss like our proposal?"* Sometimes sellers ask, *"Are we still in good shape to close this deal by the end of the month?"* The salesperson in these examples is obviously hoping next Tuesday will "work" for a conference call, or that the boss does "like" the proposal, or that the deal is still in "good shape" to close by month-end. These positively dispositioned questions do not generate more positive results, however. In fact, just the opposite happens. Positively dispositioned questions tend to cause customers to withhold information, or provide less accurate information, which is counterproductive to your selling efforts.

Possibly the most intriguing paradox in sales has to do with sellers and their attempts to communicate value. Companies are working harder than ever to create and communicate impactful messages about their respective value propositions, and salespeople have become more emphatic about the value their products and services bring to the table. Yet these claims of greatness are quickly discarded by prospective customers. In fact, it seems the more emphatic a salesperson is, the more skeptical a prospective customer becomes, which creates an interesting challenge for sellers who are desperately trying to differentiate themselves in the marketplace, only to end up commoditizing their respective value propositions.

The truth is we live in an increasingly cautious society and people are naturally skeptical. They don't just accept claims of greatness at face value. Don't take my word for it. How many pieces of junk mail have you thrown away so far this year, even though they all claimed to offer some phenomenal benefit *just for you*? For that matter, how many unsolicited e-mails have you deleted in the last few months that made raving claims about a product or service?

So, here's the paradox. To win in sales, you must communicate impactful messages about your product or service, and you must be able to differentiate yourself from the other competitive offerings in the marketplace. But, how can we accomplish these objectives if our value propositions are falling on deaf ears?

The Intangible Nature of Perceived Value

Let me ask, do you sell a tangible product or an intangible one? When posed with this question, sellers tend to reflect back to the definition of tangibility. Can you touch it? If so, then it must be a tangible product. Someone who sells laptop computers, for example, could easily conclude that their product is indeed tangible. Not only can you touch and feel a laptop computer, you can actually put it in your lap. A salesperson who distributes medical supplies could say the same thing about their new IV pumps. If you can bring one into an operating room and show it to a doctor, then it must be a tangible item.

On the other hand, most service offerings are not tangible items. A salesperson cannot bring a dozen hours of consulting time into a sales call and hand it to a prospective customer. Other familiar products, like insurance and advertising, have a similar intangibility. I mean…how often do you roll over and take one last look at your auto insurance before going to sleep at night?

One could assume that since customers cannot actually hold an intangible product in their hand, selling intangible items is probably more difficult than selling tangible goods. In fact, marketing an intangible item is much more of a conceptual sale, where you are selling the perception of value, as opposed to value itself. Think of it this way. With intangible items, if customers don't perceive high levels of value, then your chances of making a sale are greatly reduced. Consequently, a salesperson's success in the intangible sale is largely attributable to their ability to communicate concepts that will ultimately cause prospects to perceive high levels of value, as opposed to relying on the tangible nature of the product itself.

But, guess what? Even if the product you sell is tangible, the value proposition of that product is not. That's because the value proposition of most tangible items is, in fact, intangible. Can you see the paradox? Even though you can physically hold a tangible product in your hand, you are still selling its perceived value. And, if potential buyers don't perceive significant value, you are not likely to succeed in closing a sale.

Let me give you a simple example. We agreed that a laptop computer is a tangible

> Even if the product you are selling is indeed tangible, the value proposition of that product is not.

item, right? But, you can't necessarily touch the true value of a laptop computer. In other words, why are laptop computers valuable? Different users have different requirements, that's true. But speaking for myself, a laptop computer offers increased productivity when I'm away from the office. It also enables to me to connect to the Internet, stay in closer touch with clients, and communicate with other certified QBS trainers. My laptop computer is definitely a tangible item, but you can't touch the value of increased productivity. Other intangible benefits include mobility, reliability, ease of use, cost effectiveness, and of course, the ability to play computer games on long flights. All of these intangible benefits create perceived value, but you still can't hold mobility, reliability, ease of use, or cost effectiveness in your hand.

This same principle applies if you sell real estate, manufactured goods, cellular telephones, or medical supplies. Real estate, for example, is certainly a tangible item. You can touch the dirt, and you can even enter into physical structures located on the property. But people don't buy real estate just for dirt and structures. Instead, they buy because of perceived intangibles like location, usefulness, aesthetic beauty, spaciousness, growth potential, return on investment, quality of schools, and the view out the kitchen window. And, I can guarantee that if a potential buyer doesn't perceive those or other equally intangible benefits as being valuable, they will not move forward with a purchase.

The value proposition of more sophisticated products like clinical IV pumps in medical sales is equally intangible. Although an IV pump is certainly touchable, physicians don't care about product specifications. They care about the intangible aspects of these products like their impact on ease of use, clinical efficacy, patient comfort, availability of product, cost effectiveness, possible exclusions or complications, reimbursement rates, legal liability, and interoperability with other medical devices.

I would argue that even everyday products like tooth brushes, breakfast cereal, or a pair of Italian loafers are purchased based on value propositions that are intangible. How can you touch the value of having cleaner-feeling teeth, a healthier diet, or feeling stylish all the way to the ground?

Although this is rarely talked about in other sales training programs, I would argue that the inherent benefits of the products and services you offer are, in fact, highly intangible. And, in order for prospective customers to make a purchase decision, those customers must first *perceive* enough value to justify a purchase and create a sense of urgency for moving forward.

Corporate Messaging Has Become Convoluted

Once you understand that the value propositions of the products and services being offered are indeed intangible, we need to put some thought into how best to communicate a strong sense of value in these intangible benefits to prospective customers.

Most salespeople have been taught that the best way to communicate value to prospective customers is to simply explain all the wonderful advantages of their product or service. As a result, sellers tend to highlight features of their proposed solutions, followed by an explanation of their corresponding benefits. Here's what that sounds like: *"Mr. Prospect, our product was designed using high-density plastic to provide greater tensile strength when lifting heavy objects, which makes it more durable for a longer useful life."* This feature-benefit combination is fairly straightforward, to the point where a customer who was interested in durability, strength of product, or life-expectancy would probably register significant value when hearing this pitch.

With the increasing competitive pressure of today's business environment, I have noticed that value propositions are becoming more and more difficult to understand, however. Have you read any product brochures lately? Corporate marketing departments are really stretching their thesauruses. Perhaps they feel the need to *tailor vivid descriptions of their products that are both evocative and expressive, by applying verbiage that eloquently characterizes the gamut of intrinsic value using words that combine urbane sophistication with erudite refinement.* Can you dig it? Of course not—it's just a bunch of gobbledy-goop!

Product descriptions have evolved to a point where the feature/benefit combinations that are now being positioned to customers, both in written form and in product presentations, have become so convoluted and confusing that they actually erode your value proposition. To cite an example, check out the following excerpt from a recent product launch I found on the web. (I changed the name of the vendor and product to protect the innocent.)

"ABC Company's new X-1400 was designed to improve customer retention through personalized customer initiatives and increased communications, strengthen business partner relationships through increased collaboration and access to information, and improve employee productivity by connecting all the people, information, and applications employees need to do their job organized in a format that allows them to be increasingly more efficient."

Whoever came up with this "blurb" linked together some fancy words, but what does this passage really mean? To me, it doesn't pass the Layman's Test, meaning the average person can't even tell what the product does, not to mention understand what value it would provide to them.

I understand why corporate messaging is now headed in this direction. Competitive pressures in the marketplace are not receding, they are becoming more intense. If you turn the clock back thirty years, the corporate marketing function in many companies was an afterthought. Businesses wanted to be competitive, but they had no where near the market sophistication that exists today. Now, spin doctors in corporate marketing departments research what competitors are saying, and they are tasked with creating messages about their respective products and services that are even better and more impactful. Of course, when a competitor gets wind of your new messaging, they put the wheels in motion to create a next generation message that will be even more impactful. As a result, we have gotten ourselves into a vicious cycle of escalating complexity, where corporate marketers and salespeople are ferociously trying to "out-describe" each other.

Convoluted is a good word for this mess. Value propositions have become so flamboyant and verbose that the actual benefits companies want to communicate are being lost in the words. This creates yet another interesting paradox. As companies work harder and harder to communicate greater value, the messages being conveyed are becoming less and less impactful.

This phenomenon of companies all trying to out-describe each other is everywhere—even in your local grocery store. Have you noticed that it is no longer possible to buy regular dishwashing liquid? You can only buy *new and improved* dishwashing liquid, with the *advanced formula for extra-strength*. But, if you look down the isle, you will notice

> As companies work harder and harder to communicate greater value, the messages being conveyed are becoming less and less impactful.

that everyone else claims to have a new and improved dishwashing formula, too. As a result, these claims of superiority are quickly discounted by consumers because all the different products sound the same.

If you want a dose of reality, check out the websites of your top three competitors. (Be warned that this can be an enlightening experience.) I bet you will find your competitors claiming to provide many of the same capabilities that are listed on your website. And, I bet they are claiming that they do a better job than you! All these similar sounding value messages present a problem from the customer's point of view. When customers invest the time to research vendor options, only to discover that everyone's value propositions sound pretty much the same, it becomes very difficult to determine which option provides the best fit.

What vendor companies are attempting to do is differentiate themselves and cause customers to perceive greater value. The tendency, however, has been to try and communicate greater value by encouraging salespeople to be increasingly more emphatic about their offerings. But, the difference between touting something as being *really great, incredibly great, unbelievably great,* or *phenomenally great,* is negligible. Consumers today have grown increasingly skeptical, and they are quick to commoditize a salesperson's declarations of superiority. Therefore, claims of greatness are falling on deaf ears, and salespeople are left facing the challenge of how to differentiate their value propositions in an increasingly competitive marketplace.

Touting "Solutions" May Be the Problem

Like most paradoxes, there is a reason things are the way they are. As we discussed, the tendency for sellers is to try to communicate value in terms of the solutions they provide. That's because logic would suggest that the more "wonderful" a product seems, the more valuable it will be in the eyes of prospective customers.

We agreed back in Chapter 6, however, that customers are generally much more interested in solving their own problems than they are in hearing about a salesperson's potential solutions. This leaves sellers in the precarious position of trying to communicate value by touting the "wonderful-ness" of a proposed solution, when potential buyers are much more interested in their own problems, issues, and concerns. Furthermore, when sellers communicate a value proposition that is based on intangible benefits, the tendency is to try and explain value in terms of the *presence* of their product or service, basically describing how satisfied customers will be after the purchase. But with many solutions, it's difficult to characterize the value of an intangible benefit by describing it in material terms. Again, how many people go to bed at night thinking, "Boy, my car insurance policy really felt good today!"

I am not suggesting that insurance is not valuable. Insurance is absolutely valuable, which explains why you and I both continue to purchase auto, homeowner's, health, and life insurance on a yearly basis. Nonetheless, it is difficult to describe the intrinsic value of insurance in terms of how wonderful it feels once you own it. In fact, if you sat in on a sales call with a top life insurance salesperson, you would find that they spend very little time talking about how good their policies are, and most of their time talking about what can happen if someone is not appropriately protected.

Think about it this way. You don't buy life insurance just to own it. Rather, you buy life insurance because of the downside risks associated with *not* owning it.

Are you ready for another paradox about value? Truth be told, the value of an intangible benefit is best understood in terms of the *absence* of it. Upon researching life insurance options, for example, when a prospective buyer considers the impact of leaving their family without a steady income, or without the resources needed to fund a college education, or they consider the possibility of having the Internal Revenue Service lay claim to half of their estate, the value of life insurance suddenly takes on new meaning. A life insurance salesperson can try to describe how wonderful their policies are until they are blue in the face, but it's the images that get created by the absence of owning proper insurance in the time of need that ultimately send a shiver up the customer's spine.

This same principle can be applied to most products. In the case of technology, having a highly available network is certainly desirable, but *not* having a reliable network can be disastrous. Or, if you are considering the purchase of radial tires, a tread design that channels water out from underneath the tire in wet conditions is certainly a nice benefit, but it is no where near as valuable as its ability to prevent your car from hydroplaning, and skidding off into oncoming traffic.

Think about the product I sell—Question Based Selling. Our product is definitely intangible. The only way to create opportunities in my business is to help prospective clients perceive high amounts of value in the programs we deliver. But, when I talk with Vice Presidents of Sales, they don't want to hear how wonderful my program is, they want to know how QBS will address their business challenges. Even though sales VP's all have different issues, from wanting salespeople to more effectively differentiate themselves, to increased margin pressures, ramping new salespeople up more quickly, or better qualifying opportunities, the idea of not accomplishing these objectives is ultimately what creates the greatest sense of urgency to make a commitment to schedule a training event.

I suppose it's human nature to take the positive benefits of a product or service for granted. But the minute they go away, we (as consumers) go berserk. Do you own a cellular phone? I bet you rarely think about all the wonderful benefits of having a cell phone, until it's time to make an important call and you can't get a strong enough signal.

So as a salesperson, wouldn't you put yourself in a stronger position by positioning the value of your product or service in terms of the positive benefits it provides *and* the problems it solves (or prevents)? You absolutely would! I talked about this in Chapter 4 of *Secrets of Question Based Selling*, where we introduced the idea of *Gold Medals* and *German Shepherds*. Essentially, different types of buyers have different buying motivations, hot buttons, and political agendas for a decision. Rather than overcomplicate the subject of buyer motivation with sophisticated Freudian psychology, let me say again that people are motivated in two basic ways—by positive reward and by negative aversion. Hence the metaphor: while some people are motivated to run fast toward *Gold Medals*, many other people run even faster from *German Shepherds*. Consequently, if you want to expand your value proposition and enhance your ability to connect with different types of buyers, then it's up to you to make the conscious effort to position your solution in terms of *Gold Medals* and *German Shepherds* (both).

This tendency for a salesperson to position their value proposition in positive terms often happens long before the customer actually makes a purchase decision. Early on in the sales process, for example, when a seller is trying to get to higher levels within an account, they might say to their internal champion, "Mr. Customer, I would like to spend a few minutes with your CFO to show him how our products will increase productivity and maximize his return on investment." Sounds like a mini-elevator pitch, doesn't it? Here's the reverse. "Mr. Customer, would it make sense for us to spend a few minutes educating your CFO, so he doesn't take one look at the price and torpedo the idea?"

When preparing for QBS training events, I usually ask for a conference call with the client in order to customize the material for the intended audience. But, I don't ask for a manager's time so "I" can understand their business and deliver better training. That's because doing what's best for me doesn't necessarily create the desired sense of urgency. Instead, I am more inclined to ask a Vice President of Sales for time on their calendar, so we don't "completely miss the boat" at their upcoming training event. Both of these requests refer to benefits that would come from strategizing in advance. But how you ask does make a difference.

Regarding the broader issue of selling intangibles, we said that even if the product you sell is tangible, the value of your proposed solution is not. It's also true that a salesperson will convey greater value to potential buyers by communicating intangible benefits in terms of the absence of their product or service, rather than simply depending on sophisticated corporate marketing jargon to say a lot of words, but not convey a lot of substance.

Education is the Ultimate Goal

When we strategize about communicating value in the sales process, what we are really talking about is education. A large part of the opportunity to succeed in sales hinges on your ability to help prospective customers clearly understand the value being offered by your product or service. Education is a funny thing, however. One might assume that the best way to educate someone on something is simply to explain it as eloquently as possible. But as we are seeing, some things, like the perceived value of an intangible benefit, are difficult to explain.

Here's an example from my own business. In QBS, we spend a great deal of time talking about curiosity, and the role it plays in the strategic sales process. While other sales trainers ignore the subject, we have built a very successful training practice by focusing on the fundamental concepts of sales effectiveness, one of which is the fact that curiosity is the genesis of every sale. As I have said many times, if a prospect or customer is not the least bit curious about who you are or what you can do for them, then you are not likely to get mindshare in the account. Everyone agrees with this.

In my early years of training, I knew this idea was critically important, but I found it surprisingly difficult to explain the concept of leveraging curiosity to sales audiences. I stood at the podium and told them, "If you want to be successful in sales, then you have to pique the prospect's interest." Participants were polite, but I could tell the message wasn't getting through. The point finally hit home once I began explaining what happens in the absence of curiosity. "Let me put it this way," I say now, "if a prospective cus-

> Sometimes the best way to communicate something is to explain what happens in the absence of it.

166

tomer is *not* the least bit curious about who you are, or what you can do for them, you have no chance." Now, they get it!

It's another one of life's crazy paradoxes. Sometimes the best way to communicate something is to explain what happens in the absence of it. This is an important lesson for salespeople, because as educators, you will find that customers often perceive greater value when they think about not having key features or benefits. Again, thinking about all the wonderful benefits one gets from owning life insurance isn't nearly as impactful as thinking about what could happen if you were not appropriately covered in the event of an untimely death.

"...and that's what we solve!"

Here's one more ironic twist. With regard to positioning, rather than trying to articulate all the wonderful benefits your product or service offers, the best and most impactful way to express the true value of your solutions may be as simple as saying, "We solve that!"

The logic here is simple. If you agree that customers are much more interested in solving their own problems than they are in hearing a salesperson's claims, then it stands to reason that your value proposition ought to center more around their problems (P), rather than your solutions (S).

The value clients derive from QBS is quite intangible, as I have said. Consequently, benefits like a wider sales funnel, reduced buyer resistance, and differentiation are difficult to communicate without sounding just like every other sales trainer sporting a bag full of slides. Therefore, I don't spend a lot of time trying to describe the "wonderful" benefits of QBS training. Instead, I spend most of my time talking with salespeople, managers, and executives about the challenges they might be facing given the current selling climate, and problems they might be trying to solve. For example, I explain:

"QBS is very different than traditional sales methods. That's because there's a problem with traditional sales approaches. Every sales training program I am aware of is foundationed on the premise that a salesperson must first uncover a need, in order to then provide value. My guess, Mr. VP of Sales, is that you agree with this premise. Me too! But, here's the problem. Just because a salesperson in today's business environment wants to ask questions to uncover needs, doesn't necessarily mean that prospective customers will want to share information. Likewise, just because you have a good story to tell, doesn't guarantee you an audience within your target accounts.

The selling environment has also changed. Customers have less time, there are more products and services being offered, and sellers have become increasingly more aggressive. As a result, prospective buyers have become more cautious and standoffish than ever before, making it that much more difficult for salespeople to penetrate new accounts. In fact, key decision makers in important prospect accounts are often working just as hard to get off the telephone as salespeople are to stay on.

Furthermore, if your salespeople sound the same as everyone else in your market space, then they will forfeit their competitive advantage—which makes it even more difficult for them to penetrate accounts, fill the pipeline with qualified accounts, differentiate their solutions, and create a sense of urgency for moving forward.

These are very real challenges that impact sales organizations on a daily basis...and that's basically what QBS solves."

I spend most of the time talking with prospective clients about potential problems (P), rather than trying to bestow accolades on myself about the benefits of Question Based Selling. Granted, the verbiage above is a condensed version of our value proposition. But when prospective customers can relate to the verbal pictures you paint about challenges they currently face, they will naturally look to you as someone who can help them address those issues.

First and foremost, customers want to know that you under-stand their problems, issues, and concerns. Knowing this, my conference calls with sales managers and sales executives usually begin with a simple question like, "How can I help?" Most clients will men-tion a few symptoms of their

> When prospective customers can relate to the verbal pictures you paint about challenges they currently face, they will naturally look to you for help in addressing those issues.

current environment, but what they really want is someone to help think through and diagnose the root causes of the problem. That's why I take the time to lay the groundwork for QBS by first explaining that the selling environment has changed. I go on to explain that there is a problem with traditional sales methods, and I make the point that sounding just like everyone else is the quickest way to commoditize your value proposition. In a typical conference call, it's not unusual for me to spend fifteen or twen-ty minutes talking about the challenges sales organizations now face, and why continuing with an old-school approach is no longer a viable option.

The net effect is this: when a prospective client forms the impres-sion that, "Hey, this guy understands my problem," customers then begin to think, "maybe he can help us solve it!" That's when you start to establish some serious credibility as a valuable resource.

Here's the cool part. Once you articulate the customer's prob-lems to the point where you can say, "Those are the type of challenges we help customers solve," the next question customers ask is, "How?" Doesn't that sound like an invitation to engage further, to provide more detail regarding the specific aspects of your product or service? It's also an excellent opportunity to suggest possible next steps, like a face-to-face meeting. Either way, the net result of the conversation is very different than what would have happened had I gone down the more traditional path of trying to describe all the "wonderful" benefits of Question Based Selling.

This strategy applies with virtually any type of intangible sale. Take financial services, for example. With the economic roller-coaster ride people experienced in the 1990's, there is a fair amount of skepticism toward stockbrokers and financial advisers. Now, when a financial advisor calls on prospective clients, just claiming to have a track record of success is no longer enough to gain their confidence. Instead, the financial advisor must be able to articulate the challenges investors face, and facilitate a discussion about what issues might be most important to this customer. That's how to put yourself in a position to transform a customer's skepticism into a potential interest.

Let me give a few examples of what this positioning sounds like:

Financial Advisor:
"Mr. Customer, although we are in the business of providing financial products and services, just providing market advice isn't good enough for most clients anymore. People don't want to hear about the latest hot stock pick, and they don't want to be pressured into making an unwise investment by a commission-hungry broker. Instead, clients want solid thinking and sound direction. They want an integrity-based financial partner who will work to maximize their return on investment and minimize their risk. They also want someone who

will take the time to consider their current financial status as well as long term investment objectives. Mr. Customer, *that's basically what we do for the clients we serve."*

Real Estate Agent:
"Mr. Customer, I understand you're thinking about listing your home and you are currently in the process of selecting an agent. The way I see it, the real value homeowners get from an agent comes after the listing agreement is signed. In today's real estate market, selling a home is not as simple as just taking a picture and registering with a multiple listing service. If you want to get quality offers, your property has to be proactively marketed to other real estate agents and to the buying public. Leads must be monitored and followed up on, and feedback should be used to adjust to market conditions and deal with any issues a prospective buyer may have. The bottom line is, if you want results, you need to choose an agent who will put forth the effort as if they were selling their own home ...*which is exactly what we do!"*

Medical Sales:
"Dr. Prospect, there are several medicines you can choose from to fight foot fungus. The problem is, most patients don't just want a temporary solution. They want permanent relief. So, the ultimate goal is to prescribe a treatment that eliminates the symptoms of itching, chafing, burning, and peeling, with the added benefit of eradicating the underlying medical condition after a few weeks of continued usage. *And, that's basically what this new product does."*

Notice that the salesperson in these examples doesn't spend a lot of time talking about product features. Interestingly, they aren't spending a lot of time talking about the problems they solve either.

Instead, they are very specifically talking with customers about potential problems and challenges that might exist. You see, customers have challenges whether you offer a solution to them or not. And, I have come to believe that the first thing customers want to know is whether or not you understand their current situation. Of course, if any of the challenges you raise resonate with the client, then your introductory 'blurb' will undoubtedly expand into a more in-depth exchange of ideas regarding the customer's financial objectives, real estate concerns, or medical challenges.

There is another angle on this strategy of bonding with customers on their problems, issues, and concerns. One of the best salespeople I know is a real estate agent with Remax here in Atlanta. His name is Jerry Saunders. Jerry has been my agent for 16 years. And, I can tell you that, as a perennial skeptic, the last thing I want is some pushy real estate agent trying to "sell" me a house.

At the very first house Jerry took me to in 1987, he unlocked the front door, walked into the foyer, and said, "You don't want this house."

"I don't?" I asked, a bit baffled, since I hadn't even made it in the door. "Why not?"

Jerry pointed to some barely noticeable cracks in the sheetrock, and to some places where the molding had separated from the wall. A quick trip to the basement revealed the house was sitting crooked on the foundation. We left. Wow! Jerry wasn't trying to sell me just any house. He was actually trying to help me buy the right house. His credibility with me instantly skyrocketed.

Now that I have worked with Jerry several times, I have noticed a trend. When Jerry Saunders sees a potential problem, he points it out. He highlights benefits as well. But, one of the reasons he has become so successful in real estate is because he has tremendous credibility with clients, much of which comes from his willingness to talk directly about actual problems, as opposed to always focusing on the "silver lining," like so many other agents do.

The way I see it, customers will make all kinds of time to spend with someone they believe can help them address problems, issues, or concerns, but they have very little time to spend with someone who is just another sales caller. Of course, the only way for prospective customers to know whether or not you can help, is to get their problems out on the table. That doesn't happen by blasting potential buyers with the latest elevator pitch, and having your value proposition get commoditized, however. Nor does it happen because you incessantly probe customers for needs. Let me say it again. You bond with customers by talking more about what's most important to them (their problems), rather than whatever might be most important to us (our solutions).

The question you must now answer is: Do you want to be seen as a valuable resource in the eyes of prospective customers, or just another sales caller? I choose the former. The good news is, how you position your value proposition will have a lot to do with how you are perceived in the marketplace.

< ACTION ITEMS >

1. Make a list of the intangible benefits of your proposed offering. Then match this list of benefits up with the list of business issues and implications created in Chapter 4. What are you doing to communicate value in terms of the *absence* of your product or service?
2. Visit your company's website. Does it pass the Layman's Test? Then, visit your competitor's websites. How different is your messaging from other vendors? Can you point to verbiage that would indicate to a prospective customer that you understand their problem?

3. Subdivide your current value proposition into *Gold Medal* and *German Shepherd* benefits. Document which features produce a positive benefit versus those that help protect customers against negative consequences. The objective is not to threaten customers into buying. Rather, we are simply recognizing that different people have different hot buttons regarding purchase decisions, and we should take advantage of the opportunity to arm ourselves with a broader value proposition.

CHAPTER 8

Functional Equivalence is Your Enemy

If your products and services were functionally superior to all others, and they were also being offered at the absolute lowest price in the industry, then your company may not even need salespeople. All your company would need is a healthy advertising budget and a team of operators standing by to handle the onslaught of telephone orders. Don't worry though, because this scenario is not likely to happen. In our economic system, companies need salespeople because products and services that offer superior functionality are sold at a premium over less capable alternatives. Hence the old saying, "You get what you pay for."

> If the products and services being offered are functionally equivalent, the decision of which one to purchase usually comes down to lowest price.

Interestingly, the opposite is also true. If the products and services being offered to customers are functionally equivalent, the decision of which one to purchase usually comes down to lowest price. If everything else were equal, why wouldn't customers choose the least expensive alternative?

Since very few companies are in a position to consistently offer the absolute lowest price, however, it is the salesperson's job to differentiate their products and services in order to justify the difference in price.

It's important to note that competitive forces in the industry are not in your favor on this quest to differentiate your products and services. While you are out there working hard to increase the perceived value of your offerings in the eyes of potential buyers, your competitors are trying to take you down a notch, or two…or three. Ask yourself this question: who is the customer supposed to believe when one salesperson makes claims that his or her product is head-and-shoulders above the rest, while three or four competitors counter with equally compelling data showing that their products are best?

Customers are naturally skeptical anyway. If we revisit lessons learned in earlier chapters, we made the point that claims of greatness coming from a salesperson tend to be commoditized in the eyes of prospective customers. In a competitive market, everyone says their product is the best. The shame is, even if your company really does offer the best solution, if your message sounds basically the same as everyone else's, you forfeit your competitive advantage.

> True differentiation occurs when customers recognize the value of one product to be greater than the value of another, enough so to justify the difference in price.

The ultimate goal with respect to product positioning is differentiation in the marketplace, which is something that sales organizations everywhere struggle with. True differentiation occurs when customers recognize the value of one product to be greater than the value of another, enough so to justify the difference in price.

Contrary to popular belief, most customers don't opt for the cheapest alternative. Given the increased margin pressures in today's market, this may seem a bit strange. But if you look around, you will find that most people are discriminating consumers, but they don't necessarily make choices based on price alone. For example, most people don't eat the cheapest food. Likewise, most people don't buy the cheapest furniture, or wear the cheapest clothes. If you scheduled a reconnaissance visit to your target customer locations, you would find office space, government buildings, schools, operating rooms, warehouses, and manufacturing facilities, filled with products that didn't necessarily have the lowest price tag.

Most of your friends don't drive the cheapest automobile. They probably don't drive the most expensive car, either. At some point in the buying process, a customer makes a purchase decision that is ultimately based on

> Functional equivalence is your enemy, especially if you sell valuable products.

two things—perceived value and cost. If the cost between alternatives is equivalent, the customer will usually choose the product or service with the greatest perceived value. The operative word here is "perceived." Even if your solution actually would provide significantly greater value, if it is perceived as being "functionally equivalent," the purchase decision will ultimately come down to who has the lowest price.

Functional equivalence is your enemy, especially if you sell valuable products. With a few rare exceptions, we (as salespeople) don't want our solutions to be perceived by customers as being the same as our competitors. Instead, we want to differentiate ourselves, and we also want to be able to justify any differences in price. In fact, we want to create so much perceived value in the eyes of our customers that the decision to move forward with a purchase becomes a relative "no-brainer." To accomplish this objective, there are a few basic principles that sellers need to understand, starting with the fact that cost and price are not the same.

"Cost" and "Price" are Very Different

"How much does your product (or service) cost?" This is a common question that all salespeople get asked. It's a legitimate question, and one that customers should ask. Cost will always be a critical factor in the decision of whether or not to move forward with a purchase.

When sellers are asked about cost, the tendency is to respond by quoting the price. "Mr. Customer, our new Z-9000 product costs $59.00 per user, or you can purchase a 1000-user license for a bundled price of $35,000."

In theory, if the price you quote is within a range that meets the customer's expectations, then you are probably in a good position to move forward toward wrapping up the sale. Chances are good, however, that you are not the only salesperson providing a price quote. Therefore, what if the opposite happens? What if the price you quote is higher than a competitor? In that case, one might conclude that you are now at a competitive disadvantage. Again, if two offerings are seen as being functionally equivalent, very few customers will choose the higher priced alternative. Fortunately for us, things are not always what they seem.

I learned this lesson soon after I opened the southeastern regional office for NetFrame Systems back in 1992. As an innovative high-tech manufacturer, NetFrame designed and developed the super-server, which was basically a mainframe-like computer that could drive large corporate networks. Our target audience included large corporations who were adding new capabilities to their existing network, and companies who were building a network infrastructure to accommodate the growing technology needs of their business.

One option customers had was to build their network by purchasing individual file servers at a price of approximately $20,000 per machine. Customers were adding new servers all the time, and without any reason not to, utilizing individual file servers became the default decision. Then, NetFrame Systems came along offering customers another alternative—deploying superserver technology at a cost ranging anywhere from $40,000 to $160,000 per machine, depending on configuration.

Which would you have said was the more economical decision—a file server that costs $20,000, or one that might cost well over $100,000? Talk about obvious! Other server vendors quickly wrote NetFrame off as an over-priced technology not even worth competing against. They rationalized that even the most ignorant of customers couldn't justify spending five times more money for a file server. What they didn't realize was that a NetFrame superserver and an individual file server were not functionally equivalent.

The problem with choosing between solution alternatives is the underlying assumption that the products being considered are functionally the same. You've heard the old saying, "if it walks like a duck, and talks like a duck, it must be a duck." Without any reason to believe otherwise, a customer could easily assume that one server option was fairly similar to the next. Therefore, if a traditional file server costs $20,000, and the price tag of an appropriately configured NetFrame came in at around $100,000, justifying the $80,000 difference in price could seem like an insurmountable objection. My responsibility was to help clients make an apples-to-apples comparison and arrive at the best decision for their growing business.

You see, comparing the functionality and power of a NetFrame superserver to a standard file server is like comparing a MAC Truck to a minivan. Sure, they are both vehicles. But there is a big difference in capability between a passenger vehicle and an eighteen-wheeler.

To that end, the NetFrame family of superservers was designed using sophisticated multi-processor server architecture (MPSA).

MPSA enabled a fully configured NetFrame superserver to do the work of eight or ten traditional file servers. Furthermore, the customer's decision usually wasn't to purchase either one new file server or a NetFrame. Companies were growing their networks exponentially. More often the decision was either to buy a single NetFrame, or six or seven additional file servers.

Of course, when you compared the price of a NetFrame superserver to the incremental cost of adding six or seven file servers, a one-time expenditure of $100,000 suddenly became much more cost effective than purchasing individual servers. And, that was just the hardware component. Purchasing a superserver also helped to save large amounts of money on software because customers only needed to buy a single license as opposed to purchasing six or seven individual software licenses. The ongoing maintenance and operational costs for managing a consolidated platform were also significantly reduced. And, as icing on the cake, NetFrame was able to provide additional functionality. The superserver option offered clients parity checking for data integrity, a fault tolerant hardware platform, and load balancing. Now do the math!

The importance of an apples-to-apples comparison is not limited to technology sales. This same concept applies to every value-based sale. Take real estate for example. Which is a better value, a four-bedroom house listed at $250,000, or a five-bedroom house with a pool listed at $370,000? The answer, as you might guess, is going to depend on several factors, starting with the needs of the prospective buyer, the location, lot size and square footage of both houses, quality of school districts, amenities that may be included in the purchase, and the general condition of the properties.

Here's another example. Which is better, bringing in an experienced consultant to solve a business problem and paying their daily rate for a few days, or hiring an inexperienced person at a much lower rate, whose lack of experience could end up making the problem worse. We can keep going. Is it better to spend half as much to acquire a product that will last a year or two, or twice as much to purchase something that will last a lifetime?

I am not suggesting that the higher priced alternative is always the better choice. I like to get a good deal just as much as you. But, we must realize that we live in an economic system where differences in price often represent significant differences in value to the customer. That value must be factored into their purchase decisions. Our job as salespeople is to make sure prospective customers are aware of these differences in value. Otherwise, if customers assume your products and services are basically the same as the those being offered by competitors, their purchase decisions will be based on whoever offers the lowest price, as opposed to which alternative is most cost-effective.

> Is it better to spend half as much to acquire a product that will last a year or two, or twice as much to purchase something that will last a lifetime?

What's the Cost of Not Solving the Problem?

Some companies focus on selling the total cost of ownership. This is a good strategy because the true cost of a product or service is likely to include a wide range of factors other than price. These decision factors could include everything from quality of the goods, to amenities, ease of use, upgradeability, required education, management oversight, membership fees, depreciation, residual value, and the long-term viability of the vendor.

Here's a question I always ask prospective customers, "Mr. Customer, what will happen if the needs or requirements driving your purchase are not appropriately addressed?" What I'm really asking is, what's the cost of not making a good decision?

If your customer does not have a sense of urgency for making a decision, then you are not likely to make a sale. On the other hand, when a customer does have a sense of urgency for moving forward, they are generally making their decision to satisfy specific requirements—to either address an existing business issue, prevent a problem from happening, or take advantage of a potential opportunity. Sometimes, there are multiple reasons for wanting to move forward, which helps escalate their sense of urgency even further.

If you want to be perceived as a valuable resource and not just another sales caller, then it's your responsibility to help prospective customers realize that there may be a significant costs associated with *not* moving forward with a decision—whether it's not addressing a current business issue, failing to prevent an impending problem, or not being in a position to take advantage of a potential opportunity.

You can ask simple questions like, "What would be the impact on productivity if your current systems suddenly became unavailable to end-users?" Or, "What would happen if there was a disruption to your supply chain and your company was unable to ship or receive materials on a timely basis?"

You can even ask customers to quantify the risk, asking, "Have you ever calculated the hourly cost of downtime for your company?"

While some costs are empirically quantifiable, others are not. So, be sure to ask questions like, "How many people would be inconvenienced if (insert scenario)?" Or, "To what extent would your management get upset if (insert scenario)?"

Even though you may not be able to get customers to attach a specific dollar amount to these possibilities, I can guarantee most customers will recognize that there are costs associated with inconveniencing people or having management get upset.

Sometimes, the cost of not purchasing a product or service far exceeds its price. The realization, for example, that an automobile accident could result in serious injuries or a law suit that could cost many thousands of dollars

> Sometimes, the cost of not purchasing a product or service far exceeds its price.

suddenly makes the annual automobile insurance premium of a few hundred dollars seem cheap. Likewise, the cost of not having the appropriate support on your computers in the event of a system shutdown could be exponentially more expensive than the price of the annual maintenance contract.

Be Careful Trying to Justify a Higher Price

When evaluating different product or service options, often the better option has a higher sticker price. As in the case of a super-server, it is absolutely possible to cost justify these price differences by helping customers understand that the sticker price is only one component in the total cost-of-ownership equation. But, you must be very careful how you position your product when you justify it as a higher price alternative.

When there is a cost difference between your solution and another vendor's, customers are going to require you to justify your price. "Why is your product more expensive than your competitor's?" they will ask.

The natural tendency for sellers who are trying to justify a higher price is to explain to customers why they should pay more. As a result, sellers make the argument: "Our product may be more expensive, but it's worth it because...."

Unfortunately, this explanation is a losing argument. In particular, I have a huge problem with a salesperson acknowledging that their product or service *is* more expensive. With a few exceptions, like jewelry, designer clothing, and other luxury items, we live in a world where if a product doesn't make money or save money, then justifying a purchase is going to be difficult. Therefore, if you position your solution as being "more expensive" than other competing products, you run the risk of customers thinking you provide similar value at a much higher cost. How could customers justify paying a higher price for a product or service that essentially sounds the same?

I would argue that if you offer valuable solutions at a competitive price, then you should be very aggressive on the issue of cost, which includes positioning your product or service as being less expensive, not more. Customers are trying to choose the solution that is most cost-effective, and they understand that doesn't necessarily mean the lowest priced alternative. Therefore, your strongest position is to say with conviction, "Our product is the most cost-effective alternative that has the ability to provide _____." You should be able to support this positioning with data that makes an apples-to-apples comparison and gives the customer a broader perspective regarding total cost of ownership.

Here's what this positioning sounded like in the NetFrame sale:

Customer: *"How can we justify spending $100,000 on a NetFrame, when we can buy a standard file server for $20,000?"*

Seller: *"Mr. Customer, it's true that the price of a superserver is greater than the price of a standalone PC server. A NetFrame superserver will cost your company*

	significantly less money over the life of the product, however."
Customer:	*"Less money?"*
Seller:	*"Absolutely. As I understand it, your current plans are to add six or seven file servers over the next six months, at a cost of about $20,000 per machine. Since a NetFrame superserver can drive that much traffic on a single machine, you can justify the decision on hardware savings alone. Factor in the savings you get from not having to purchase multiple software licenses, coupled with reduced maintenance costs, less complexity, less downtime, and data protection, and cost savings becomes the primary reason most customers choose NetFrame!*

One of the clients I recently trained, a Maryland-based company called Immersion Medical, sells clinical simulation equipment to hospitals and teaching facilities. They developed and patented a touch sensitive technology called Haptics, which enables doctors, residents, and nurses to learn and practice clinical procedures using technology that gives audio, visual, and touch sensitive feedback to simulate real life scenarios. Wouldn't you want your physician to try an invasive procedure like a colonoscopy on a simulator first, before attempting it on you? Put it this way: you wouldn't want to be flying at thirty-thousand feet in a 747 with a pilot who hadn't practiced their skills on a flight simulator first.

Doctors and clinicians love these simulation devices. In addition to speeding up the learning curve, Haptics technology tends to reduce error rates, which reduces the number of patient complications, the costs of those complications, and the potential for legal liability. An Immersion device also increases the productivity of the medical staff and saves time, which translates into more hospital revenue and increased patient satisfaction. Sounds like a slam-dunk sale, right? Well, not necessarily.

I asked the Vice President of Sales at Immersion to send me some sample proposals prior to their QBS training session. It turns out their simulators range in price from $15,000 at the low end, to over $100,000, depending on the recommended configuration. So, when the inevitable question comes up about how much a simulator costs, an Immersion rep might quote a figure in the middle of that range, saying that such-and such device costs $28,000.

And, that's what happens. They quote a price. Proud of their product, the Immersion salesperson confidently says, "This product costs $28,000." To a doctor who has seen the demonstration, that may sound quite reasonable. But doctors usually don't purchase medical equipment for hospitals. It's the other way around. Hospitals purchase medical equipment for their doctors.

The proposal document then floats around the hospital as the purchase is being considered. At some point, the price quote finds its way to the Chief Financial Officer's desk, since he or she is the person who ultimately signs off on purchases of capital equipment. Guess what happens when a CFO sees that a simulator is going to "cost" the hospital $28,000. Request denied!

You have to know that CFOs are business people. Their job is to manage the bottom line of the business—in this case, a hospital. To them, the decision is simple. If it doesn't make our hospital money or save us money, we shouldn't do it. From a business perspective, that logic makes sense. With the constant pressure to reduce costs and the continued erosion of medical reimbursement rates, why would a CFO agree to purchase a medical device that ends up costing their institution money?

For Immersion, and so many other companies, when the news comes back that the buyer decided against the purchase, the focus of the sale turns to a discussion of how to overcome the cost objection.

Let me suggest an alternative. The next time a prospective customer asks you how much your product costs, you should respond by telling them how much your product saves. I am not telling you to withhold your price. Rather, I'm suggesting that you should put the price in perspective, so your advocates within the account can make a compelling argument, one that will get the purchase approved. Here's what that sounds like.

Doctor: *"How much does one of these simulation devices cost?"*

Salesperson: *"Doctor Jones, that's actually the best part. If you take into account the increased productivity gained by ramping clinicians up more quickly, coupled with lower error rates, fewer complications, and higher reimbursement rates from JAHCO accreditation, this unit could save the hospital $200,000 over the next two years…at a price of only $28,000.*

I might even go on to ask, "How many lawsuits would need to be avoided to justify a cost of $28,000?" In reality, a single legal action would pay for this product many times over. Saving thirty minutes a week in the operating room would more than pay for this machine as well. In addition to justifying the cost, the hospital would become the beneficiary of many other intangible benefits, like higher employee morale, a reputation for having state of the art technology, and happier patients.

At the end of the day, there is a huge difference between a product that costs $28,000 and one that saves $200,000. Ironically, the product being considered in both scenarios is the same. The only difference is the way that product is being positioned, which has a lot to do with the seller.

I asked the sales team at Immersion, "If your product was offered free of charge, would you be able to sell more units?" The answer was a resounding, "Yes." The thought was that they would sell exponentially more units. So, what if your product was offered at a price that was even better than free? In the case of Immersion, if simulation technology could provide a $200,000 benefit, isn't that the same as giving the product away for free, and then handing the hospital a check for $172,000. Who wouldn't want one if that were the case? By the way, even if the cost savings in these projections were halved, the hospital would still get the product for no cost, with a bonus of $72,000 in additional benefits. Such a deal!

One more note on cost versus benefits. Cost is a topic that sometimes doesn't get addressed until much later in the sales process. Sellers often feel that they need to hold their pricing close to the vest, because cost is thought to be the final objection on the way to making a sale. I feel exactly the opposite. To me, cost is the number one reason people buy from you. Again, if it doesn't make the customer money or save them money, they shouldn't move forward with a purchase. But, if you can show a customer that your product is a money maker (or saver), why withhold this information until the end?

Let me give you a "for instance" using the simulation example above. Immersion wants to show their product to as many doctors as possible. So, they set up live demonstrations in hospitals, hoping to get slivers of doctors time between cases. As anyone who has ever sold in the medical arena knows, doctors are a tough audience.

They don't have much time for, and even less patience with, sales presentations. Therefore, when you finally do get a doctor's attention, sellers end up racing through their presentations hoping to make a good impression.

Racing to communicate as much value as possible in a limited time window is not a formula for success. I would much rather do something, or say something, that will grab the doctor's attention, in order to then have an opportunity to educate them on the value of my product or service.

For example, suppose a doctor comes around the corner, sees me (the Immersion rep) and says, "I've got two minutes, what have you got?"

I would say, "Doctor Johnson, this is a clinical simulation device that could save you an average of three hours a week, and your Endoscopy lab approximately $200,000 over the next two years."

Most doctors will say, "Show me how it works." Doesn't that sound like an invitation? When skeptical prospects suddenly become interested and invite you to engage, the dynamic of the conversation changes instantly—now you don't have to race!

I have always been very aggressive on the issue of cost, and you should be too! Think about it this way. If I offered to sell you a one-hundred dollar bill, for a cost of only five dollars, would we still be arguing over price? If you offer valuable products at a competitive price point, then you should be able to look a customer in the eye, and say with confidence, "Mr. Customer, our

> If I offered to sell you a one-hundred dollar bill, for a cost of only five dollars, would we still be arguing over price?

product is the most cost effective alternative that (*insert compelling argument*)!" This is very different than telling customers your product or service is indeed more expensive, but worth it because…

Help Customers Register More Value

I made the point earlier that value is something that must be perceived. We can expand this point by agreeing that prospective customers must perceive significant value in your solutions or it will be difficult for them to justify a purchase. Likewise, if prospects don't register a difference in value between your offering and your competitors', it will be equally difficult to justify any difference in price. Your job is to cause customers to register enough value to justify a decision in your favor. Let's talk about how that happens.

Perceived value only gets registered when it is conveyed against the backdrop of something that is truly important to the customer. Your product or service might have some very interesting features, but customers will only register value if those features address a specific need. This is where the needs development process and your product's value proposition come together, in order to hopefully cause prospective customers to recognize greater value.

The first question we need to consider is a familiar one. How many reasons do you want customers to have to buy from you? Most salespeople want customers to have multiple reasons to move forward with a purchase. Having numerous reasons to buy from you increases the customer's sense of urgency, which in turn, shortens the timeline for making a decision. It's also an advantage to have multiple differentiators—which increases the perceived value of your product or service, and justifies any differences in price between your proposed solution and lower-end alternatives.

> Perceived value is only registered when it is conveyed against the backdrop of something that is truly important to the customer.

As the sales profession has evolved, sellers have unfortunately been taught that the best way to build value is by using benefit statements. Tell customers about a feature of your product, and then follow up with a quick 'blurb' about how that feature will benefit them. The thought was, the more benefit statements you can communicate to customers, the more value you accumulate on the way to making a sale.

What traditional approaches failed to realize is that customers are not always listening to these benefit statements. They might hear the words, but if the messages sound the same as what every other vendor is saying, customers don't register the intended value.

In my view, it's critical that salespeople talk about value in terms that are impactful to their customers. We already determined back in Chapter 6 that customers are much more interested in their own problems (P), than they are in hearing about a salesperson's solutions (S). Therefore, it stands to reason that customers would register more benefits if the value of those benefits was being communicated against the backdrop of their key business issues or decision criteria. Of course, different issues are important to different customers, which is why you must invest the time to "arm" yourself with a repository of potential business issues and implications. Knowing what things might be important to potential customers (and why) enables you to facilitate a more robust needs development conversation, thus laying the groundwork for greater value.

If we refer back to the NetFrame analogy, one of the competitive advantages NetFrame had over lower-end PC servers was the ability to provide parity checking for data integrity. The more traditional feature/benefit positioning would have been to say, "Mr. Customer, the NetFrame family of superservers offers parity checking, which will protect the data on your networks, much like mainframe computers have been doing for years, so you no longer have to worry about the integrity of your business information."

It's a simple format. Basically, we provide such-and-such capability, which is good for customers because of this-and-that. The problem with this format is that the value of a highly differentiable feature can easily get lost in the blandness of the message.

Instead, I used a more compelling argument which started with the following question: "Mr. Customer, would you consider the data on your corporate networks to be mission critical to your business, or would you call this a recreational serving environment?"

Predictably, customers would say, "Yes, the data on our file server is very important to our business."

I further emphasized the point by confirming, "So, if something were to corrupt or destroy the data on your existing network, that would be a problem?"

"That would certainly be a problem," customers said.

"Small problem? Or, potentially a huge problem?"

"Losing data could cripple our business!"

"So, protecting your data is a definite requirement, right?"

"Absolutely!"

This series of questions suddenly put me in a strong competitive position when it came time to compare a NetFrame superserver with less expensive PC-based solutions. You see, one of the phenomenons that occurs with electronic devices is the random corruption of data when a single bit, in an eight bit field, spontaneously flips from a "0" to a "1," or from a "1" back to a "0." To address this issue, NetFrame's architecture had the unique ability to add a check digit onto the standard eight-bit field that continuously verified the integrity of the information. Frankly, it was the same capability mini-computers and mainframes had been using for years, but PC servers couldn't provide this capability because on a standard EISA, ISA, or Micro-channel bus architecture, there was no ninth-bit. Therefore, getting customers to agree upfront that protecting the data on their network was absolutely critical gave us a significant competitive advantage. Meanwhile, buying a PC-based solution that couldn't protect the customer's data suddenly became a much less attractive option.

Another issue I asked about during needs development was, "Mr. Customer, how important is it to minimize downtime?" I also made it a point to raise the issue of growth, asking, "How many incremental file servers do you plan to deploy in the next six to twelve months?" Of course, these were two other areas where NetFrame had a significant advantage over PC servers.

Now that I have impressed you with my technical prowess, here's the point. Customers are going to put you on the spot with questions like, "Why should I spend $100,000 on a superserver, when I can purchase a low-end PC server for $20,000?" Here are some thoughts on how best to respond.

First, it's important to acknowledge the customer's option to buy the lower price product. Then, it's incumbent upon you, as the salesperson, to put the decision in perspective with regard to the customer's requirements. Sometimes, I even use a little tongue-in-cheek positioning. For example, "Mr. Customer, you can purchase an individual PC file server at a cost of around $20,000. That's true. It's also true that you can buy a decent Volkswagen for $20,000, or a piano…but none of these options will protect your data. Plus, if you continue to grow as planned, purchasing multiple PC servers that won't protect your data, minimize downtime, or aren't able to scale to accommodate future growth, might actually be your most expensive alternative."

In addition to knowing what's important to your customers, and why those things might be important, it's vital to know where you have the greatest opportunity to create competitive separation. Identifying multiple business issues and implications can increase the prospect's sense of urgency and give them many reasons to move forward toward a purchase decision. But, identifying key differentiators between your product and competitive offerings is the real secret to justifying any difference in price. That's where you come in, as the valuable resource who can remind customers why they are even making this decision. "Mr. Customer, I understand that budgets are tight, but if your needs are to protect network data, accommodate future growth, minimize downtime, and reduce complexity, then buying something that doesn't accomplish these goals is *not* your least expensive option."

> Identifying key differentiators between your product and competitive offerings is the real secret to justifying any difference in price.

Helping customers understand that lowest price does not always mean least expensive makes a strong argument, given that customers are usually trying to accomplish specific objectives with their purchase decisions.

What if You Sell a True Commodity?

We've talked about the need to differentiate your solutions from the rest of the "noise" in the marketplace. But, what if your product or service is *not* different than other solution alternatives? What if the products or services you sell are exactly the same as your competitor's?

Probably the best example of this can be seen in the financial services industry. Stockbrokers sell commodities. For all practical purposes, you can buy the same stocks, bonds, and mutual funds from your financial advisor that you can purchase from twenty other brokers down the street. In fact, the lines of delineation between financial specialties are quickly being erased as clients can now buy stocks from their banker, and do their banking with their favorite brokerage house. Let's not forget the insurance segment of the market, which is chock-full of large insurance companies who would also like to manage your investments. Oh, and by the way, the larger banks and brokerage houses are now offering insurance.

Someone in the financial services industry could argue the point that not all financial services products are commodities. Merrill Lynch, for example, offers an in-house family of mutual funds that are only available through a Merrill Lynch associate. Likewise, Bank of America has certain account features that are only available to their best customers. But, these unique offerings are statistical outliers compared to the broader range of financial alternatives that are now, for all practical purposes, available anywhere.

Real estate is another commodity industry. With a few exceptions, the inventory of homes on the real estate market is the same for every real estate agent in the surrounding area. In fact, with real estate, you are actually competing with other agents to sell the exact same house, for about the same price!

Even if the product you sell isn't a true commodity, it can still seem the same to target customers. Property and casualty insurance is a good example. If you locked insurance agents from Allstate, Nationwide, and State Farm in the same room to have a friendly debate on which company offered the best insurance, they would probably rip each other's eyes out before admitting their policies and premiums were basically the same. I am not saying there aren't differences between these companies. I am saying, however, that to the average consumer, the differences between the products being offered by competitive insurance firms are negligible.

With most commodity purchases, customers don't investigate all their options anyway. The last time you made a stock purchase, did you study the prospectus of every company in the industry before telling your broker to put you "in" for a hundred shares? What about the last time your purchased homeowner's insurance? Did you examine the legal terms and conditions of all the different companies and their policies before choosing an insurer? Of course you didn't! Most consumers don't. Most narrow their options down to a few manageable alternatives that would accomplish their objectives and gives them the confidence that they are making a sound decision. This process provides us with an important clue for how salespeople can be successful in an environment where the sale does not hinge upon your ability to differentiate a specific product. And, if differentiating the product in a commodity business is no longer the goal, then our focus must shift to a discussion about what we can do to cause prospective customers to feel more comfortable when it comes to choosing to do business with you.

Note that just because the product you sell is similar to, if not the same as, your competitor's, does not mean there aren't significant differentiators that will ultimately determine the outcome of the sale. Rarely do consumers throw darts at a board to choose an insurance agent or financial advisor. For that matter, rarely do companies, hospitals, or law firms randomly select their suppliers. Instead, they make calculated choices based on three decision factors: relationship, service, and price.

Let's start with price because it is the *least* important of the three differentiating factors. When the products or services being offered are functionally equivalent, the decision usually comes down to lowest price. Price becomes the differentiating factor. I made this point already. But with commodities, price usually isn't the differentiator because costs are basically equivalent. You can buy the same hundred shares of Coca-Cola stock from Merrill Lynch or Morgan Stanley Dean Witter, at basically the same cost. Allstate and State Farm may quote different insurance rates for specific line items, but on balance, competition in the marketplace drives their cost structure to be very similar to comparable offerings.

When price and function are essentially equivalent, then relationships and service become very important. Consistent top performers in sales are masters at creating and managing effective business relationships. Granted, they might be friendly and outgoing people, but customers don't buy just because a salesperson is friendly. Mastering the business relationship is the key to being successful in a commodity sale.

Prospective buyers want to feel comfortable before, during, and after the transaction. If you have a personal relationship with a prospective client already, then you may be ahead of the game in terms of establishing credibility and building trust with that person. If your father-in-law is President/CEO of an important prospect account, call him! Or, if you have an existing relationships that can be leveraged to create referrals into a new account, by all means, use them. Sellers don't always have the opportunity to leverage existing relationship, however. And customers don't always have a salesperson they can trust. In cases where a relationship does not already exist, service becomes the single most important differentiating factor when choosing between comparable options.

As a consumer yourself, if you contacted two salespeople, and one invested the time to meet with you personally, and then followed up with a professionally drafted proposal that was tailored to fit your needs, you would be impressed—especially if the other salesperson was late, lax, or unprofessional. At that point, choosing a salesperson would be easy.

Does extra effort on the part of a salesperson guarantee them the business? No, there are never any guarantees that you will win a sale just because you invest lots of time. The purpose of providing good service before the sale isn't to create a sense of obligation, or make customers feel they "owe" you the business. Rather, service is an important differentiator because the level of effort and commitment salespeople show before the sale is usually a good indication of what customers can expect after they make the actual purchase.

> Exemplary service leads customers to believe their salesperson, advisor, or consultant cares enough to invest the time and effort to make them successful.

We've been talking about supporting a value proposition where intangible benefits must be perceived as valuable by prospective clients or customers. That's where good service comes in. When the level of service before the sale is exemplary, customers tend to assume that the quality of the product will be higher as well. They also tend to assume that turnaround times will be shorter, mistakes will be less frequent, and the overall business relationship will be more satisfying and productive, not to mention more prosperous.

Exemplary service leads customers to believe their salesperson, advisor, or consultant cares enough about them and what's important, to invest the time and effort to make them successful. For customers, this translates into a higher degree of confidence when moving forward into a business relationship. Of course, excellent service can take different forms. Good follow up skills, for example, can be critical to building a customer's confidence. Delivering more than what's expected can also make a huge difference in the outcome of a sale. Sometimes, it's just the little things, like sending a relevant newspaper clipping or magazine article with a small note attached that says, "This made me think of you."

Is taking the time to provide exemplary service worth the investment in your business? Not knowing your specific business environment or situation, I can't answer that question from a distance. But, if you sell in a competitive industry, where comparable products are being offered at competitive prices, I would bet that the sellers who are willing to go the extra mile are winning most of the sales.

Put Yourself in a Strong Negotiating Position

Differentiating yourself, your solutions, and your company is not only important, it's a prerequisite to having a strong negotiating position at the end of the sale. Too often, a seller's message gets commoditized during the sales process and customers end up basing their decision on who offers the lowest price. "You better start sharpening your pencil," customers will say.

At QBS Research, Inc., we receive lots of inquiries from sales managers who want to improve their sales organization's negotiation skills. The first question I always ask is, "What problem are you trying to solve?" Sometimes, it's increased margin pressure. In other cases, the length of the selling cycle has expanded, and decisions are dragging on way too long. Behind each of these requests is a common theme—for some reason, sellers are finding themselves (or putting themselves) in a weak position at the end of the sales process.

The truth is, if your value proposition gets commoditized during the sales process and your product is seen as functionally equivalent, justifying a difference in price between your offering and lower-end alternatives will be difficult. It will be equally difficult to create the sense of urgency necessary to motivate customers to move forward with a favorable decision. Unfortunately, neither of these issues (getting commoditized in the sales process, or customers having a low sense of urgency) will be solved by having your salespeople attend a negotiating skills class. And, while I agree that the art of negotiation is one of several strategic disciplines sellers can learn, trying to fix the wrong problem is not the answer.

I made the point in my second book, *It Only Takes 1% to Have a Competitive Edge in Sales*, that larger sales are typically won as an accumulation of smaller successes. If you notice, most sales are not decided at the end of the sales process. Rather, you win or lose as you go. Therefore, the goal is not to arrive at the end of the sale, and then start negotiating the deal. That's too late. By then, initial impressions have long since been formed, and your competitive position has already been established. The real opportunity to be successful stems from being proactive early in the sales process, in a way that puts you in a stronger position when the time comes to negotiate the terms of a transaction. How can you be proactive? Basically, the QBS methodology is a study in how to do just that—how to step outside the box of traditional thinking, and put yourself in the strongest possible position throughout the sales process.

At the end of the day, very few products that are superior in function are also being offered at the absolute lowest price. As a result, your company needs salespeople who can differentiate the value of your products and services as compared to competitive solutions—enough so as to justify a favorable decision and create a sense of urgency for moving forward with a purchase. Fortunately, whether or not this happens has a lot to do with you!

< ACTION ITEMS >

1. Create a total cost of ownership model that prospective customers can use to compare your proposed solutions to other competitive alternatives. Be sure to focus on "total expense," which should include ancillary costs like installation, ongoing maintenance, early replacement, and any service fees that customers may incur. Be sure to also include any costs that can be avoided by implementing your solution.

2. Revisit the repository list of business issues and implications that you created earlier, and prioritize which ones offer the greatest opportunity for differentiation between your product offerings and the competition. Also, identify which ones offer a cost advantage.

3. Write down on a piece of paper the three or four things you currently do to provide exemplary service. Have a roundtable discussion with your sales team about how else you can deliver excellent service before, during, and after the sale, in ways that will exceed your competitor's best efforts. Be sure to stretch on this one, because they may be reading this book, too!

CHAPTER 9

The Convergence of Sales & Marketing

I don't mean to be the bad guy, but if we are going to continue being candid and pragmatic, let me just say that a disconnect exists between the field sales organization and corporate marketing in many large corporations. Although this problem isn't necessarily new, the fact that sellers now face increasingly difficult market conditions has widened the disparity, thereby creating a strong sense of urgency to meld these two distinct cultures back together into a cohesive and consistent strategic vision for the company.

Perhaps you have experienced symptoms of this problem in your own organization. Usually, it starts with someone in a position of authority, who is no longer satisfied with the company's current position in the marketplace and wants to breathe some new life into the sales process. Either sales numbers have fallen off, the vision for the company has stagnated, or some competitor keeps winning important deals. This dissatisfaction with the status quo often manifests itself in two ways on the revenue side of the business: 1.) by directing the corporate marketing department to update and enhance the current message, or 2.) by putting increased pressure on the field sales organization to produce results.

From a salesperson's perspective, applying more pressure to perform doesn't change the value of the products being sold, nor does it enhance your competitive position in the marketplace. Therefore, sellers figure it's better to just keep their heads down and finish out the sales year. Meanwhile, the market-

> "Why can't marketing come up with a product strategy that gives us a real advantage in the marketplace?"

ing staff is hard at work developing a new and improved corporate message. They have been asked to put together a comprehensive market analysis, interview focus groups, and build tools and collateral to support the sales effort.

After months of anticipation, the company's new market messages are unveiled. These announcements are often scheduled to coincide with a national sales meeting or mid-year kickoff, and they are generally accompanied by some carefully orchestrated pomp and circumstance to create a sense of excitement with prospective customers, which hopefully will give the sales organization some much needed momentum in the marketplace.

Unfortunately, the honeymoon on these much anticipated rollouts is often short-lived as hype and momentum tend to wear off relatively quickly. After the big meeting, sellers generally experience an initial burst of activity, but the effects fade in both their mind and the customer's. See, your competition is smart. Most of the time, your adversaries are working just as hard to counter with their own enhanced positioning in order to take away your advantage. Within a quarter or two, whatever short-term advantage you may have had reverts back into a longer-term competitive battle to win business. As a result, any boost in productivity from the national sales meeting has flattened back out, and the pressure being placed on the sales organization begins to mount once again.

Not surprisingly, the sales team is unwilling to accept full responsibility for sluggish results. It's easier just to blame the product, or in this case, the positioning strategy—especially midway through the year when business is slow. Of course, when executive management hears there is a problem with the product or messaging, they take the marketing people to task by once again directing them to create *even more impactful* messages. And, back to work they go, analyzing market segments, interviewing focus groups, and developing new collateral.

A few months later, the cycle repeats. Corporate marketing unveils a new positioning strategy that creates some initial momentum. Predictably, the sales organization gets a short-term boost in productivity, but the value of the new and improved messaging wanes over time as competitors catch up. All this effort, and you're back to square one.

This corporate merry-go-round has caused growing resentment over the years between the field sales organization and corporate marketing. Frustrated salespeople, battling on the front lines of the sales process, pound the table and say, "Why can't marketing come up with a product strategy that gives us a real advantage in the marketplace?" Sales organizations are quick to criticize marketing for isolating themselves inside the "ivory tower," (otherwise known as corporate headquarters), rather than being in close touch with customers and what's really happening out in the marketplace.

> "Why can't salespeople beat the bushes a little harder and execute the current strategy, rather than worry about what's happening back at corporate?"

Meanwhile, the corporate marketing people think, "Why can't salespeople beat the bushes a little harder and execute the current strategy, rather than worry about what's happening back at corporate?" Marketers have also been known to criticize the field sales organization, suggesting that they are too busy chasing deals to understand the bigger picture.

As a salesperson myself, I should make the point that I am not *down* on marketing people. In fact, just the opposite. Corporate marketing departments serve many important functions that are critical to the success of the sales organization, and the business overall. Besides, I have found that being on the good side of the marketing department has certain advantages, starting with the fact that a talented marketing person can be worth their weight in commission checks. I have also learned through the school of hard knocks that a significant divergence in strategy (or execution) between corporate marketing and the field sales organization can undermine your largest deal in a flash.

My objective here is not just to highlight the problem and then wish you the best of luck. Instead, what if it was possible for the field sales organization and corporate marketing to be on the same page relative to developing a strategy that gives you a differentiable advantage in your respective marketplace? Not only is this possible, I think the convergence of sales and marketing is becoming more and more critical to the success of companies who want to grow their business.

Formulating a Cohesive Strategy

One of the first things that pops into my head when I think about the corporate marketing function is the "elevator pitch." I already made reference to the fact that if you are selling into a competitive market, there is nothing you can say about your product or service in three minutes or less that your competitors aren't also saying about their solutions. Customers have already heard all the buzzwords, and the amount of gobbledy-goop that exists as a result of companies all striving to out-describe each other is overwhelming.

This begs the question: Why do companies continue to invest millions of dollars to create a more impactful elevator pitch about their product or service, when claims of greatness are the quickest way for a salesperson to commoditize their value proposition in the eyes of prospective customers? In addition to sounding the same as your competitors, claims of greatness are also a turn-off. They tend to make sellers sound braggadocious, causing prospective buyers to be even more standoffish—which is not good for the marketing effort, and definitely not good for sales.

> The key to having a cohesive go-to-market strategy is making sure the field sales organization and corporate marketing group are both heading in the same direction.

The key to having a cohesive go-to-market strategy is making sure the field sales organization and corporate marketing group are both heading in the same direction. There are many opportunities to parallel these organizations, starting with the need to maintain a customer-centric focus.

If you want salespeople and your company to be customer-focused, then you must turn your attention back to what's most important to the customer—their problems. Particularly when a salesperson first engages, prospective customers are much more interested in their own problems (PAS), than they are in hearing about a salesperson's solutions (SPA). We talked about the strategic differences between PAS and SPA back in Chapter 6. Hopefully, this discussion puts the final nail in the coffin with respect to opening sales calls with the traditional elevator pitch, and blasting customers with an introductory blurb that focuses on the benefits provided by your solutions (S), as opposed what is more important to customers—their problems (P).

At some point during every QBS Methodology training class I deliver, one of the students asks, "Are you teaching the PAS model to our marketing people back at corporate?" Regrettably, the answer to this question is usually, "No." Once in a while, someone from corporate marketing will sneak into one of our courses, but for the most part, it has been my experience that marketing people generally don't attend sales training courses. There must be some unwritten law that sales training is only for salespeople.

Sadly, most sales training *is* just for salespeople, with material that focuses primarily on tactics and strategies that sellers can use in their daily routines. QBS is more of a positioning strategy, however, where we teach sellers how to engage more prospects in more productive conversation throughout the sales process. We also wrap the sales process around concepts like strategic effectiveness, differentiation, the importance of bonding with customers on their problems, and how to avoid commoditizing your value proposition with a pitch that makes you sound just like everyone else. Interestingly, positioning strategies like these usually don't even come up in traditional sales courses. But, if you want your sales team to be customer-focused, then the messages coming from corporate must support a PAS positioning strategy, as opposed to burdening salespeople with more and more SPA.

Another strategy to help bridge the gap between sales and marketing is the realization that different types of customers have different buying motivations. In my first book, I introduced this idea by explaining how people are motivated to make decisions as a result of one of two things—either to take advantage of some potential positive reward or result, or to avoid some potential negative consequence or circumstance. To transform this concept into a visual image, I created a simple metaphor to reinforce the point.

Remember? While some people are motivated to run fast toward *Gold Medals*, many other people run even faster from *German Shepherds*. These two motivating influences come from two very different buying motivations—pain and desire. We touched on this earlier.

All too frequently, sellers are being sent out into their respective territories to look for problems, issues, and concerns (i.e. *German Shepherds*). Then, when they uncover a problem, they start telling the customer about all the wonderful *(Gold Medal)* benefits they provide. Unfortunately, these two buying motivations don't match, which can undermine the value of your company's message and reduce your probability of success in making a sale.

As the sales profession has evolved over time, sellers have gravitated more to probing for potential problems and the existence of pain (i.e. *German Shepherds*). Corporate marketers, on the other hand, who want their company's products and services to be seen in the best light, tend to focus more on positioning their offerings in terms of providing *Gold Medal* benefits. Can you see how these two groups are working in different directions?

Fortunately, positioning *Gold Medal* benefits is neither better or worse than positioning for *German Shepherds*. In fact, you probably have an opportunity to leverage both. In addition to helping customers realize some very positive benefits, most companies also help protect customers from experiencing some fairly negative outcomes. Understanding this makes your strategy relatively simple. If you want to sell to people who are trying to avoid potential problems, then you should be sure to position the *German Shepherd* aspects of your product or service. Additionally, to motivate people who have a desire to take advantage of exciting new opportunities, you would want to sell the *Gold Medal* aspects of your solutions.

Since most customers are motivated by a combination of *Gold Medals* and *German Shepherds*, wouldn't you want the entire sales organization to position your solutions both ways?

Managers can't just wave a magic wand and tell salespeople to go out and be more strategic, however. Without a catalyst for change, salespeople are going to continue probing for pain, by focusing on the *German Shepherds* customers would want to avoid, and corporate marketing is going to keep positioning value in terms of *Gold Medals,* citing all the wonderful benefits customers will gain from purchasing your product. Therefore, intervention is needed. A cohesive positioning strategy is something the entire revenue side of a company must support. This ultimately starts at the top, with someone who understands that the company's sales approach and market messages must match.

If you want to maximize your perceived value in the eyes of target customers, then I strongly encourage you to re-examine the way your product or service is being positioned, so your sales team can bond with customers on what's most important to them, which includes *Gold Medal* and *German Shepherd* motivations (both).

Develop a Pull Strategy versus a Push Mentality

The pattern I talked about earlier, with salespeople and companies all trying to out-describe each other, has contributed to an increase in customer resistance. As salespeople push harder and harder to penetrate new prospect opportunities, customers have become more cautious, hesitant, and standoffish than ever before. In an attempt to overcome their reluctance, sellers have countered by being even more aggressive and tenacious. Not surprisingly, this push to win business is causing prospective customers to recoil even further, and we are now stuck in another vicious cycle.

Having been in sales for twenty plus years, one of the observations I would make is simply this: the harder you push, the harder your prospects and customers will push back. Customers are no longer willing to endure a steady stream of salespeople trying to pressure them into buying their products and services.

As salespeople push harder to penetrate new opportunities, customers have become more cautious and standoffish than ever before.

At the risk of stating the obvious, you don't want customers pushing back harder and harder. That's because it's very difficult to sell to someone who is holding you off at arm's length. Therefore, I am not a fan of sales approaches that aim to "push" customers toward a commitment. Instead, I would much rather use more of a "pull" strategy—one that causes prospects and customers to *want to* engage in a mutually beneficial business conversation about their needs and how my solutions could provide value.

The question now is, what causes prospects and customers to "want to" engage in a productive conversation about their needs and your corresponding solutions? Actually, there are two things: curiosity and credibility. We talked about this earlier in Chapter 4.

Think about it this way. If a prospective customer is not the least bit curious about who you are, or what you bring to the table, then you are not likely to garner time with them. The same is true with credibility. If a potential buyer sees you as just another cold-caller, and not a credible resource who can help them understand requirements and make good decisions, then you will have a very difficult time securing a commitment.

Fortunately for us, it is possible to pique a customer's curiosity *and* cause them to see you as a competent and credible resource. By doing so, you earn the right to engage them in a productive conversation about their needs and your corresponding value. This approach is more of a pull strategy. When customers begin to form the impression that you might actually be a valuable resource, they will pull you into more in-depth conversation about their goals and objectives. This brings us back to the issue of whether it's better to be statement-based or question-based.

In my view, the problem with a statement-based approach is blatantly simple. Most customers don't want to be *told* what to do. People don't want to be pushed, persuaded, or otherwise convinced, either. Therefore, after companies spend millions of dollars to craft their next generation market messages, and salespeople take these value statements out into their respective territories blasting customers with claims of superiority, customers who don't want to be pressured, push back. You do the same thing when the telephone rings at your house during dinner and you hear an aggressive salesperson on the other end of the phone.

A pull strategy, on the other hand, requires a question-based approach, which is obviously my preference. After all, I wrote the book on the subject! I should make the point, however, that Question Based Selling is *not* just about asking questions. While needs development is an important part of the QBS methodology, strategic questions can be used for so much more than just gathering information. Strategic questions are also your best tools for piquing a prospect's curiosity and establishing credibility—two of the main prerequisites for engaging potential buyers in productive conversation. In fact, I would argue that piquing a prospect's curiosity and establishing credibility should be two of the main objectives shared by both field sales and corporate marketing.

Supporting the Field Sales Organization

Your product, service, and company may be very well positioned in the marketplace, but at the end of the day, if the customer doesn't have a need, you can't offer any value. That's why understanding customer needs is such a crucial part of the strategic sales process.

Whose job is it to uncover needs? It's the salesperson's job, of course. Your extended sales force may also have a role in needs development if you leverage reseller partners or channel relationships. Too often, however, companies load their sales force up with product brochures, and send them out into their geographies to probe for needs. The problem with that strategy is this: just because a salesperson goes out into a territory wanting to ask questions, doesn't mean potential customers will "want to" share their problems, issues, and concerns with you. Sound familiar? Likewise, just because you have a good story to tell, doesn't guarantee you an audience within your target accounts.

I think we agree how important it is to understand customer needs but, needs development is not the beginning of the sales process. Simply put, if a prospective customers does not want to share information with you, then it doesn't matter what you ask—the needs development conversation isn't going anywhere. Fortunately, the opposite is true. If a prospective buyer *does* want to share important information with you, then you won't have to work so hard to have a productive conversation about their needs and your solution alternatives. The question now is, what is corporate marketing doing to support the field sales organization's efforts in causing prospective customers to "want to" engage?

The answer to this question remains unclear for many companies. Corporate marketing departments historically have been tasked with creating product strategies and generating positioning statements, among other duties. These responsibilities are important, but providing more product literature or next generation value messaging doesn't address the single biggest challenge sellers currently face; which is, securing mindshare within target prospect accounts. Herein lies another opportunity for companies to step outside the box of traditional thinking and separate themselves from the rest of the "noise" in the marketplace. The only catch is, your corporate culture must be receptive to the idea that the marketing objectives of the corporation should reflect and support the challenges salespeople face in the field.

> Providing more product literature or next generation value messaging doesn't address the single biggest challenge sellers currently face.

The convergence of field sales and corporate marketing is hardly a new idea. Most people would agree that these two areas of the business should be on the same page relative to product positioning and overall go-to-market strategies. But, there is a big difference between wanting these two disciplines (sales and marketing) to be in sync and actually making it happen. The key to congruence is getting beyond the philosophical discussion, and into a more specific "laundry list" of specific initiatives that can be integrated into a company's corporate culture, especially on the revenue side of the business. Let me give you a few ideas to get the conversation started.

- Corporate marketing must support PAS. We have invested a significant amount of time and energy discussing the differences between PAS positioning and the traditional SPA approach, starting with the fact that you bond with customers on their problems (P), not your solutions (S). If the sales organization is going to successfully culturalize this concept of PAS, then corporate marketing must be equally customer-centric. This means building your company's positioning strategy around the business issues that are important to customers, and the underlying implications that are ultimately driving those needs. This could begin with something as simple as changing the first paragraph of your literature from saying, *"Our company provides products that will...,"* to instead read, *"Customers in today's business environment face many challenges. Those challenges include..."* Remember, the messages you convey about your product or service are only meaningful if they are being communicated against the backdrop of something that is important to your customers.

- Maintain a corporate repository of business issues and corresponding implications. To be perceived as a valuable resource, sellers must be knowledgeable in their respective disciplines and industries. Knowledge of the product is always important, and mechanisms for product education are already in place at most companies. What about "problem education?" Sellers should also have pretty good insight into the problems, issues, and concerns their customers face. Therefore, in addition to positioning in a PAS model, companies should create and maintain a master list of business issues that different types of customers might be facing, and the underlying implications of those issues. These business issues and implications can then be mapped back to the solutions your company provides. This is one of the most important action items salespeople are tasked with after finishing a QBS training course, and there can be significant benefit from not making every employee in the company have to reinvent their own wheel.

- Integrate *Gold Medals* & *German Shepherds* into your corporate messaging. Traditionally, sellers go out into their territories looking for pain. When they uncover a need, however, they pull out a product brochure or corporate slides that talk about all the wonderful benefits their product or service provides (pleasure, if you will). But, these two things (pain and pleasure) don't necessarily match. As we discussed, different types of buyers have different buying motivations. To alleviate pain, prospects will seek relief. To satisfy a desire, prospects will attempt to improve their existing condition. The key is to position your product or service for both *Gold Medals* and *Germans Shepherds*, which starts long before salespeople in the field start calling prospective customers.

- Identify the right questions. Companies invest significant amounts of money telling salespeople what to say, but they spend almost nothing teaching sellers what to ask. With the QBS Methodology, there are many opportunities to leverage strategic questions throughout the sales process. But, why should each salesperson have to create their own individual strategy? For example, I teach salespeople to initiate their needs development conversations with a series of short-answer, diagnostic questions.

> Companies invest significant amounts of money telling salespeople what to say, but they spend almost nothing teaching sellers what to ask.

Essentially, this is a stepping-stone strategy in QBS that gives sellers an opportunity to gain credibility early in the discovery process, thus earning the right to probe more deeply into the customer's specific problems, issues, and concerns.

What questions can be asked to accomplish this objective? In every sale, there are certain pieces of information a seller needs to know about the customer (how many employees they have, how many remote office locations they support, or their monthly utilization of product). I made the recommendation back in Chapter 4 that you should create a repository of questions that could be asked, rather than hoping the right questions will pop into your head when talking with prospective customers. It's always easier to choose from an existing list, than to invent a new set of questions on every sales call. Corporate marketing can and should be directly involved in this process of helping the field sales organization identify the right questions to ask at the right time.

- Develop curiosity strategies for specific marketing initiatives. This is so important, let me say it again—curiosity is the genesis of every sale. If a prospective customer is not the least bit curious about who you are, or what you can do for them, you are not likely to succeed in securing their time or attention. So, what are your salespeople doing to leverage curiosity in the sales process? And, what is corporate marketing doing to support the sales organization by creating curiosity strategies that can be used to drive new announcements or specific initiatives? If it's true that good ideas can be shared, then we shouldn't put the responsibility for securing mindshare with prospective customers solely in the laps of individual salespeople. Note that curiosity is a strategy that can be leveraged with voice-mail, e-mail, mass mailings, seminar invitations, and advertising campaigns. Curiosity can also be leveraged to make sure the right people are involved in key steps throughout the sales process, like attending product presentations or during contract negotiations.

- Build a luke-warm calling template. In "live" QBS training courses, I make the point that sellers should stop making cold calls. Cold calling in today's business environment is highly unproductive, and produces a very low return on invested effort. I am not suggesting that sellers should stop initiating contact with new prospects. Creating new business opportunities is an important part of the sales function. The key is to turn your cold calls into luke-warm calls (Chapter 12, in my first book). I am not a big fan of scripted calls, however, because the customer on the other end of the phone isn't likely to follow a script. But you can absolutely build a template model for your sales calls, and document each of the component steps of the call. Creating a high-percentage blueprint to follow makes it easier for salespeople to repeat their successes. Corporate marketing should be involved in this effort to build a repeatable model, because they will certainly be integral in providing much of the content that will be discussed during the actual sales calls.

The convergence of sales and marketing is no longer a diplomatic nice-to-have; rather, it's an essential ingredient in growing your business. That said, corporate infighting is the enemy, and companies can no longer tolerate a mentality where the superficial goal is just to appease the other party, while everyone strives to achieve their own internal agendas. The business climate is such that companies who are unable to achieve a cohesive go-to-market strategy will soon find themselves at a significant competitive disadvantage.

Ironically, the reason this disconnect exists between field sales and corporate marketing isn't necessarily because of an underlying power struggle or a fundamental disagreement in philosophy. In most cases, when a gap exists, it's because the field sales organization and the corporate marketing department have evolved as separate entities. For years, these two disciplines have operated independently, figuring that the marketing department "markets," and the sales organization "sells." In many companies, sales and marketing even report up through different channels, since they have traditionally served different functions for the company. But at the end of the day, the people working at corporate headquarters and the salespeople in the field are ultimately on the same team, and they deserve to have a cohesive strategy.

Earlier I told you that QBS students often ask, "Are you teaching QBS to our marketing people back at corporate?" What's the answer to this question at your company? To me, sales training courses should *not* just be for salespeople. They should be for everyone who touches the sales process, including our friends and partners back at corporate headquarters.

< ACTION ITEMS >

1. Assign someone in corporate marketing the task of documenting the sales process. Independently, assign the same task to someone in the field sales organization. Then compare results. Don't be surprised if they don't match. In most cases, they won't. The exercise of writing it down, however, will give you a baseline from which you can work toward converging the way field sales and corporate marketing view the strategic sale.

2. At every internal meeting you attend, make it a point to ask, "What problem are we trying to solve?" Too often, the idea machine is hard at work producing solutions without first understanding the problem. This question can serve as a useful tool to help culturalize the PAS model throughout the organization.

3. Inventory your sales training experiences to date. What sales training courses have your salespeople attended? Who else in the company has attended this training? Evaluate and develop a plan outlining which sales courses would help people in sales support, sales operations, and marketing to better support the sales team.

CHAPTER 10

Ask and You Shall Receive

Everyone agrees that asking questions is a key ingredient in the formula for being successful in sales. Sales managers all encourage their sales teams to ask lots of questions. Sales trainers pound the table telling salespeople to ask good questions. Even the Bible says, "Ask, and ye shall receive." Therefore, logic would

> There is more to being a top performer in sales than just randomly asking a bunch of questions.

suggest that Question Based Selling is definitely on the right track with the notion that salespeople are supposed to ask good questions. True. But, there is more to being a top performer in sales than just randomly asking a bunch of questions.

As I have said many times, just because a salesperson wants to ask questions, doesn't necessarily mean potential customers will want to answer. The fact is, we live in a society that is more cautious than ever before, and people are reluctant to share important information with someone they don't yet know or trust. We talked about this earlier with regard to needs development. Even though sellers have been taught to probe for needs, we are quickly realizing that prospective customers don't want to be "probed."

I am not suggesting that you should stop trying to uncover new opportunities or understand the customer's needs. Needs development is, and will always be, a critical component of the strategic sales process. But, there may be an opportunity to put some "methodology to the madness," and as a result, put yourself in a position to leverage strategic questions to gain a competitive advantage. There may also be an opportunity to control your own destiny knowing that what you ask it, and how you ask, will ultimately determine how much information you receive from prospects and customers.

For example, when I engage new prospects in a conversation about their needs, my first needs development question is always the same. At the appropriate time in the conversation, I simply say, "*Can I ask you a couple specifics about* _____?" Word for word, this is my first question. Why? There are two reasons. First, prospects and customers want salespeople to be respectful of their time and space, right? Getting permission to ask questions is highly respectful of the fact that you understand customers are under no obligation to respond. Don't worry, because if a prospect is going to share any information at all with you, they will surely say, "Yes." It's actually a low risk opening question. Secondly, in addition to gaining permission to proceed, being respectful changes the dynamic of the conversation. Once you have been invited to ask questions, the prospective customer is much more likely to open up and volunteer information, than if you had just plunged forward with your own agenda.

Another QBS technique we talked about earlier was using diagnostic questions as a strategy for kicking off the needs development conversation. Knowing that people are naturally reluctant to share with someone they don't yet know or trust, there is significant risk in asking for too much, too soon. Open-ended questions, therefore, can be great conversational tools, but they only work if a customer already wants to share information with you. Assuming that prospects already want to share information is a mistake, however. I'm sure you and I both are equally cautious about sharing information with a salesperson we've just met.

> Open-ended questions can be great conversational tools, but they only work if a customer already wants to share information with you.

What we, as salespeople, really want to talk about is the customer's needs. We want to understand their problems, issues, and concerns. We also want to know about pending projects, deadlines, budget constraints, maintenance headaches—basically, we want to understand the issues that keep them up at night. The challenge is getting customers to "want to" share this information with you.

Given the risk that open-ended questions pose, my logical mind said, why not try something different? So, after some early experimentation years ago, I discovered that credibility was an important prerequisite for engaging customers in a productive business conversation. And, the most effective way (I found as a salesperson) to establish credibility early in the needs development conversation is by opening the dialogue with a series of short-answer, diagnostic questions. This technique has since become an integral part of the QBS methodology.

Here's what this approach sounds like when you put it all together. At the appropriate time in the conversation, when you would normally want to ask about the customer's needs, you simply say, "Mr. Customer, can I ask you a couple of specifics about your current _____?" 99% of the time, customers will say, "Sure." Now you have permission to proceed, which creates a window of opportunity to initiate the discovery process and establish credibility using diagnostic questions.

How many diagnostic questions should you ask? Generally, five or six will do the trick, assuming your questions are indeed relevant to the customer's situation. The real value of this technique is that it gives sellers an opportunity to accomplish four very strategic objectives in a very short window of time (generally less than sixty seconds), which paves the way for a more robust exchange of information for needs development. Briefly, those four objectives are:

Strategic Objectives of Diagnostic Questions

1. Diagnostic questions give you a vehicle for opening the needs development conversation in a non-threatening way.
2. In a short amount of time, you gain some valuable information about the prospect's current status or situation.
3. Asking relevant and intelligent questions gives you an opportunity to establish credibility in the eyes of target customers.
4. Accomplishing objectives one through three makes it easy to expand the conversation into more depth concerning the customer's issues and implications.

We discussed each of these objectives in detail back in Chapter 4. The point of reflecting on them again now is to reinforce the strategic importance of asking the right questions at the right time. The rest of QBS's needs development strategy is simply a function of facilitating an exploratory conversation about "what" is important to the customer (potential business issues that might exist), and "why" those issues are important (specific implications that are ultimately driving the need). I am going to stop here, since my goal is not to re-explain what has been already been covered in previous QBS material (see Chapters 8 and 9, *Secrets of Question Based Selling*).

I do want to reaffirm the value of having a needs development strategy that can be duplicated and repeated to maximize your sales team's probability of success when interacting with prospective customers. I also want to point out that strategic questions are no longer just tools for gathering information. I tell students in QBS courses all the time: "Too many salespeople are out there probing for needs." Therefore, if the only thing you use questions for is gathering information and uncovering needs, then buckle your seatbelt because you may have a huge upside opportunity.

More than Just Gathering Information

Question Based Selling was built on the premise that what a salesperson asks, and how you ask, is more important than what you can ever say. This premise comes from my belief that whatever a seller could possibly say about their product or service is essentially valueless unless it gets conveyed against the backdrop of something that is important to a customer. I have also come to believe that questions can put salespeople in a unique position of strength with regard to qualifying opportunities, enhancing relationships, understanding the decision process, smoking out potential objections, expanding the opportunity, diffusing conflicts, and increasing the prospect's sense of urgency for moving forward with a purchase decision. Used strategically, a sound question-based methodology can give you a significant competitive advantage.

To support the culturalization of QBS across the broader sales organization, I want to invest some time to review several key questioning strategies we teach in our "live" QBS Methodology training programs. Of course, your industry and your specific customer situations will dictate the execution of the various QBS

225

techniques. My purpose here is simply to "arm" you with a set of questioning skills that will help you facilitate more strategic conversations with prospective customers—the goal being to leverage relationships and move opportunities forward toward a mutually beneficial business transaction.

Controlling Your Sales Conversations

If the decision was totally up to you, who would you want to be in control of your sales conversations, the customer or yourself? When I pose this question during a "live" QBS training program, salespeople in the audience are quick to say that they want to be in the driver's seat. That's what I would choose as well. From a salesperson's perspective, there are certain goals and objectives we would like to accomplish during a sales call, and maintaining control helps keep the conversation on track, right?

If we surveyed your customers, however, and asked them who they want to control conversations they have with salespeople, what do you think they would say? Do you think the typical customer wants a salesperson to be in control, or do you think customers would rather be in control of the conversation themselves? I can guarantee that most customers do not relish the idea of being "controlled" by a salesperson.

Now we have a problem. Sellers want to control their conversations, but customers also want to be in control. So, who do you think will ultimately win this battle? Ironically, that depends on you and whether you are perceived by customers as a truly valuable resource, or just another sales caller.

Here's the real question. Is it in the customer's best interest for you to be "in control" of your sales conversations? Because if it's not in the customer's best interest for you to be in control, then you probably won't be. The good new is, since you are knowledgeable about your business, you know how your product or service can provide value. Therefore, by keeping the conversation on track, as opposed to having it wander off in different directions, you make better use of the customer's time. Hence, it's in the best interest of your customer for a knowledgeable salesperson to be in control of the sales conversation.

This brings us to the next question, which is: What's the best way to actually control a sales conversation? Oddly enough, it all comes down to punctuation. Yes, it's that simple. The two most common ways to end a sentence are with a period or a question mark. We've all known this since the second grade.

Well, I have found that there is significant risk in trying to control a conversation using periods. Here's a simple example. Suppose you are standing around the water cooler at the office talking with a colleague about one of their hobbies. Realizing that topics of conversation tend to exhaust themselves, you reach a point in the dialogue where you want to move on. Here's what that might sound like if you used a period. "Well, that's very interesting, Richard, but let's talk about something else now."

Can you feel the harshness of this statement? Whether or not you meant to be harsh, it sounded like you weren't very interested in whatever your friend had just communicated. Poor conversationalists rely too much on statements, which is

> Poor conversationalists rely too much on statements, which is one of the reasons they often have a difficult time leading conversations and interacting with others.

one of the reasons they often have a difficult time leading conversations and interacting with others.

But, what if we replaced that period with a question mark? Let's re-examine the same scenario. You are talking to a buddy about one of their hobbies. When you reach the point in the conversation where you want to change topics, you simply say, "John, your love of gardening is very interesting. Do you also like to travel?" You could ask all kinds of other questions like, "Are you an avid sports fan? Have you ever been to the Middle East? Where did you go to school?" Or, "Do you have any children?"

Using question marks puts you in a unique position of strength. As we say in QBS, he who asks the question has the power in the conversation. Think about it this way. The person who asks the question gets to choose the topic of the conversation. They also get to choose the pace. If you want to speed a conversation up, simply ask a question that moves the dialogue along. If you want to slow it down, you can ask a question that takes the conversation into more depth. It's what great conversationalists do!

In your sales conversations, you won't necessarily be talking with prospective customers about gardening, travel, children, or the Middle East. You will be discussing the customer's business issues, some of which may come up naturally in the conversation without your prompting. But, who will raise other important business issues if the customer doesn't bring them up on their own? If not you, then you leave the door wide open for competitors to come in and take your opportunity.

In fact, as a salesperson, you should always be thinking about changing the topic during their conversations with prospective customers. I'm not suggesting you should randomly jump around in your conversations. Rather, I'm saying that you should always look for opportunities to talk *beyond* the broader issue, in order to explore the underlying implications that are ultimately driving the customer's need. In the now-famous water pump analogy, for example, I didn't want to talk with homeowners about having a flooded

basement. Instead, we wanted to talk with them about the implications of having water where it shouldn't be. These implications
could include everything from
potential mold or mildew
problems, to unpleasant odors,
structural damage, cost, safety
risks, potential heath hazards,
damage to personal property, insurance hassles, avoiding recurrence, inconvenience, clean-up, not to mention being unable to utilize the space.

> As a salesperson, you should always be thinking about changing the topic during your sales conversations with prospective customers.

It all comes down to a single question: How many reasons do
you want prospective customers to have to move forward with a
favorable purchase decision? Personally, I want customers have lots
of reasons to buy from me. I'm guessing you do as well. Therefore,
if you "arm" yourself with a mental repository of what might be
important to prospective customers, and you are able to control the
dialogue with strategic questions, then you put yourself in a strong
position to increase the depth of your sales conversations, as well as
raise your perceived value in the eyes of your target market.

Ask, "How do you mean?"

The most valuable question I used as a salesperson, and still use
today as a sales trainer, husband, father, neighbor, friend, and
Sunday school teacher, consists of four easy words: *"How do you
mean?"* If someone says something to you or asks something of you,
when you respond with these four simple words, you will be surprised how much information you receive.

Some people who hear me talk about this technique, say, "Gee,
Tom, the question, 'How do you mean?' seems grammatically chal-

lenged." Yes, I know. Every time I sent my first book out to be proofed, my editor crossed out the word 'how' with her red pencil. She even wrote me little notes saying, "What do you mean?" is more grammatically correct.

While a grammarian could take points off for breaking the rules, I have a specific reason for asking "how," instead of "what." If you ask, "What do you mean?", people tend to go backward in the conversation and restate what they just said. But I don't want to go backward in the conversation. I heard what the other person just said. My goal is to get to the next level of detail. I don't worry about grammatical correctness in this case anyway, because when I say, "How do you mean?", most people don't hear those words. Instead, they hear my meaning—which is, "I am very interested in what you just said. Could you please tell me more?" Let me ask you: Do people like it when we are very interested in what they just said? Yes, they do. So let the sharing begin.

You may recognize this technique as part of the larger QBS strategy of asking *Global Questions*. Most people, when they are asked a question, share only some portion of their true thoughts, feelings, and concerns. Global questions, as conversational tools, give salespeople an opportunity to expand the depth of communication by saying, "Tell me more." But, rather than commanding someone to, "Tell me more," I ask global questions like, "What happens next?" Or, "Who else needs to be involved?" Or, (feel free to use my personal favorite), "How do you mean?"

"But, Tom," you say, "I'm not sure these questions are consistent with my style." For the skeptics in the audience, I suggest you try it one time. The next time someone tells you something, or asks you a question, simply respond by saying, "How do you mean?" Then button up. When customers start sharing volumes of valuable information with you about their problems, issues, and concerns, it's amazing how quickly this technique will become second-nature. It's easy to adopt something that works.

Let me make one more point about this technique—to solve a problem before it happens. Say an issue like cost comes up in one of your sales opportunities, which it will, and the customer says, "I appreciate your efforts in putting together a proposal, but I'm concerned about cost." You do some quick thinking back to your QBS training and ask, "How do you mean?"

Suppose the customer, with somewhat of a quizzical look on their face, turns to you and says, "What do you mean, how do I mean?"

Oh, no! Are you stuck? If the gimmick or trick didn't work, then yes, you might be stuck. But, this technique is not a trick. Here's why I would not be stuck, and you should not be either. At the point where the customer says, "What do you mean, how do I mean?", you simply say:

Seller: *"Mr. Customer, when someone says to me that they are concerned about cost, that could mean any number of things. They might be concerned about the budget, the approval process, the timing of the transaction, or a comparison with another solution. You said you were concerned, but rather than guess, would you mind if I asked, what specifically are you concerned about?"*

By employing this simple technique, you might even be accused by prospects and customers of sounding "down to earth" or being *easy* to deal with. Wouldn't that be a nice contrast to the normal environment of high pressure sales?

Use Humbling Disclaimers

Salespeople are constantly being encouraged to ask lots of questions. They are especially encouraged to ask qualifying questions to understand decision timeframes, identify key players, and find out about the customer's budget. But, have you ever noticed that there is a fine line between asking qualifying questions, and probing for too much information? Moreover, if a customer decides that they do not wish to share sensitive information with you, then it doesn't matter what you ask.

To minimize the risk of being shut down by potential buyers, we teach a technique called humbling disclaimers. A humbling disclaimer gives sellers an easy way to diffuse the invasive feeling that can otherwise come from the probative nature of questions. That's a lot of words, I know.

> Have you ever noticed that there is a fine line between asking qualifying questions, and probing for too much information?

Budget is a good example. Salespeople want to ask about the budget. Does the customer have money to spend? Is this deal even worth pursuing? Everyone knows that understanding the customer's budget is one of the most important qualifying criteria regarding a pending sales transaction. But, just because sellers want to ask about the customer's budget, doesn't mean customers will willingly share this information. Consequently, salespeople end up coming back to their managers saying, "I asked about the budget, but the customer is playing it close to the vest."

Perhaps we shouldn't be surprised when customers are reluctant to share budget information with salespeople. If you were a customer standing on the showroom floor of a car dealership, looking at a shiny new sports car, and an eager salesperson scurried over and asked, "How much money have you got?", you probably wouldn't want to share that information with them.

It's one of the metaphysical laws of the universe—people are reluctant to share budget details with a salesperson. Still, salespeople are expected to find out about the customer's budget, but when you ask directly, they don't always share, and everyone gets frustrated.

In my simple way of thinking, when something is not working as well as expected, I am inclined to try something else. Therefore, knowing that customers are reluctant to share budget information, I use a questioning technique called *humbling disclaimers*.

Note that budget information is not something you would generally ask about at the very beginning of a sales conversation anyway. But, at the appropriate time in the dialogue, here's the question I would ask: "Mr. Customer, I don't want to step out-of-bounds and bring up something I'm not supposed to ask about, but do you mind if I ask the budget question?"

Technically, the answer to this question is either, "Yes," (you may ask about the budget), or, "No," (you may not). But most customers won't respond with a simple yes or no. In fact, you will be surprised how often people, who would otherwise play it close to the vest, will open up and start sharing their financial landscape relative to the opportunity.

Of course, it's possible that a customer could respond by saying, "Sure, you can ask about the budget, but we don't share that information with vendors." In that case, you weren't going to get specific information about their budget anyway. But, that doesn't mean you are finished. I recommend you follow up by saying, "That's fine, Mr. Customer. I understand there may be some reluctance to share confidential information. But, could I ask you this? If you like our solution and we put together a $40,000 proposal, do you have the financial where-with-all to pull the trigger on a purchase decision, or do we need to go through some other approval process?" Even if a customer doesn't want to share specific budget numbers with you, they will usually give some indication about where the sale stands relative to the approval process. This is an important point, because if you can cause customers to share even tidbits of information about their financial condition, it is easier to broach the subject again down the road.

Humbling disclaimers are also valuable strategic tools for expanding your needs development conversations. Have you ever been in the middle of a needs development discussion when you start to feel yourself running out of runway? Responses to questions get shorter as the customer's patience wanes, and there is a sense of awkwardness as you realize the customer is starting to feel as though they are being "probed" for information. At that point, you basically have two options. One is to abandon the needs development process and jump directly into your sales presentation. The other option is to do something that extends the length of your runway in the conversation. You can do this using a humbling disclaimer. Let me give you an example.

At the appropriate time in the dialogue, you simply say, "Mr. Customer, I appreciate you telling me about your current manufacturing systems and the upcoming re-engineering project. And, while I don't want to ask too many questions, I would like to understand how this project could impact your long-term growth plans. Do you mind if I ask a couple of specifics about your current systems configuration?"

Here are some other examples of humbling disclaimers:

"I'm not sure the best way to ask, but would you mind…"

"Without stepping on anyone's toes, could I ask you about…"

"At the risk of being too forward, could we spend a minute ... "

"I don't want to say the wrong thing, but..."

To appreciate the significance of this strategy, let me give you a quick lesson in human nature. And, I would recommend that you take this to heart, because understanding this one idea can create a huge strategic advantage for any salesperson who competes for mindshare

> If you are respectful of the customer's right not to share information with you, it is amazing how much information you can get.

in today's business climate. Here's the lesson: If you are respectful of a customer's right *not* to share information with you, it is amazing how much information you can get. Humility is a very attractive human quality. Therefore, by strategically injecting small doses of humility into your questions (using humbling disclaimers), you can significantly enhance the quality of the responses you receive.

Neutralize Questions to Smoke-Out Possible Objections

One of the consistent threads that connect top performing salespeople is their ability to manage or prevent obstacles that may arise during the sales process. So, here's my question to you. If there was a problem brewing somewhere in one of your accounts, would you want to know about it? Most of us would, because we realize that a problem cannot be solved unless we know about it. No one wants problems, but if something is happening, I absolutely want to know about it. That's why I don't ask "hopeful" questions.

Back in Chapter 4, we talked about the fact that sellers have been conditioned over time to ask positive, hopeful questions, in the hopes of receiving more positive responses. Positive sales questions sound like this:

"Would next Tuesday work for a conference call?"

"Does your boss like our proposal?"

"Do you think we're still in good shape to wrap this deal up by the end of the month?"

Asking positive questions to receive more positive responses is a strategy that usually backfires. In fact, just the opposite happens—asking for good news, or what we (as salespeople) want to hear, tends to cause prospective customers to respond with less information and less accurate information. The reason is simple. People don't like to share bad news. It's easier for a prospect or customer to avoid an issue, rather than confront a salesperson with the news that an obstacle has come up in one of their sales. If you really want to know where you stand in your deals, you must be willing to inquire about potential obstacles. Otherwise, you may never know they exist. That's why in Question Based Selling, we teach salespeople to *neutralize the disposition* of their questions.

> Asking for good news tends to cause prospective customers to respond with less information and less accurate information.

In the study of interpersonal communications, every question asked has a certain "personality" or disposition that can be characterized as being either positive, negative, or neutral. You see, I don't ask questions about a sale to get the answer I "want to" hear. Instead, my purpose in asking is to solicit accurate information about the status of a sale, which includes a proactive effort on my part to uncover potential obstacles as well.

As an example, if I wanted to ask a prospective customer about the status of a sale, I might ask, "Mr. Customer, are we still in good shape to wrap this deal up by the end of the month, or do you think something could cause this transaction to get pushed out?" Notice this question actually *invites* the customer to share bad news, if there is any. Under different circumstances, another way to neutralize your question would be to say, "Is there anything that would prevent you from moving forward on this deal?" Notice these questions aren't just asking for good news—they are seeking the whole story.

An adaptation of this strategy is simply to reverse roles in the conversation. Ask your customer, "Mr. Customer, if you were the salesperson on this account, what would you be doing differently?" In fact, this is a good question to ask coworkers, your manager, and your employees. You can even ask your best friend, your kids, or your spouse. "If our roles were reversed, and you were me, would you be doing anything differently?" I have found that this simple request for information will generate some of the most valuable and accurate feedback you could ever receive. The question is, do you want to hear it?

Understanding the Decision Process

In addition to knowing where you stand in the sale, sellers are also supposed to qualify sales opportunities on the forecast. Is this a thirty percent opportunity, or an eighty percent one? What are the chances we can close this transaction in the current month or quarter? What is the financial approval process? Who else in the account needs to sign off on a purchase order? What are the next steps? Is there anything we can do to accelerate a decision?

Salespeople ask customers these qualifying questions, and they, in turn, are being asked these same questions by management. In fact, as opportunities move through the sales process, we must continue to qualify them, knowing that having complete and accurate information about the status of a deal should make the target of closing the sale easier to hit.

The problem is, customers know salespeople are paid on commission, which means they assume that your income will go up if you make a sale, and down if you don't. So, after a salesperson has asked these qualifying questions a few times in the same account, there is a risk of starting to sound like a self-serving money-grubber who is only interested in closing the deal.

To avoid sounding like a money-grubber, I encourage sellers to focus on the broader decision process, not just the immediate sale. For example, my first qualifying question might be to ask the customer, "What is the typical process for making this type of decision?" Notice I use phrases like, "typical process," and, "type of decision." I use those phrases on purpose, because they take the pressure off. Even if a deal is up in the air, customers can still talk abstractly about the *typical* process for this *type* of decision.

Salespeople must also be sensitive to the fact that big decisions can be overwhelming to a customer, which often creates emotional hurdles that can stymie a decision. One way to help your customers not to feel so overwhelmed is to use a divide and conquer strategy, where you ask questions about the smaller individual components of the larger sales process. For example, you might ask, "Ms. Customer, have you already talked to your bank about financing?" Or, "Where are you planning to warehouse the equipment when it arrives?" You could also ask, "When would you like to take delivery?"

In the same vein, a medical equipment salesperson might ask a doctor, "Do you have any surgery cases scheduled in the next few days?" An advertising salesperson could ask, "How far along is the art design for your new advertising campaign?" A real estate agent might ask a prospective homeowner, "Have you thought about how you would furnish this house?" If the potential buyer hasn't even "thought about" furnishings, then you are probably not close to making a sale. On the other hand, if they have already measured for a new dining room suite, that might be a signal they are indeed ready to move forward with a purchase.

As you talk with prospective customers, be sure to ask just as many questions about what will happen *after* the purchase as before. Decision makers need to know that you are not just focused on the sale itself, but on a successful implementation, and on the longer-term well-being of your customers. Therefore, I always make it a point to talk with customers about issues beyond the purchase, because it increases their comfort level for moving forward, and it also tends to create some nice add-on opportunities after the initial sale is closed. In fact, the McDonald's Corporation taught the sales world an important lesson when they trained their employees to always ask, "Would you like some fries with that shake?"

Testing Your Champion's Confidence

In large corporate sales, having a strong internal champion can be the difference between winning the sale and coming up empty. To win, someone inside the account must be willing to carry your company's flag up the hill, and recommend your solution to upper management or to a decision committee. This person's ability to be an effective advocate of your product or service will greatly impact your probability of success in making a sale.

Even if you sell outside the corporate environment, someone still has to champion your proposed solution. A doctor, for example, might want to check with other physicians in his or her practice before making a financial commitment. In real estate or insurance sales, husbands and wives often check with each other before signing on the dotted line.

In a sale that involves multiple players, someone must be able to "sell" your proposal to their peers or to management. This causes me to wonder: How many sales training courses do you think the typical internal champion in your accounts have attended thus far in their career? In most cases, the answer is zero. Therefore, if you don't invest the time to coach your champions, which includes boosting their confidence and making them better advocates of your message, your competitors will. My intent here is to challenge the traditional mindset of just trying to sell a product, and get into the broader objective of teaching champions in your accounts how to become more effective advocates of your message.

> When someone confidently endorses your product or service, these recommendations from internal champions are worth their weight in commission checks.

One of the most important aspects of coaching your internal champions is preparing them in advance for how best to take your value messages forward. If you think about it, an internal champion can commoditize your value proposition just as quickly as anyone, which would undermine your selling efforts. Fortunately, the opposite is also true. When someone confidently endorses your product or service, these recommendations from internal champions are worth their weight in commission checks.

Just telling an internal advocate what to say is usually not enough, however. It's too easy for someone just to bob their head up and down, and say, "I've got it!" What if they don't have *it*, or what if they only retain some portion of *it*? What if the way they are positioning your proposed solution is simply not compelling? This is where the use of strategic questions can really help.

Whenever I strategize with internal sponsors, one of my goals is to find out how prepared they are to deliver an impactful message about my product. I also want to see how they will handle potential objections that could get raised by their boss, or by someone in purchasing or on a decision committee. I find these things out by giving my internal champion a verbal exam, which will tell me how much additional coaching is needed, if any.

Of course, you don't just start pummeling your internal advocates with test questions. First, you must obtain their buy-in to participate in this type of exercise. That's easy. Simply say, "Mr. Customer, I work with a lot of people who recommend our product or service. Would you like some tips on what other people are doing to secure approval from management, or do you want me to back off and let you handle it?" Again, if you are respectful of the customer's right *not* to engage, it's amazing how willing people are to participate.

"Sure, I'd love some ideas," most of them will respond.

"OK," I say, "But in order to know where I can be of the most assistance, why don't you think of me as your boss, and make your presentation to me?" How they position your message will give you some immediate insight into the value of their recommendation. If their presentation is powerful, give them a verbal pat on the back and count yourself lucky. On the other hand, if their message needs work, you now have a pretty good idea where your champion could use the most help. Sometimes, I even go so far as to bring up possible objections. "What would you say if your boss raises the issue of cost?" Or, I'll say, "What if someone on the committee raises a question about postponing the decision? How would you respond to that?"

You would much rather have your internal advocate sputter and pause in front of you, than get stuck when they are in front of the big boss. These practice sessions essentially give you an opportunity to smooth out any rough edges, and they also prepare your internal champions to think on their feet when objections do get raised. As an added bonus, when you invest the time to make sure your internal advocates are prepared to present a stronger message, their confidence in making the recommendation for your product or service will increase significantly. At that point, the outcome may be a foregone conclusion, because when a confident champion delivers a strong recommendation, your probability of success is greatly enhanced.

< ACTION ITEMS >

1. Find out how your sales team is currently leveraging strategic questions to pique the customer's curiosity, establish credibility, broaden the needs development conversation, keep the conversation on track, expand opportunities, smoke out potential objections, understand the decision process, and coach internal champions to make a stronger recommendation.
2. Make it a practice to hold loss review meetings. While it is beneficial to learn from your successes, it is also very possible to learn even more from what could have been done differently. Take a recent scenario and ask what you or the sales team could have done differently in each of the areas mentioned in this chapter.

3. Since strategic questions are not reserved for business situations only, make it a point to become conscious of the different types of questions you ask, and how other people respond to them. If you can cause people to "want to" engage in more productive conversations, you will not only accomplish your sales objectives, you will have a more fulfilling life.

CHAPTER 11

QBS Escalation Strategies

In today's economic climate, passive behavior on the part of a prospect or customer is a salesperson's enemy. The reason is simple: a passive customer is much less likely to make a commitment to buy than someone who has a sense of urgency to move forward with a purchase decision.

In Question Based Selling, I talked about the fact that there are five prerequisites for closing a sale. The first prerequisite is relatively obvious. In order to move forward with a sale, prospects must have a recognized need. The operative word here is "recognized." The fact that you think the customer has a need is irrelevant. The real question is, do *they* think they have a need? The second prerequisite for closing a sale is customers must see your proposed solution as a viable alternative. Once again, the operative word is "viable." The fact that you offer valuable solutions doesn't necessarily mean they are viable options in the eyes of your customers. Third, the value of your product or service must be great enough to justify its cost. Fourth and fifth, you must be dealing with someone who has the authority to pull the trigger on a purchase, and the customer must have a sense of urgency for moving forward. Each of these prerequisite conditions must be fully satisfied to close a sale. In this chapter, we want to focus on the last prerequisite I mentioned—creating a sense of urgency.

Have you ever been in the situation where a prospective customer had a definite need and you offered a viable solution at an affordable cost, but for some reason, the customer did not have a sense of urgency for moving forward? As a result, your proposal just sat on the decision maker's desk for weeks? This passiveness on the part of prospective customers is one of the greatest challenges sellers face in today's increasingly competitive business environment.

Sellers have a definite sense of urgency to finalize transactions. If for no other reason, the salesperson usually stands to receive a nice commission check or bonus. But customers don't always have the same sense of urgency, for several reasons. In some cases, companies are under pressure to reduce spending and conserve resources. Other customers have been burned by previous decisions, and they want to avoid making another mistake. Whatever the reason, potential buyers don't always share our same enthusiasm for wrapping up a sale, and they are not likely to act just because an eager salesperson pushes them to make a decision.

> Buyers don't always share our same enthusiasm for wrapping up a sale, and they are not likely to act just because an eager salesperson pushes them to make a decision.

Is it possible to increase a customer's urgency for making a decision? The answer is, yes. In fact, knowing how to escalate a customer's sense of urgency without making them feel pushed is one of the soft skills that separates top performing salespeople from the rest of the field. As I have said many times, the harder you push, the harder customers tend to push back. But, we don't want customers pushing back. Instead, we want to cause them to "want to" move forward toward a mutually beneficial business transaction.

How can you accomplish this feat? There is no magical formula. Some customers are not going to move forward with a purchase no matter what you do. For those sales situations that are teetering on the brink of a "go" or "no go" decision, however, a proactive strategy on your part may be the difference between closing a sale and having an opportunity slip away. With that in mind, let me review with you five QBS strategies that were specifically developed to address this issue of escalating the customer's sense of urgency.

A word of caution before we begin. When sellers approach the end of the sale and suddenly discover that their prospect does not have a sense of urgency for pulling the trigger on a decision, the tendency is to try and turn the customer around. By then, it's often too little, too late. That's because "urgency" is not something that gets created in the late stages of a sale. Rather, the customer's sense of urgency is something that should evolve over the course of the entire sales process, sometimes even starting with the tone that gets set during the initial sales call.

Curiosity Always Kills the Cat

Curiosity is a key ingredient in the strategic sales process because it impacts the customer's sense of urgency. When someone becomes curious about something, it is natural for that person to focus all their attention on whatever they have become curious about. Meanwhile, everything else fades into the background. As sellers, we want to generate that kind of focus with regard to moving sales opportunities along. Therefore, curiosity becomes a very important strategic lever for salespeople who want to secure the time and attention of key decision makers within target accounts.

Let's start with something easy—voice-mail, which we talked

about a little earlier. Essentially, there are two reasons prospects and customers respond to voice-mail messages. One is obligation; the other is curiosity. Very few prospects feel obligated to return sales calls; in which case, your opportunity to receive a return call hinges on whether or not your voice-mail message piques the prospect's interest.

Since we already talked about curiosity-inducing voice-mail messages in the context of penetrating new account opportunities, let me give you an example of how curiosity can be leveraged to increase a customer's sense of urgency later in the sales process.

I recently had the opportunity to work with IBM's Global Services team in Atlanta, Dallas, and Toronto. One of the reps on the team, Scott Felcher, asked me about the best way to follow up with prospective customers after sending a proposal. Scott said he didn't want to seem over eager with regard to making a sale, and he didn't want customers to feel like he was too aggressive. On the other hand, he didn't want to ignore the opportunity, and risk having it slip away. Scott was basically using the approach he had always been taught—to send a proposal and then follow up with a professional sounding voice-mail message that sounded something like:

Before: *"Hi Mr. Customer, this is Scott Felcher with IBM Global Services in Atlanta. I'm calling to follow up on the proposal I sent you last week, and I wanted to see if you had any questions. When you get a minute, could you please call me at (770) 863-1000…or I will try you back in the morning. Again, my name is Scott Felcher, with IBM Global Services, and you can reach me at (770) 863-1000."*

I listened to Scott's typical message and then asked, "How's your call back rate?"

Scott admitted that it could be higher. That's no surprise, really, when you step back and listen to what this voice-mail message actually communicates. To me, this message does nothing to create a sense of urgency. In fact, it lacks a sense of purpose, like he just wants to check in and see what's going on, dude!

There are a couple other problems with this voice-mail message. For example, the phrase, "I'm calling to follow up to see if you had any questions," is risky because it's not true. A salesperson isn't calling to see if the customer has questions, they're calling to find out the status of the sale. I also recommend against telling customers that if you don't hear from them by a certain time, you will "try them back." You risk making customers feel that they are being hounded.

Pressuring customers for a commitment was not Scott's intention. Unfortunately, his words could easily be misconstrued, however, especially if the other sixty-seven salespeople who called previously were high-pressure types. Consequently, Scott admitted that his follow-up efforts via voice-mail had been relatively unsuccessful.

My suggestion (to Scott) was to a leave voice-mail message that created a greater sense of urgency—one that would cause even skeptical customers to call back sooner. Together, we updated his message. Now, after sending a proposal, Scott leaves the following voice-mail message:

After: *"Hi Mr. Customer, this is Scott Felcher calling from IBM Global Services in Atlanta. I sent you an electronic copy of the statement of work yesterday as we discussed, but after reviewing it again this morning, I have some concerns relative to the verbiage in the contract. If you get a chance today, would you call me back at (770) 863-1000, so we can eliminate any problems before they occur? Thank you."*

If you were the customer, would you respond to this voice-mail? See how this is not just another "follow up" call from an eager salesperson wanting to check on the status of their commission. Frankly, I never make calls just to "follow up." Most customers don't want to be pursued. Instead, this revised message has a greater sense of purpose which will predictably create a greater sense of urgency. In this voice-mail message, the seller has "some concerns" relative to the contract and is calling to avoid a potential problem before it occurs. Of course, the customer is going to return this call!

My first objective when leaving voice-mail messages is to pique the prospect's curiosity, in order to generate a return call. If a prospect or customer becomes curious about who you are or what you can do for them, they will absolutely return your call. Once they call back, your next move is easy—you simply tell them why you called. Curious customers want to know two things early on in the conversation. They want to know who you are and why you are calling. So tell them.

In this case, Scott was calling because he had some concerns about the contract. "I do?" he wondered as we strategized together. "What exactly am I concerned about?" Scott asked. Good question, which brings us to the second part of this two-pronged voice-mail strategy.

Instead of responding to Scott's question directly, I asked him a few basic questions. "Scott, does the typical IBM services contract have multiple pages? Are there terms and conditions, or other legal mumbo-jumbo that might be confusing to a customer? Does the statement of work ever need to be clarified or adjusted to accurately reflect the customer's requirements?"

"Scott," I said, "Aren't you concerned about every contract you send out? For instance, aren't you concerned that the statement of work accurately reflects the customer's expectations, and that they fully understand the otherwise confusing nature of contractual language?" He nodded and smiled, as a look of clarity slowly began to creep into his expression. "You should never have to fake being concerned about your customers," I added. At this point, executing the rest of the conversation is relatively simple:

Customer: *(returning call): "Hi Scott, I am returning your voice-mail message. What's up?"*

Seller: *"Thanks, Mr. Customer, for calling me back. Have you had a chance to review the agreement?"*

Customer: *"I looked at it briefly. Why?"*

Seller: *"Well, these contracts tend to be very confusing. I work with them every day, and it's still a challenge. So, I wanted to be proactive and clarify a couple of points that may not be self-explanatory, in an effort to save you some time and hassle down the road. Do you happen to have the paperwork in front of you?"*

Ninety percent of the game when it comes to closing a sale is getting customers to focus on the details of the transaction long enough to become comfortable with the deal.

> Ninety percent of closing a sale is getting customers to focus on the details of a transaction long enough to become comfortable with the deal.

Particularly when the sale involves a written agreement, it is very important to review contractual language with the customer. All we're doing here is adjusting our voice-mail strategy to create the desired sense of urgency to make this happen sooner, rather than later. After all, if you don't get an opportunity to stand up to the plate, you won't get a chance to swing at the ball.

One more note about curiosity-inducing voice-mail messages: The opportunity for self-critique doesn't begin unless you are willing to write your voice-mail messages down on paper. Have you ever listened to your own voice on tape? Most people say their voice sounds much different than they expected. The same is true with voice-mail messages. If you want to improve your strategic effectiveness with regard to your voice-mail messages, then you must invest the time to put your voice-mail messages on paper, and examine your wording.

Let me give you some quick pointers about what to look for when analyzing your voice-mail messages. When you see your voice-mail messages written down, the first test is to ask, if you happened to be a key decision maker in an important account, and you were on the receiving end of a steady diet of voice-mail messages from salespeople, would you return this call? Secondly, you should be able to physically point to the word or phrase that is going to pique the prospect's curiosity. If you can't, then perhaps your message is doing more to satisfy a customer's interest, rather than create it. Lastly, sellers are quick to leave voice-mail messages that say, "I was calling to introduce myself," or, "I wanted to take a few minutes of your time." Now we know what the salesperson's objectives are in the call. But, what's in it for the customer?

Sometimes even a little thing like asking a customer to return your call by a certain time helps to escalate their sense of urgency. For example, it's not unusual for the last sentence in my voice-mail messages to say, "So, if you get a chance, please call me back at (770) 840-7640. I should be in the office today until around 4:30pm." When my prospect cleans out their voice-mail box, they make a written note to call Dan, call Richard, call Susan, call Jim, call Robert, and call Tom Freese (*before 4:30pm*). Now, which name sticks out on their memo pad as having the greatest sense of urgency? Usually, it's the one that seems time sensitive, which is why I let customers know that, "I should be in the office today until around 4:30pm."

Focus Beyond the Transaction

For customers, the sale doesn't end when the purchase order gets signed. Frankly, a purchase order is just an administrative stepping stone on the way to the customer actually using your product or service. The real value of your proposed solution, and the anticipated benefits that drove the justification for the purchase, are often not realized until long after a sale is consummated. Therefore, it is incumbent upon sellers to focus on the broader scope of the project, which extends well beyond the initial purchase. This idea of focusing beyond the transaction can also be a powerful strategy for increasing the prospect's sense of urgency for moving forward with a favorable decision.

Focusing on the implementation schedule, for example, is a good way for sellers to talk about the status of a sale without the risk of customers feeling pressured regarding the initial order. In fact, customers want you to be interested in their long term success regarding the implementation of your product or service. Here's a sample dialogue to illustrate the point.

Seller:	*"Mr. Customer, can we put the transaction aside and spend a few minutes talking about your plans for implementation?"*
Customer:	*"Sure, let's do that."*

Seller: *"Given that we are coming up on the end of September, if you choose to move forward with this product, when would you want the system to be fully operational?"*

Suppose the customer chooses January 15th as their target "live" date. If this conversation occurs in September, January might seem like a long way off—in which case, the customer may not be in a hurry to make a decision. They think, why worry about something that is not going to happen until next year? Hence, we need to think about escalating the customer's sense of urgency, in this case, by working backward from the implementation date.

Seller: *"If January 15th is your target date, should we allow a couple of weeks for testing before the equipment actually goes into production?"*

Very few physical products are put directly into production on the day they arrive. Instead, most customers will want to allow time for equipment to be staged, assembled, installed, inspected, and tested, before being deemed ready for service.

Customer: *"We will need approximately two weeks to stage the hardware, another two weeks for assembly and installation, and then thirty days to test normal operating procedures with the new equipment."*

Seller: *"Do we need to allow for vacation time during the holidays?"*

Customer: *"Good point. Not much happens around here in the second half of December."*

Your next move is critical. Once you identify the different elements of the implementation and the lead-times involved, you can very easily work backward to build a timeline that essentially narrows the window for making a decision, thus increasing the prospect's sense of urgency for moving forward. For example, you might summarize by saying:

Seller: *"Well, Mr. Customer, if the goal is to bring your system "live" on January 15th, and we need to allow four weeks for staging and installation, thirty days for testing, plus we're going to lose two weeks at the end of December, then the equipment needs to be on-site the first week of November. Factoring in the typical lead times for ordering, we would need to have a commitment from you no later than mid-October to comfortably meet your implementation schedule. That means we have less than thirty days to make a decision."*

Can you see how a project that was going to happen "sometime next year" suddenly turns into a decision that needs to be made in less than thirty days? As an added bonus, your willingness to help customer's define the timeline for decision actually provides a valuable service for them. By working backward through the details of the implementation schedule, you are helping the customer plan ahead and make sure their project goes smoothly, which is much more valuable than just pestering them to hurry up and finalize a transaction.

Even if you don't sell "systems," as in this example, the technique of focusing beyond the transaction to increase the prospect's sense of urgency still applies. Most purchase decisions have certain timing and logistical considerations that could affect the customer before, during, and after the sale.

If you sell real estate, for example, in addition to talking with clients about financing options and scheduling the actual closing date, you could also facilitate a discussion about their upcoming move. Have they booked a moving company? Do they want to be settled before school begins? If you sell medical supplies, you can talk with doctors about the impact of pending legislation on reimbursement rates, which may very well impact their sense of urgency to move forward with a purchase.

What's the Cost of Not Moving Forward?

Instead of consummating a sale, what if your customer chooses to wait? For whatever reason, they just don't feel an urgency to move forward with a decision. What then? Do you turn up the pressure on the account thinking that pushing harder will increase your probability of success? Or, do you back off, hoping the customer will suddenly realize how much value they are missing? Dealing with this lack of urgency has become a common challenge in our current economic climate, especially now that customers are more cautious in their decision-making and more judicious with their budgets and spending than ever before.

Too often, a seller will try to break the log jam by offering special discounts in an attempt to increase their prospect's sense of urgency. Financial incentives clearly have their place in your overall sales strategy, but dangling a financial carrot out in front of customers isn't always enough to make them comfortable with your product, or overcome current feelings of complacency.

In truth, when customers feel there is no downside to delaying a purchase, it is easy for them to postpone. At that point, it's pure economics. If the cost of moving forward outweighs the cost of waiting, customers will be tempted to delay the decision. Fortunately, the opposite is true. When the cost of delaying a purchase exceeds the cost of moving forward, then wrapping up the sales transaction becomes relatively simple. It's just a matter of fueling the customer's sense of urgency by giving them enough reasons to buy from you.

> It's pure economics. If the cost of moving forward outweighs the cost of waiting, customers will be tempted to delay their decisions.

So, how many reasons do you want prospective customers to have to buy from you? Ideally, you want customers to have many reasons to support a purchase decision, because the aggregate of these reasons creates a greater sense of urgency for moving forward. We talked about this in Chapter 6 when we examined the differences between SPA and PAS positioning.

Our initial goal with the PAS model was to differentiate ourselves from the rest of the "noise" in the marketplace. With the increasingly competitive nature of sales, doing something that commoditizes your value message also tends to lower the customer's sense of urgency for making a decision. That's why starting with the elevator pitch is so problematic, as we discussed.

Instead, we talked about bonding with buyers on their problems, in order to uncover opportunities to then provide valuable solutions. We also talked about expanding the opportunity by getting beyond the basic issue into a more in-depth discussion of the specific implications that might be driving the need. Helping customers to see these more detailed implications tends to increase their urgency for change.

So, let's revisit our water pump analogy one more time. If you remember, I made the point that you don't want your conversations with homeowners to be limited to the fact that they have a flooded basement. You want to talk with them about all the different implications of having water where it shouldn't be. The more implications raised in the needs development conversation, the better. In addition to expanding the opportunity, uncovering multiple implications helps customers realize that there may be a significant cost associated with *not* moving forward with a purchase decision. In the case of a flooded basement, a customer who chooses to wait could face any number of undesirable evils including mold, mildew, structural damage to the foundation of the home, and so on.

When calculating the cost of *not* moving forward with a decision, you must also help customers realize that the longer these problems go unresolved, the more costly the situation becomes. If you lay the groundwork properly, identifying multiple implications early in the sales process can have a significant impact on the customer's sense of urgency later on, especially when they realize that maintaining the status quo will only cause these problems to get progressively worse.

Escalating to Higher Levels Within Your Target Accounts

Buying decisions often need to be escalated to someone in a higher position of authority within the account before approval can be given to move forward with a purchase commitment. Granted, not every deal needs a manager's stamp of approval, but escalating decisions to higher levels is certainly a common theme in sales.

The most effective way to escalate an opportunity and secure the necessary approvals is to have a strong internal advocate who will champion your proposed solution. But, these people who serve as internal champions don't just appear out of thin air, they need to be developed. The fact that someone likes your solution doesn't necessarily mean they can make a strong case to justify it internally.

Whenever I worked an opportunity that involved many players, one of my early qualifying questions was, "Who else will need to sign off on this decision?" I didn't want to get to the end of the sales process and discover that a key decision maker had been left out of all our discussions. I understood that high level executives don't always participate in every step of the sales process. I simply wanted to know who would be involved in the evaluation and what their role would be with regard to the purchase decision. Once you know who the players are, you can begin developing internal advocates.

Some sellers look for the opportunity to hand-pick someone in their accounts to fulfill the role of internal champion. Me, I prefer to shoot for the masses. Who says you can't have a handful of internal advocates in your accounts? In my view, the best case scenario would be to have three of four internal champions who could recommend your product or service to senior management.

The key to developing internal champions is to build their confidence in you, as well as their confidence in your proposed solutions. How do you build an internal champion's confidence? The answer is by addressing their specific hot buttons.

Whenever multiple people get involved in a purchase, they are bound to have different agendas for the decision. It's human nature. If you sell technology, for example, an operations manager might be most concerned about productivity and systems quality. Meanwhile, the education coordinator might zero-in on other features like ease of use or new employee ramp up, while the security officer fixates on issues regarding data integrity and system firewalls. You will find that people who have different hot buttons also have different urgencies when it comes time to make a decision. My objective as a salesperson was to try and make champions out of each—first, by understanding their specific hot buttons, and then,

> We must remember that most internal champions haven't ever attended a sales training course that teaches them how to position your product or service.

by tailoring my value proposition to address a broader range of implications. If their concerns are all met, guess what? Everybody wins!

Ultimately, you want load internal advocates up with as much ammunition as possible to recommend your solutions. But we must remember that most internal champions haven't ever attended a sales training course that teaches them how to position the value of your solutions. Do you know what that makes you? A sales trainer! Since most large purchase decisions are made behind closed doors, your success will largely depend on your internal champions' confidence and their ability to deliver a powerful recommendation for your product or service. Therefore, it is incumbent upon you, as the salesperson, to teach your internal champions how to be more effective advocates within your target accounts.

Bringing a Sales Manager or Executive into Your Deals

Sometimes, it's possible to escalate the customer's sense of urgency by introducing a higher level manager or executive from your own company into the equation. Their presence in the sale can be a good way to shake loose any lingering concerns or outstanding issues. Use some discretion about who you choose to invite into your sales, but generally speaking, the higher level of authority the better.

If you introduce an authority figure from your company into one of your deals, there are a couple of rules of thumb. First, you can't let a manager from your company come in and say something that you should have said. This only erodes your credibility. Granted, people in positions of authority can make commitments a salesperson normally can't make, and that's fine. That's why they're being brought into the account. In the best case scenario, however, your manager or an executive from your company shows up and reiterates key points you already made. Demonstrating a unified front can do wonders for a salesperson's credibility and ultimately cause customers to feel even more comfortable working with your company.

The second rule of thumb for bringing an authority figure into a deal is simply this: You shouldn't let anyone near your account until you have had an opportunity to strategize with them in advance. I don't care if the president of your company wants to meet your best customer. Put it this way: It only takes a couple of inappropriate words to derail a pending deal. I once had a senior executive say to a potential buyer, "Our next generation product has fewer problems!" With that, the customer postponed the decision until next release, which wasn't scheduled to happen for another nine months.

Fortunately, high level managers also have the ability to say things that can help close deals. Sometimes, an opportunity is teetering on the brink of closure, and the customer just needs some reassurance to make them feel comfortable that they are indeed making the right choice. When customers need reassurance, the four most powerful words your sales manager or executive can say are: "How can I help?"

Whenever I brought my managers into a sale, I briefed them in advance on the status of the opportunity, as well as any issues that were outstanding. We also strategized about our objectives for the call, and who was going to say what. Of course, I opened the meeting and introduced everyone, since it was my account. But after my introduction, I specifically coached my sales manager or executive to open with four simple words, "How can I help?"

Here's how this works. Suppose you're the account rep and you bring your sales manager in to call on the decision committee. You play host, probably facilitating some general chit-chat until the meeting is called to order. At the appropriate time, you introduce each of the participants in the meeting, and summarize a brief history of what has brought you to this point in the sales process. When you are finished, your manager should chime in, like this:

Sales Manager: *"Thank you, Mr. Customer. I have heard a lot about your project over the last several weeks and I appreciate your time today. I am also familiar with some of your immediate objectives and (salesperson) has done a good job keeping me posted on the status of your account. My ultimate goal is to be another resource for you and your team. So, perhaps I should start by asking: How can I help?"*

Bingo! While these four words seem simple enough, they accomplish two very strategic objectives in the meeting. First, most customers will respond by giving your manager an updated status on where they stand relative to purchasing your product or service. Basically, they will paint a verbal picture of the current issues and what else needs to happen to bring the sale to fruition. If you were the sales manager, wouldn't you want that kind of detail before you started addressing specific issues? This opening is also a good way to get customers actively involved in the discussion, as opposed to having them sit quietly while your sales manager drones on and on.

The second, and more important objective, is the impression your sales manager or executive will leave with customers. At the end of the day, customers want to feel comfortable that they are making the right decision. In that vein, those four simple words ("How can I help?") will do more than anything else your manager could say to leave a positive impression long after the meeting or teleconference ends. Customers want to know that someone in a position of authority cares about their long-term success and is willing to help if needed. Once you succeed in kicking the meeting off in a non-threatening way, customers tend to open up and relax, which makes it much easier to address any obstacles that might be in the way of finalizing a mutually beneficial sales transaction.

What we are basically talking about here is empowering other people to become part of your extended sales force. We want to create internal advocates who can carry our messages forward, and we want decision makers to feel comfortable enough with our product or service to pull the trigger on a purchase decision. And, since we all have monthly and quarterly sales objectives, we want these things to happen sooner rather than later.

< ACTION ITEMS >

1. Create 3 x 5 cards that have the words, "How can I help?" Affix those cards to your telephone and take them with you on customer visits. Make it a habit to gravitate to these four words when you open conversations with prospective customers. After all, customers need to feel comfortable that you care about what happens to them before, during, and after the sale.

2. When strategizing with your sales team, make a list of impending events that could increase a prospect's sense of urgency for

moving forward. Basically, why should customers make a decision now, instead of waiting until later?

3. Create a justification model that documents potential costs of *not* solving the identified problem. What are the risks of maintaining the status quo? What are the costs of moving ahead with a decision for a product that doesn't adequately address key business concerns? Some people need to see numbers on paper before these downside risks fully register.

CHAPTER 12

Leveraging Your Extended Sales Force

There is an old adage that says, if you want something done right, do it yourself. There's a lot of truth to this statement. But if you are a salesperson, this theory has a serious flaw. In the profession of sales, it is very difficult to succeed without the help of others. Most salespeople, in fact, are part of a larger team, which consists of sales support professionals, marketers, advertisers, managers, operations people, strategic business partners, and internal advocates. That's right! Even folks who don't work for your company are part of your extended sales team. And their ability to communicate the value of your product or service will have a direct correlation to your success. We talked about leveraging internal champions in the previous chapter. What we haven't talked about yet is the broader opportunity of leveraging partner relationships to strengthen your value proposition and get deeper, wider and more strategic within your target accounts.

Strategic partnerships take different forms, depending on your industry and the type of products you sell. Companies who sell through distribution channels often have a network of value added resellers (VARs). VARs serve as an extension of the vendor's internal sales organization, and resell products into their local customer base. Other companies leverage agent relationships, where a pre-determined commission or fee is paid to agents for revenue they generate. Some companies also have OEM (other equipment manufacturer) relationships with providers where some or all of a product is embedded into another company's branded offering, thus benefiting both parties in the marketplace.

For our purposes here, let's just say that a strategic partner is someone who has a vested interest in your sales success. More specifically, it's an individual or company who stands to make a profit if and when a customer chooses to purchase your product or service.

Building an effective distribution channel within a targeted market is a critical part of the overall sales strategy for many companies. Strategic partners create additional leverage by giving vendor companies a way to broaden their internal sales organizations to penetrate more prospect opportunities and close more business. Simply put, it gives you more feet on the street.

Of course, the hope is that your partners will be effective with regard to uncovering new prospect opportunities, and then moving those opportunities forward toward closure. But, where do these "effective" partners come from? Should we look for partners who are effective already, or are effective partnerships something that needs to be developed? Although the concept of strategic partnering is relatively new over the last decade or two, we can learn some very important lessons from the history of how business relationships have evolved over time.

The Evolution of Sales Partnerships

In years past, most vendors went out looking for established companies they could partner with. Particularly in technology, which was my primary sales background, salespeople were sent out into their respective territories to sign up established resellers, in an effort to broaden their coverage base. In some cases, finding new partner opportunities was part of the compensation plan. If a reseller liked what they heard about your product or service, they signed the necessary agreements, everyone shook hands, and a partnership was born. Once, I signed up five new partners in a single month and got paid a significant sum of money for doing so.

Back at the home office, senior management was licking their chops. "If we sign up tons of new partners," they surmised, "and they all go out and sell lots of product, we will be rolling in dough!"

There were several problems with this mentality. While it was possible to get an initial boost in productivity from some partnerships, just because the paperwork got signed, didn't necessarily mean sales increased. In fact, it was not unusual for resellers to sign on the dotted line and then sit back, and wait for leads to come from the host vendor. As you might guess, settling into a demand fulfillment role didn't increase sales volumes.

Furthermore, if you sold in a competitive industry, you were probably not the only company looking for strategic partners. Everyone else wanted additional leverage in the marketplace too! Therefore, established resellers were being aggressively courted by all of the name-brand vendors, since each wanted to become a dominant part of their reseller's go-to-market strategy.

Not surprisingly, top resellers were reluctant to limit themselves to a single vendor. In fact, the tendency is just the opposite. Resellers figured that, "If we represent every vendor, we can offer the broadest range of products and services to our customers." Of course, this mindset quickly diluted the reseller's expertise for any one solution. It also diluted the impact of the messages being communicated. In other words, the strategy of saying to prospective customers, "We can sell you anything, just let us know what you want," doesn't do much to create demand for a particular product or service.

Since it is virtually impossible for resellers to have a prospering business relationship with everyone, vendor companies basically had two options—either sever ties with underperforming resellers, or take steps to try and bolster their sales productivity.

Unfortunately, arrogance in a robust economy sometimes gives way to ignorance. Meaning, during the boom years, it was easiest just to dissolve relationships where reseller partners were not performing according to expectations. This "churn and burn" mentality often backfired, however, when partners, who were cut off by a host vendor for non-performance, resurfaced as an authorized reseller aggressively representing a competitive product. Vendor companies have also realized that there are a finite number of resellers within any specified geographic territory, and only a small fraction of those will meet performance expectations on their own volition. As a result, vendors are starting to turn their focus toward trying to develop more effective business partners, as opposed to just cutting ties with them.

> During the boom years, it was easiest just to dissolve relationships where a reseller partner was not performing according to expectations.

Developing Effective Market Partners

If one of your goals as a host vendor is to increase market leverage, then it is incumbent upon you to take steps to enhance your reseller partner's effectiveness when representing your company, products and services. Most partners want to do a good job. They want to be successful in providing valuable solutions to their customer base, and they want to earn a reasonable profit in the process. Therefore, the success formula for leveraging strategic partners is actually very simple. If you can make partners *more* effective with respect to selling and delivering your products and services, then both you and they will make more money and have more satisfied customers.

> If you can make partners more effective with respect to selling and delivering your products and services, then both of you will make more money and have more satisfied customers.

The problem is most reseller partners are spread relatively thin in terms of their ability to allocate time and attention to host vendors. In addition to selling your products and services, chances are good they represent a number of other vendors who also want a significant share of their time and attention. Some of you may have exclusive relationships within a distribution channel, meaning your partners are one-hundred percent focused on your solutions. This is the exception rather than the rule, however. For most vendors who sell through partners, competing for mindshare is the name of the game.

It comes as no surprise then, that every other vendor you compete with has the same goals. They want partners to find new prospect opportunities and lead with a proposal that features their solutions. They also want partners to stay focused on pending deals as they move through the sales process, which includes being proactive and ready to address potential obstacles or objections that may arise. Additionally, they want resellers to stay current on product updates or specification changes when they are announced. We talked earlier about the problems of having similar-sounding messages when positioning our solutions to target customers. The same phenomenon exists in the channel, where there is more "noise" in the marketplace than ever before. Therefore, since you are not the only vendor competing for mindshare, perhaps we can apply the same QBS techniques we have been talking about in this book to secure more time and attention from your target partners.

Over the past few years, the mentality with regard to developing business partner relationships has started to change. Instead of simply discarding less productive partners as underachievers, vendor companies are now looking for ways to nurture existing channel relationships in order to create additional leverage within key markets. This requires a proactive effort on someone's part, however, to raise the level of advocacy in terms of favoring your solutions.

Host companies that recognize the importance of strategic partner relationships have started investing significant efforts into developing more productive business partner relationships. Consequently, partners now receive countless invitations from vendors wanting them to participate in all kinds of relationship-building events that range from product seminars to user-group meetings, happy-hour receptions, trade shows, conference calls, lunch-and-learns, and vendor-sponsored golf outings. As a result, there are an enormous number of distractions pulling partners away from their core business—to the point where a partner salesperson could easily fill their calendar with relationship-building events and never sell anything.

Here's another chance to step outside the box of traditional thinking. Perhaps it's time to question the return on investment on some of these events. A golf outing, for example, is a great way to make a friend, but eighteen holes of golf doesn't make a business partner salesperson more effective when it comes to positioning the value of your product or service. Likewise, I never had much success with lunch-and-learn events. You know, where the vendor rep brings in lunch in exchange for having the partner's sales organization sit through a thirty-minute vendor presentation. If you are the only one hosting these lunches, they could probably be effective. But, your competition is also trying to appeal to these partner's culinary weaknesses, and after a while, the sales team is only there for the free lunch. Think about it this way: What's the likelihood that the messages you present on Monday will remain "fresh" in your partner's minds by Wednesday or Thursday, after two or three other lunch-and-learn events?

Even when you do get quality mindshare from a strategic partner, you must be sure your value proposition doesn't sound just like every other vendor's. I've said it before, and I'll say it again—in a competitive market, companies tend to have similar-sounding value propositions, and if you sound the same as everyone else, you forfeit your competitive advantage. The same thing occurs when you're working with partners. If your value message gets commoditized in the eyes of the partner's sales team, and they, in turn, commoditize your value proposition to prospective customers, everyone loses.

If differentiation is truly one of the keys to success in selling, then perhaps it's time to examine what we are doing to help strategic partners be more effective in terms of differentiating the value of our product or service. In QBS, one of the ways we accomplish this is by steering the conversation away from a discussion of product features. I would much rather teach partners how to be more effective salespeople, particularly with respect to positioning the value of our product or service. Did you catch the significance of that last statement? I am suggesting that perhaps we should spend less time trying to sell strategic partners on the value of our solutions, and more time teaching them how to successfully

> Perhaps we should spend less time trying to sell partners on the value of our solutions, and more time teaching them how to successfully position our value proposition to prospective customers.

position our value proposition to prospective customers. In other words, if you want to develop more productive partner relationships, then you should spend less time being a salesperson, and invest more time being a sales coach. If you do, you can show partners how to earn more money and have more satisfied customers.

Let Partners in on Your Secrets

It has always been difficult to duplicate the success of top performing salespeople. Companies all over the world struggle with this. That's because it has always been difficult to identify and then replicate the skills that separate top performers from the rest of the masses. Wouldn't it be terrific if we could figure out how to make everyone on your company's sales team so incredibly effective that they delivered stellar results on a monthly, quarterly, and annual basis? Wouldn't it be doubly great if there was something you could do to cause your extended sales team of partners to be equally effective?

My life's work in developing Question Based Selling and the QBS methodology has been a study in sales effectiveness. That has always been my focus, and now it's my expertise. Back when I was a territory sales rep, I was constantly adjusting my approach in order to increase my own probability of success and reduce the risk of failure—which became two of the premise concepts I introduced in my first book, *Secrets of Question Based Selling*.

Basically, I focused on the softer skills (things like relationship development and communication), in an attempt to identify what was working well, and repeat those successes. I also wanted to identify what wasn't working to minimize any risk of failure. Now that these concepts have been formalized into the QBS methodology, it has become clear that the soft skills in professional sales are not only identifiable, they are also transferable. This begs the question, what are you doing currently to enhance the softer skills of your extended sales force—your partners?

Historically, host companies have done little to nurture or enhance the professional selling skills of their vendor partners. Most of the effort with regard to educating partners has been invested in transferring product knowledge. The mentality

> Most of the effort with regard to educating partners has been invested in transferring product knowledge.

being, "If we find good distribution partners, and train them on all the features and benefits of our products and services, sales results should take care of themselves."

But what makes a good partner? Generally speaking, a good partner is thought to be someone who will sell lots of your product or service. To me, this thinking seems superficial. It dismisses any responsibility on our part to work with partners to enhance their sales effectiveness. Instead, I encourage vendor corporations to think strategically about how to make partners more effective, so they can sell significantly more of your product or service.

The notion of increasing your partner's sales effectiveness brings us back to some familiar themes. What vendors really want is for partners to create business opportunities that otherwise wouldn't exist. This includes identifying potential customers, uncovering needs within those accounts, and differentiating the value of your solutions. We also want partners to expand the size and scope of opportunities by getting deeper, wider, and more strategic within their customer accounts. These, too, are high level concepts. How (exactly) can partners create more business opportunities that otherwise wouldn't exist, and what should they be doing to uncover needs or differentiate your solutions in an increasingly competitive business environment?

I am going to let you in on a little secret. I enjoyed a fair amount of success in my career as a salesperson, finishing my last seven years in corporate sales over 200% of quota. But it wasn't because I was a better salesperson. It's because I was a better coach. It's true. My success as a salesperson was largely attributable to the fact that I invested a tremendous amount of time and effort teaching my extended sales force how to be more effective salespeople.

Truth be told, the same techniques we've talked about thus far apply to your partner's sales force, too. Think about it, what if it were possible to increase your partner's strategic effectiveness with regard to voice-mail, to the point where they had an eighty to ninety percent call back rate? Wouldn't that increase their value to you as part of your extended sales force?

What if it was easy for partners to establish credibility in the eyes of prospective customers, especially early in the sales process? Instead of making claims that commoditize your value proposition, what if your partners learned how to bond with potential customers on their problems (P), as opposed to starting with the traditional elevator pitch? In addition, what if it were possible for partners to learn how to manage the scope, focus, and disposition of their questions in order to escalate the value of their sales conversations, and expand the needs development process?

I can keep going! What if it were possible for your strategic partners to create a sense of momentum in and around the sale by showing prospective customers that the trail to success has already been blazed? What if your partners could escalate their points of contact to more strategic levels within the account, in order to deal with decision-makers who have the budget, authority, and strategic vision to pull the trigger on a purchase?

What if it were also possible for strategic partners to deliver more impactful product presentations or at least be in a position to reiterate the same value messages that are being communicated by the host vendor? What if your "good" partners were able to effectively position your solutions against other competitive products or services in the industry, and then be proactive in recognizing potential obstacles and handling objections?

What if your strategic partners could also close more deals? What if they were able to position the value of your product or service in a way that would increase the customer's sense of urgency for wrapping up business in the current quarter or month? What if they could set expectations properly in the negotiation phase of the sale, in order to consistently secure a lucrative profit in the face of ever-increasing margin pressures?

What if *all* of these things could happen at the same time? The answer is they can, if your strategic partners possess the selling skills these actions require. The question now is, how can your partners acquire these skills?

Earlier, I made a point that it's difficult to find good salespeople in today's economic climate. Where would you look for them? Most of the large corporate sales schools are now closed, and most of the sales training material that's currently available was developed twenty plus years ago. Finding effective business partners is just as difficult as finding good salespeople. Professional selling skills are not something that you "find" anyway. Techniques and strategies that produce a successful sales approach must be developed though training and implementation.

Who is responsible for developing your partner's selling skills? Well, there are a couple of options. One is to take the older-school view and just assume that it's every man for himself. More contemporary thinking would suggest, however, that if you want your business partners to be more productive, then you must be proactive in helping them to increase their sales effectiveness.

Seeking More Than Just Mindshare

Would it surprise you to learn that approximately one fourth of the events we now deliver are for QBS clients who bring us in to train their extended sales force? It's a natural next step. Once a client's internal sales team has been exposed to the QBS methodology, almost without fail, someone will ask, "What about our channel partners? Wouldn't they also benefit from Question Based Selling?"

It's a good point. Ideally, you want everyone on your sales team to be on the same page relative to positioning your products and services. This includes your extended team of distribution partners and value added resellers. The good news is, everything we teach in QBS relative to increasing the strategic effectiveness of your sales team, also applies to strategic partners.

The trick is to invest in effectiveness training, not just product training. To me, sales effectiveness training comes in two distinct forms. One is what we have been talking about—working with strategic partners to develop their softer skills, which is critically important. If you aren't willing to make your partners more effective in representing your solutions, then you leave the door wide open for competitors to take away partner mindshare.

The second form of sales effectiveness training centers around industry knowledge. Partners get deluged with product information from host vendors. The thought is, the more partners know about the products they represent, the more effective they will be in communicating value to prospective customers. I do not dispute this. But, what's even more important than product information is having a clear understanding of the typical problems and challenges customers in your industry are currently facing.

Remember that when a partner rep first engages a new account, literally one hundred percent of those prospects will be forming an impression. What impression would you like prospective customers to form about your business partners? Do you want them to be seen as a valuable industry resource, or just another sales caller? I assume the former. That's good, because customers have all kinds of time for someone who can help them, but they have very little patience for dealing with someone who is just another salesperson.

In our pump analogy from earlier, if we were selling water pumps through a distribution channel, we would want business partners to be knowledgeable about the products and services we offered. But we would want them to be even *more* knowledgeable about the problems customers could face with respect to having a flooded basement. We would want them to know, for example, that in addition to removing the water, there may be a host of other implications driving the need. We would want them to know that flooding creates all kinds of other problems like mold, mildew, unpleasant odor, structural damage to the foundation of the home, safety and health hazards, damage to personal property, insurance hassles, recurrence, clean up, and not being able to utilize the space.

Having industry knowledge is important because sellers, whether you are a vendor or partner rep, still bond with potential customers on what's most important to them—their problems. But, this requires an educational effort to sensitize partner representatives on potential issues that may exist, the implications of those issues, and how your product or service could benefit the customer in specific situations.

Again, those happy-hour receptions and afternoon golf outings might be great for building relationships, but business partner reps won't learn how to become more effective salespeople on the golf course. The better alternative might be to divert some of the marketing dollars that would otherwise be used to fund these relationship-building events, into a skills development program that would increase the strategic effectiveness of your extended sales force, and produce a significantly higher return on investment.

> Happy-hour receptions and afternoon golf outings might be great for building relationships, but business partner reps won't learn how to become more effective salespeople on the golf course.

Critics of this idea to invest in your partner's strategic effectiveness may raise the point that a partner's newfound selling skills could be used to sell other products, not just yours. That's true. It would be virtually impossible to restrict someone's sales ability to a single line of products. I don't worry about this; in fact, I have the opposite philosophy. Even if partners do apply their selling skills to other products, people tend to remember that you were the one who helped to make them become more successful, which usually pays big dividends in terms of increased partner loyalty.

Cooperative Marketing

As you can tell, I prefer taking a much more proactive role in a business partner's development, rather than just signing them up and hoping for the best. Working with partners to develop their sales effectiveness through training is one way vendors can provide value. Another way for vendor reps to participate with partners is in the planning and execution of the sales process.

Now, I am not suggesting that you should attend every sales call your partners make. That defeats the purpose of having partners, and reduces the leverage you are attempting to gain by having an extended sales force. But there are times in the sales process where vendor participation can pay off, whether it's early on to penetrate new accounts or later in the sales process to help finalize a transaction.

Frankly, much of my own education in dealing with business partners came from the school of hard knocks, and there is no question that I learned some of the most valuable lessons when I sold superservers. At NetFrame, I was most comfortable playing the role of product expert. Don't get me wrong, I wasn't a true "tech head," but I was significantly more knowledgeable about superserver technology than most partners. That was understandable since my focus was relatively narrow, as compared to our business partners who usually represented numerous different vendors.

As the product expert, I was generally brought into the sales process as part of an escalation strategy. At the point when the conversation with a prospect went beyond a reseller's expertise, I was being called in to answer questions or handle objections. It sounded like a good plan, but we quickly discovered that this strategy was inherently flawed. Bringing me in to handle objections actually created two problems. First, by the time I got involved, customers had (in many cases) already formed the impression that NetFrame was expensive, technically complex, and difficult to manage. So, my first contact with the customer was often to fend off objections—most of which came up because the partner was not able to adequately differentiate the value of a superserver. I quickly realized that it was more difficult to undo an unfavorable impression, than it was to properly set the customer expectations in the first place.

The second problem our reseller partners had was penetrating new accounts. They had good intentions, but with so many companies calling on identified prospect opportunities, they were not getting enough appointments, and creating even less business. I will say it again—if you don't get an opportunity to step up to the plate, you won't have a chance to swing at the ball.

To address these issues, we started experimenting with a cooperative marketing program that helped reseller partners penetrate more new prospect opportunities, as well as set the proper expectations in the sales process. Ironically, I started asking resellers to *hold off* on their attempts to explain superserver technology to prospective clients. This went against traditional logic, where reseller partners were otherwise encouraged to fan out across a geographic territory and spread the word about the vendor's products and services. But since I did not have the bandwidth to attend each and every partner sales call, we initiated a procedure by encouraging reseller partners to set up conference calls as the starting point in the NefFrame sales process. After all, there is a big difference between starting an opportunity off on the right foot and having customers form negative impressions that are difficult to overcome.

The plan was actually very simple. At the appropriate time in their conversations with potential customers, reseller partners would mention superserver technology as something that should be considered, and then suggest the following:

Partner Rep: *"Mr. Prospect, one of the most exciting technologies we offer is the NetFrame family of superserver products. NetFrame Systems has developed a more powerful, more secure, and more cost-effective platform for driving large corporate networks. This could become a strategic advantage for your company, especially given your growth plans in the coming months."*

Prospect: *"Tell me more about NetFrame."*

Partner Rep: *"I would be happy to tell you about NetFrame, but I am not the expert on superservers. Could I make a suggestion instead?"*

Prospect: *"Sure."*

Partner Rep: *"Let's pull out our calendars and set up a three-way conference call with Tom Freese, the Regional Manager for NetFrame Systems in the Southeast. That way, in just a few minutes, you can hear the details about NetFrame and decide whether or not you want to pursue this technology for your environment."*

In addition to securing a high percentage of meetings, this technique proved to be a powerful curiosity-inducing strategy. Reseller partners loved the idea because they could bring NetFrame up in their calls without having to worry about getting stumped with technical questions. And, anything that might take the conversation beyond the reseller's expertise became the reason to set up a conference call with me. For customers, it was easy to say yes, because agreeing to a conference call required minimal commitment, and most people did want to learn more about superserver technology.

I didn't expect reseller partners to be product experts, but I did want to gain leverage—in this case, by asking partners to set up conference calls with potential customers. Of course, this gave me a chance to qualify opportunities and position the value of our solutions, and I could do many more conference calls than face to face meetings.

My goal was not to try and sell superservers over the telephone. That would not have been feasible because a telephone conversation could never replace an on-site presentation or demo. Rather, my objective was simply to help our business partners sell more NetFrame. If a customer wasn't interested or qualified, then a conference call limited my time investment in marketing to that account. On the other hand, when we did uncover a qualified opportunity, it was easy to suggest an appropriate next step, like an on-site presentation.

Most importantly, I found that when we didn't invest the time to hold a conference call in advance, results were poor. Even if a reseller was able to secure an on-site presentation, customer attendance was sparse—one or two people with a superficial interest—quite the opposite of what happened when we invested the time to get customers excited in advance. Also, by the time we arrived on site, customers who liked what they heard on the conference call invited other key influencers and decision-makers to attend the presentation, so the room was often filled with all the people who would ultimately need to sign off on the purchase.

Do you know what this type of cooperative marketing strategy really does? It allows everyone to make better use of their time, and it also shortens the sales process. If an opportunity is qualified, the customer gets excited on a conference call, and you suggest possible next steps. If they are not qualified, you save the customer's time and the reseller's time, and you also save a lot of unnecessary trips. You still gain leverage from partners out in the territory, and you have a more direct impact on the execution of the sales process. Truly, everybody wins!

One more note about dealing with business partners. I made the point earlier that prospective customers have all kinds of time to spend with sellers who can actually help them. Most business partners feel the same way. If you are just pestering people to sell greater volumes of your product, you can expect minimal interest and high resistance from your partner base. On the other hand, if you prove that you not only add value in the sales process, but you can also help partners become more successful salespeople, then you can expect significant mindshare and leverage from your base of business partner relationships.

< ACTION ITEMS >

1. Survey your existing business partners to find out what type of strategic sales training they have had to date. Product training doesn't count. Has anyone made an investment in teaching them how to differentiate your value proposition, or are they positioning your product or service with the traditional elevator pitch?

2. Calculate how much money your company spends on partner events like user-group meetings, happy-hour receptions, product seminars, trade shows, dinners, lunch-and-learns, and golf outings. Compare that to how much is spent developing your partner's strategic selling skills. Then, convene your sales team and make a collective decision regarding the value of these investments, and opportunities to reallocate funds in ways that will increase your sales results.

How to Pick a Sales Trainer

In the prologue of this book, I made the observation that by the time someone graduates from college, they have completed seventeen or more years of formal education, but they didn't attend a single class on how to raise a child, and they weren't taught anything about how to sell. Oddly enough, these are two of the most important functions an adult will perform in their lifetime.

Everybody sells! But, sales training generally isn't part of our formal education curriculum. Perhaps that makes our decisions about sales courses even more important later on as we move through our professional business careers. That said, what we have really been talking about in this book is not just training. We have been talking about the possibility of change—making a conscious decision to do something different that will enhance the strategic effectiveness of your sales organization and ultimately, your bottom line results.

Sales managers essentially have two options. One is to ignore changes in the marketplace and continue using the current approach. For most sales organizations, however, the status quo is your enemy. It is unrealistic to expect competitors to just sit back while your company enjoys a strategic advantage. History has proven that natural market forces will prevail, and we now know that if you are not aggressively working to improve your position in the marketplace, then you are probably falling behind.

> Natural market forces will prevail, and if you are not aggressively working to improve your position in the marketplace, then you are probably falling behind.

The other option managers have is to embrace change as a strategy to stay ahead of an evolving sales environment. Embracing change means taking a proactive role in the ongoing development of your sales organization. It also means stepping outside the box of traditional thinking with regard to giving your sales team a competitive advantage in your respective industry. Of course, sales training and continued development are important elements in any skills-based initiative.

Sales training can be a double-edged sword, however. Most sales managers would say they absolutely want to improve the strategic effectiveness of their sales teams. The question is, how? Many of the brand-named sales training programs that are currently being offered were originally developed way back in the 1970's and 1980's, even though the business environment has changed dramatically in the last twenty years. One has to wonder, then, why would you want to train new salespeople with an old-school mentality that may not even be applicable given today's economic climate? Likewise, sending experienced salespeople back to the same sales training courses they have already attended is another miss. If they had embraced those ideas the first time around, they would still be using them.

Choosing a sales methodology is risky business anyway, because the cost of making a mistake is enormous, starting with the fact that sales training is not cheap. I'm not just talking about the cost of the training itself. In addition to whatever fees are being charged for the training course, you also have to consider the cost of taking your sales people out of the field for "*x*" number of days. There may also be a significant investment in travel if your team is geographically dispersed, and then you have the logistical considerations for hosting a group event at a convention center or upscale hotel.

Choosing the right training program is another challenge. At the end of the day, you don't want to spend a lot of money and have the training go poorly. What if the content does not

> Choosing a sales methodology is risky business, because the cost of making a bad choice is enormous.

meet your expectations, or the trainer is not well received by your salespeople? In fact, your biggest risk may be the opportunity cost, knowing that it is very difficult to recover from a bad training experience. Given the pace of today's business environment, companies cannot afford to lose ground, and there is a huge difference between having a productive sales team and one that is floundering. Sales managers also know that their credibility is at stake, and choosing the wrong sales methodology could cost them their job!

This brings us to the explanation of why I am even writing this section on how to pick a sales trainer. Trust me; it's not to sell you on Question Based Selling. You have already formed an impression about QBS, and we are in the fortunate position of already having an established track record of success. Instead, I wanted to take this opportunity to make some editorial comments on the training industry from my own observations and experiences as a salesperson, a manager, and now, a sales trainer.

Which Problem are You Trying to Solve?

The type of sales training you should choose really depends on what problem you are trying to solve. Sometimes, sales managers are looking to improve their team's organizational effectiveness. Essentially, they want to define and implement a company-wide sales process that fosters a greater sense of structure and consistency with regard to qualifying opportunities and utilizing sales resources. If your objectives for training are to redefine the sales process, courses like Miller-Heiman's Strategic Selling™, Holden's Power-Based Selling™, or Siebel's Target Account Selling™ are popular choices.

At this point, however, most sales organizations have a defined sales process in place, and their salespeople already have a relatively good picture of "what" they are trying to accomplish in managing their territories. For example, let me guess: *Step One* in your company's current sales process has something to do with identifying new prospect opportunities, right? *Step Two* is making the initial contact, hopefully to penetrate accounts at the appropriate decision levels. Then, there's *Step Three*, which usually refers to the discovery phase where you uncover needs and qualify the opportunity. Am I close? There is nothing wrong with having a predefined sales process or wanting everyone to be on the same page relative to steps of the sale. Having structure is certainly better than having a random approach across your sales organization.

I should warn you that some companies are not ready to hear what I am about to say, however. But, here goes—*just following the steps of a predefined sales process is not enough to differentiate you from other salespeople.* If you sell in a competitive marketplace, then your competitors have a defined sales process in place too, and I would bet their approach is very similar to yours. For example, I bet that Step One in their sales process is to identify new prospect opportunities. Step Two is penetrating new accounts, and so on. This raises the question, why would you want to train your salespeople to sound just like everyone else? As we have discussed, teaching your salespeople to sound just like everyone else is the quickest way to commoditize their value in the eyes of prospective customers.

I made the point earlier that most sellers already have a pretty good idea of "what" they are trying to accomplish in the sales process. Consequently, process definition is not the problem facing most companies. The real challenge now is execution, which includes increasing the strategic effectiveness of the sales organization.

Most managers I meet aren't wondering "what" objectives their salespeople should be trying to accomplish. Rather, they are focused on "how" to deliver on these objectives. And, it's the successful execution of the sales process that will ultimately separate top performing salespeople from their less effective competitors.

Therefore, the desire for sales training has shifted from simply defining the sales process to actually enhancing the selling skills and strategic effectiveness of the entire organization. As I said in Chapter 2, salespeople want to know "how" to penetrate more new accounts, given that potential buyers are more cautious and standoffish than ever before. And, when they reach a customer's voice-mail, they want to know *how* to get more return calls. Once they make it past the gatekeeper, they want to know *how* to pique the prospect's interest, and *how* to uncover more needs. They also want to know *how* to differentiate their value proposition from competitive alternatives, *how* to deal with possible objections, and *how* to increase the prospect's sense of urgency for moving forward with a decision.

So, what problem are you trying to solve? Are you seeking to more specifically define the steps of your company's sales process, or are you more interested in raising the strategic effectiveness and productivity of the broader sales organization?

What about a Motivational Speaker?

Is it possible for a sales effectiveness program to be motivational? The answer is yes, absolutely! If you teach a group of salespeople how to be more effective, they will certainly get excited. It's always more exciting to win! But, that does *not* mean motivational speeches will increase your sales effectiveness.

For me, listening to motivational speakers is great fun. Having been in corporate sales the bulk of my career, I have had many opportunities to listen to professional athletes, astronauts, politicians, celebrities, news anchors, explorers, and people who have overcome physical disabilities, talk about highly motivating personal life experiences. Most of these speakers share a success story that contains an underlying moral lesson. After they talk, we feel motivated because we think, "If that person can do it, I can too!"

The problem with a purely motivational experience for salespeople occurs when your team returns to their respective territories. No matter how interesting the speaker was, if your salespeople revert back to using their same old approach, they will likely get the same results—in which case, whatever enthusiasm that was created by the motivational speaker will wear off relatively quickly.

I am not speaking out against the idea of hiring a speaker for your next sales meeting or conference. As an author of three books, I am asked to deliver a fair number of sales talks and keynote speeches myself. You must realize, however, that the objectives of a sales talk are very different than the objectives of a sales methodology course. The goal of a training program is ultimately to change behavior. After two or three days, you want salespeople to recognize opportunities to adjust their current approach, and you also want them to adopt the strategies and techniques they have learned to execute more effectively throughout the sales process. Such behavioral changes that impact sales productivity are not likely to occur as the result of a one or two-hour sales talk, however. Therefore, let's agree that the objective of a sales talk or keynote address is to simply energize the audience, as opposed to actually changing behavior.

Since I have never climbed Mt. Everest or played professional sports, my goal when delivering sales talks is to energize audiences with a vision for how they can be more successful, as opposed to telling stories of personal achievement. Even if you can't change the world in a one or two-hour talk, we can absolutely cause people to start thinking outside the box with respect to differentiating themselves in a competitive business environment.

Weeding Through all the Different Choices

Choosing the right sales methodology for your company is critically important. So is choosing the right sales trainer. But there aren't a lot of Consumer Reports articles on how to make a good choice. Therefore, allow me to offer you a couple quick tips on what to look for, as well as some hard questions you should definitely ask potential trainers.

The first thing to look for in a sales trainer is how they sell themselves. What are they doing when they approach their own clients and customers? This is not as simple as just asking for a resume or references. Remember, everyone looks good on paper! Instead, you want to get a sense of their personal philosophy toward selling.

> Sales trainers have to market their own services, and how they approach the sales process themselves should give you a good indication of what they will be teaching your salespeople.

Sales trainers have to market their services to prospective clients, just like you, and how they approach the sales process themselves should give you a good indication of what they will be teaching your salespeople.

For example, when you interview a potential sales trainer, start off by saying, "Tell me about your sales development programs." Then, sit back and listen carefully to how they respond. If their answer takes the form of a standard elevator pitch, where they start by claiming to have a wealth of knowledge and experience, followed by a dissertation about all the "wonderful" benefits their programs offer, you should *run* as fast as you can in the other direction.

I know from practical experience that there is nothing a sales trainer can say about themselves or their material that, in the first few minutes of a conversation, will sound dramatically different than what every other sales trainer claims. Everyone touts their ability to help clients penetrate accounts, uncover needs, close more sales, and blah...blah...blah. Let me remind you, if a salesperson sounds just like everyone else, then they forfeit their competitive advantage. Do you want a trainer who commoditizes their own value proposition teaching your salespeople how to sell?

Would you want a trainer who commoditizes their own value proposition teaching your salespeople how to sell?

A good salesperson communicates their value against the backdrop of what's important to the client, rather than just spewing benefit statements. Therefore, you would want a sales trainer to respond with a quiet confidence, saying: *"Mr. Customer, I would be happy to tell you about the sales development programs we offer."* Then, you want them to ask, *"Would it be OK if I asked a couple specific questions about your sales organization, to better understand your objectives in terms of sales development?"* I find that most clients are actually relieved when I ask specific questions about their sales organization, because they want sales training to be tailored around their specific needs.

The next question you should ask a prospective trainer is: *"What makes your material different from other sales training programs?"*

Again, if the goal is to have a competitive advantage in the marketplace, you don't want more of the same old, same old. You want something that will give your sales team a measurable advantage. Therefore, if a sales trainer is truly able to offer a unique solution, they should be able to articulate what makes their material different from other sales training courses.

> If you don't have a clear understanding of what is specifically different about a certain sales training program, you should be very worried.

Don't be surprised if this question is difficult for sales trainers to answer, which makes it even more important to know if what you are getting is truly different, or just more of the same.

The goal of these interviews is not to put sales trainers on the defensive by asking difficult questions. The goal is to a have a better sense of what you are actually buying, so you can avoid a potential mistake. Think about it like this: If you don't have a clear understanding (in advance) of what specifically is different about a certain sales training program, then you should be very worried.

Ironically, a great many sales trainer "types" hang their hat on career longevity. "We have trained thousands of salespeople over the last fifteen or twenty years," they say. While I agree that experience is generally a good thing, so is adapting to changes in the marketplace. Therefore, when you hear these claims, be sure to ask, *"What (specifically) in your approach has changed over the last fifteen or twenty years?"*

Refuse to accept an ambiguous answer on this one. If their material has indeed evolved over time, a trainer should be able to cite specific examples of how their approach has been updated to adjust to changing market conditions. Ironically, I have found that most of the brand-name sales training courses are still teaching the same basic theories about selling as when I took them many years ago.

Now, it's up to you to decide whether you believe the selling environment for your industry has changed over time, or stayed pretty much the same. In my view, the business climate has changed dramatically, and managers need to be very cognizant with regard to what gives their sales team the best advantage moving forward.

In addition to differentiating their training programs, an effective sales trainer should also be able to articulate specific techniques and strategies that will provide an immediate boost in productivity. Sales managers want results. Therefore, if we're honest about it, what happens during the actual course is somewhat irrelevant. The key to increasing productivity is a function of what happens when participants go back out into their respective territories and put the concepts they learned into practice.

Be persistent on this issue, too. What (specifically) will your salespeople learn that will provide an immediate impact on results? It's a fair question. With what's at stake, you cannot accept a vague response like, "We provide a cohesive set of paradigms that empower sales professionals to...blah, blah, blah." That's great, but philosophical generalities don't increase productivity! Get clarity on what someone is planning to teach your salespeople and how it will impact their performance immediately after the training.

Always Ask for a Money-Back Guarantee

If the goal of sales training is ultimately to produce results, then you should ask for a performance guarantee. Traditionally, corporate sales trainers don't guarantee their services. But, why not? If a sales manager is going to put their reputation on the line and invest significant time and money, it seems to me that sales trainers should be willing to stand behind their product.

For example, every QBS program that we deliver comes with the following guarantee: *If the sales people who attend QBS Methodology training don't come away saying that Question Based Selling was the very best sales training they have ever experienced, then it will cost you nothing!* You should demand a similar pledge of assurance from whichever sales trainer you consider.

Granted, sales trainers cannot control external factors (like how their material gets reinforced after the training), but they *can* absolutely stand behind their courseware by guaranteeing audience buy-in. Put it this way, if a sales trainer is unable to gain the confidence of the audience,

> If a sales trainer is not willing to stand behind their material, then why would you want to put them in front of your sales team?

then it is highly unlikely that the training experience will have a positive impact on performance. And, since the sales trainer is in the best position to know their material relative to the objectives of your sales organization, it seems reasonable that clients should absolutely expect a money-back guarantee if the feedback from the training is not "off the charts" positive. Said differently, if a sales trainer is not willing to stand behind their material, why would you want to put them in front of your sales team?

Tailoring Course Content is Critical

Truth be told, there's a lot of "fluff" in the world of sales training. I may be preaching to the choir here, because most salespeople and managers I meet have already experienced plenty of sales training classes that didn't deliver the advertised return on investment. Most of us would agree that sitting through a two or three day class just to get one new idea seems like a colossal waste of time.

Every sales trainer is going to claim their programs are great. But, let's define great. Are you teaching high-level philosophy on how to be successful as a person, or are you giving salespeople specific tools and strategies that will give them a competitive advantage? Does your material talk generically about sales, or is it customized to address the specific challenges sales organizations face, in the specific markets they target? It's no longer enough to offer generic sales training classes to a client company. You must deliver valuable content that gives them a competitive advantage.

In addition to understanding a trainer's basic philosophy on sales and what makes their programs different, you should have a clear picture of how they plan to customize their material given the nuances of your specific business environment. Selling technology is different than selling real estate. Likewise, you wouldn't want a trainer to show up at your pharmaceutical company and use examples about life insurance. Instead, you need to understand how the trainer is planning to customize their material around specific "what if" scenarios that affect your salespeople on a daily basis. Professional athletes, for example, train to perform under certain conditions, and in specific situations. So do airplane pilots, soldiers, and firefighters. They train with specific scenarios in mind to create a heightened sense of preparedness that enables them to perform at the highest levels when needed. If we apply this logic to sales training, we should be giving salespeople the same level of heightened preparedness. So, do yourself a favor. Make sure your chosen trainer invests the time to customize their program and materials to address the specific "what if" scenarios that are, in fact, applicable to your business.

Require a Longer-Term View

A truly effective sales development program requires a long-term outlook. Too often, sales training courses are evaluated on content alone. Are the concepts being taught relevant to our business objectives? Will salespeople get some new ideas or just more of the same? While I agree that course content is definitely important, what's even more important is finding a program that will produce a lasting impact on your sales team. If a sales training course is indeed worthwhile, you want the material to generate a measurable increase in sales performance over an extended period of time.

Managers know most salespeople don't have photographic memories. Consequently, most training courses have a certain *half-life*, which means participants retain only some portion of the material that was covered. Let me ask: How much time did it take you to forget half of the material that was covered in your last sales training course? Without reinforcement, much of the information that gets communicated during the course of a training class will dissipate naturally over time. This is why reiteration of key techniques, as well as reinforcement of desired behaviors, should be part of the implementation plan when selecting a sales methodology.

Another challenge for sales managers is that you can't expect to completely change the culture of a company with a two or three-day sales training course. Human nature says that people will gravitate to whatever feels most comfortable, which includes returning to selling habits that have been grooved over many years. And, just because someone agrees with the logic presented in a training class, doesn't necessarily mean those ideas will produce a lasting change in behavior.

Increasing your sales effectiveness, therefore, requires more than just an intellectual decision of how to approach the sales process. It requires a personal commitment from salespeople to step outside their comfort zone and change selling behaviors, as well as a corporate commitment to support these desired changes. The operative word here is "support," which includes having a plan in place to reinforce the training long after the class has ended.

In my view, the single most important ingredient to successfully implementing a sales methodology is fostering an ongoing transfer of knowledge. Salespeople can learn from a trainer, but they can also learn from each other. Therefore, the opportunity to create lasting changes in behavior hinges on the client's ability to create an internal network of coaches and mentors who can reinforce the material that was communicated during the actual training. But, these internal resources need to be coached along the way, which is why it's important to look for a program that takes a longer-term view, offering advanced development programs as well as train-the-coaches opportunities that can reinforce desired techniques and strategies, and take your company's in-house expertise and understanding of the material to a deeper level.

In short, you shouldn't be talking with sales trainers about a specific course or event. Instead, you should talk with them about what will happen after the training to create lasting changes in behavior, and produce the desired return on investment.

Outside Trainers Are Not the Enemy

Some of my best friends, and biggest supporters of QBS, have come from in-house education departments at large corporate client accounts. The sequence of events is predictable. Someone takes the risk necessary to bring Question Based Selling in for a "pilot" event, the feedback from the training is "off the charts" positive, and suddenly, we're friends for life.

I have noticed, however, that some corporate educators are turned off by outside trainers. I'm not sure if it's about protecting their own turf, or because they feel threatened by an outsider, but rejecting innovative ideas just because they were not "invented here" is a dangerous practice in today's business environment. I had one experience where a director of corporate training got upset because the feedback from QBS methodology training was "too positive," when compared to other sales training courses they had been delivering in-house.

Having a negative attitude toward outside sales trainers is problematic because it creates an adversarial relationship. I just talked about developing mentors and coaches, so you can tell I am a supporter of in-house expertise. I can understand why corporate educators might feel most comfortable with their own programs. We already agreed that people tend to gravitate to whatever they feel most comfortable with. But, this protective mindset might actually work against you if your in-house training programs are not continuously being enhanced to stay ahead of your competition.

I sometimes hear from corporate educators the argument that a program like Question Based Selling may be "too advanced" for inexperienced salespeople. They would much rather see a basic "Sales 101" curriculum for new salespeople, the idea being that newer salespeople could come back and receive QBS training at a later date. I would counter by taking the position that teaching salespeople to sound different than your competitors doesn't require them to have experience. In fact, think about this: Why would you want to train a new salesperson to commoditize your value proposition in the eyes of prospective customers, when you could teach them how to differentiate themselves and your solutions in an increasingly competitive marketplace?

Ultimately, sales managers are trying to increase their relative effectiveness and gain a competitive advantage in their respective markets. But, companies do not always have internal training programs that can accomplish these objectives. Therefore, there is room, in my view, for outside trainers to work in conjunction with corporate educators to provide quality programs that result in a win/win relationship, as opposed to being perceived as a political threat.

Sales Excellence is a Choice

Some people have a special gift for sales. They were born with an innate ability to communicate, and success tends to follow them into every endeavor. Other people are gifted athletes. In every sport, there are top performers who don't have to work that hard to make the game look easy. I'm sure that there are also gifted doctors, attorneys, accountants, architects, engineers, and teachers, who all have the ability to make their professions look easy.

> In every sport, there are top performers who don't have to work very hard to make the game look easy.

The way I see it, gifted salespeople are the exception rather than the rule, however. Most accomplished performers in every profession have had to *earn* their success. This is definitely the case in sales. At some point, top performing salespeople have had to make a conscious decision to become the best in their field. Being the best in sales requires an ongoing commitment to developing product knowledge and industry expertise. It also requires sellers to be strategic in their positioning, so they will be perceived by customers as an invaluable resource, as opposed to just another sales caller.

I believe sales effectiveness is a learned behavior. Many times, I have taken a struggling sales team, and with a few adjustments in strategy, greatly enhanced their performance. It is equally rewarding to take a team of experienced professionals, who have been fairly successful in their careers, and raise their sales performance to the next level. In fact, in all the years I have been training salespeople, I have never met a top performer who didn't want to improve their skills, in order to become even more successful.

We have spent a great deal of energy in this book focusing on the softer skills and on sales effectiveness. Essentially, the goal has been to make you and the rest of your sales team more productive throughout the entire sales process. The key to success at this point is a choice, one that starts with you making a conscious decision to differentiate yourself and your sales team from the rest of the "noise" in the marketplace. From there, your success will likely be driven by your ability to implement the techniques and strategies talked about in this book, and your personal commitment to becoming a student of the sale throughout the rest of your professional career.

< ACTION ITEMS >

1. Make it a point to interview the person who would be training your salespeople. Don't just talk to a representative who sells training for the company. If they are unwilling to let you interview the actual person who will deliver the training, then you should respectfully say, "No, thank you."

2. Develop a set of interview questions to ask prospective sales trainers, and then invest the time to ask these questions. Make sure the answers you receive are congruent with your objectives for the training as well as your overall business philosophy. These questions should include:

"What (specifically) is different about your training programs than other courses currently being offered?"

"How long has your program been in existence? Has anything changed in your methodology over that period? What?"

"How has your program adapted to changing market conditions?"

"What are you going to teach my salespeople that's different from how our competitors are currently selling?"

"What (specifically) about your training is going to give us an immediate increase in productivity?"

"Are you willing to offer a written performance guarantee?"

3. Lastly, I recommend that you kick, scream, and fight to do everything possible to give your salespeople the very best sales education available, whether your company develops training programs in-house or you use outside vendors.

QBS TRAINING FOLLOW-UP QUESTIONS

Here are some "test" questions sales managers can ask their sales teams to reinforce the material that has been presented.

1.) What are the risks of starting off your sales conversations with the traditional elevator pitch?

2.) What is your strategy for gaining credibility early in the sales process, and earning the right to ask probative questions into the customer's problems, issues, and concerns?

3.) What's the very first question you will ask to kick-off your needs development conversations?

4.) Provide a sample voice-mail message you might leave a new prospect that will pique their curiosity enough to generate a return call. What about a sample voice-mail you might leave an existing customer, or internal resource at your company?

5.) Show me your repository of business issues and implications. Or, if you don't have a written list, be prepared to name an impressive sampling off the top of your head.

6.) What are the three biggest obstacles in your typical sale? What is your strategy for managing them?

7.) What are you doing in your current position to be proactive in your job, as opposed to reactive?

8.) Show me copies of two recent proposals (on pending deals) and explain how you plan to cost justify them to the customer. Tell me what you want your internal champion at the account to say to their CFO to show him or her that your proposed solution will either make them money or save them money.

9.) What QBS strategies are *not* working for you? What are you doing instead?

10.) If you were a sales manager (one or two levels above your current position), what would you be doing differently to increase the effectiveness of the sales organization?

Notes

Notes

Notes